A DAILY DOSE
OF THE
AMERICAN
DREAM

Stories of Success, Triumph, and Inspiration

☆ ☆ ☆

Alan C. Elliott

RUTLEDGE HILL PRESS®
Nashville, Tennessee

Published in Nashville, Tennessee, by Rutledge Hill Press® Inc., 211 Seventh Avenue North, Nashville, Tennessee 37219.
Distributed in Canada by H. B. Fenn & Company, Ltd., 34 Nixon Road, Bolton, Ontario L7E 1W2.
Distributed in Australia by The Five Mile Press Pty. Ltd., 22 Summit Road, Noble Park, Victoria 3174.
Distributed in New Zealand by Tandem Press, 2 Rugby Road, Birkenhead, Auckland 10.
Distributed in the United Kingdom by Verulam Publishing, Ltd., 152a Park Street Lane, Park Street, St. Albans, Hertfordshire AL2 2AU.

Jacket and page design by Harriette Bateman
Typography by E. T. Lowe, Nashville, Tennessee

Library of Congress Cataloging-in-Publication Data

Elliott, Alan C., 1952-
A daily dose of the american dream : stories of success, triumph, and inspiration / Alan C. Elliott
p. cm.
Includes index.
ISBN 1-55853-592-6: (HB)
1. Success-United States.   I. Title
BJ1611.2.E42   1998   98-5133
158.1—dc21   CIP

Printed in the United States of America

1 2 3 4 5 6 7 8 9—02 01 00 99 98

*For
Annette,
Mary,
and William,
who made me the
richest man in
the world.*

Contents

PREFACE   9

ACKNOWLEDGMENTS   10

January   13

February   44

March   73

April   104

May   134

June   165

July   195

August   226

September   257

October   287

November   318

December   348

INDEX   379

Preface

The purpose of this book is to show you by example how ordinary Americans have accomplished extraordinary successes—in business, life, or in service to others.

You hold in your hands a packet of idea-seeds that will help you march forward in your life. If you take these messages to heart, they will change you from spectator to participant in the American Dream. Arranged in a daily reading format, these are entertaining, informative, and sometimes humorous stories about people just like you who became innovators, inventors, entertainers, business leaders, scientists, educators, dreamers, and overcomers.

Be warned. There are no magic pills that will make you a success overnight. You must take an active role in your own success. Andrew Carnegie's motto was "Anything in life worth having is worth working for!" If your goal is to have a successful marriage, you must work for it. If you want to become wealthy, you must work for it. If you want to be an entertainer or sports hero, you must work for it. If you want to serve humanity, you must work for it. Since you must work, make the most of it. Work smart as well as hard, run with enthusiasm, be patient, be persistent, and relish the journey.

Each story contains a quote, an anecdote, and a challenge. As you read each story, pause a moment and ask yourself how the story might apply to your own life, business or circumstance. Benjamin Franklin once said "Experience is a dear teacher." If you can learn from someone else's mistake, you may be able to avoid making your own costly mistakes. Or, you might be able to translate someone else's technique for success into your own. Let these stories help you formulate your own American Dream. Then, jump into the fray and begin your journey toward success.

May your dreams come true!

Acknowledgments

Many people helped me gather this information and put these stories together. Thanks to my researchers, Beverly Woodward and Angie Hoffman. Thanks for the many people or associates of the people mentioned in this book that took time to personally correspond or talk with me. Readers who plowed through the stories to help make them better and more readable include Patsy Summey, Betty Brooks, Evelyn Langston, Mary Spencer, Ron and Linda Cawthon, Wayne Woodward, and Lori Moores. Thanks to Nicholas Smith for his efforts in making this second edition possible. Special thanks to my wife, Annette, for her encouragement, invaluable advice, and patience.

— ALAN C. ELLIOTT

A DAILY DOSE

OF THE

AMERICAN DREAM

☆ ☆ ☆

Sonny Bono

"Some people were under the misconception that Son was a short man, but he was heads and tails taller than anyone else." — Cher

Following his untimely death on the ski slopes in January 1998, Sonny Bono was remembered by four-term congressman and fellow actor Fred Grandy. "One thing you can say about him: He succeeded in two of the hardest industries in this country, show business and politics, two industries that tolerate almost anything but failure." Most people agree that Sonny Bono did not have the appearance of success. His former wife, Cher, once called him the strangest-looking man she'd ever seen. But what Sonny lacked in appearance, he made up for with determination and savvy.

Early in his singing career, Sonny had to borrow $175 to have his first hit song, "Baby Don't Go" recorded. The investment proved a wise move, and that initial success allowed him to write and record a number of other hits, including "I Got You Babe," which reached No. 1 status. In total, Sonny and Cher sold more than 40 million records. Sonny claims that his stand against drugs ended his career as a rock star, so he moved on to variety television. *The Sonny and Cher Comedy Hour* consistently ranked among the top ten television shows of the day, but the couple's break-up ended the series' popularity. When Sonny was unable to establish a new career as an actor, he reinvented himself as a restaurateur. Following a fight with city bureaucracy over restaurant sign, he decided to enter politics and became mayor of Palm Springs. He then ran unsuccessfully for the U.S. Senate in 1992 and then won a seat in the House of Representatives in 1994.

CONSIDER THIS: The road of life has many turns. Don't give up. When one road becomes blocked, look for another that may lead to a new, even more exciting adventure.

George Lucas

*"I set out to make a film for a generation growing
up without fairy tales."*   — George Lucas

Growing up in Modesto, California, George Lucas watched
every adventure serial he could find. These short action films
were stories of good versus evil, full of fights, chase scenes, and
suspenseful cliff-hangers. When George needed inspiration for
his own films, he returned in his mind to the films that excited
him during his youth. Lucas graduated from the University of
Southern California and, with his friend Francis Ford Coppola,
formed a production company called American Zoetrope. His
first feature, a science-fiction story called *THX-1138*, was the
origin of the now famous THX "The audience is listening" advanced theater sound logo. In 1973, Lucas's film *American Graf-
fiti* was successful enough to give boosts to the careers of Ron
Howard and Richard Dreyfus.

His third film catapulted Lucas to instant fame. Working with
a brilliant team of up-and-coming special-effects wizards, Lucas's
new company, Industrial Light and Magic, created the dazzling
effects for *Star Wars*. The sci-fi fairy tale, which merged cutting-
edge effects with a strong story of good versus evil inspired by
the early serials, took the world by storm. Lucas followed with
The Empire Strikes Back and *Return of the Jedi*, and again used the serial formula successfully in the *Indiana Jones* trilogy. In 1992, with
six mega-blockbusters under his belt, he received an Academy
Award, the prestigious Irving G. Thalberg Life Achievement
Award. Although he stumbled with a few of his later productions, Lucas continued to do his best work when he told stories
using the technique that first inspired his love of film.

CONSIDER THIS: What makes you excited and passionate
about your work? Use the energy you feel in your own life to
get your message across to others.

Ray Kroc Found a Winner and Multiplied It

"Common sense is instinct, and enough of it is genius." — George Bernard Shaw

Ray Kroc wanted to be a winner. For fifty-seven of his years he made a good living but never hit the jackpot. However, he kept his eyes open for an opportunity. As a salesman for a milk shake company, he was impressed by an order from a small hamburger stand in California that needed to make forty-eight shakes at a time. When he investigated, he found two brothers, Maurice and Richard McDonald, turning out hamburgers as quickly as they could be made. They had simplified the standard restaurant operation. As one of the brothers recalled: "Out went dishes, glasses, and silverware. Out went service, the dishwashers, and the long menu. We decided to serve just hamburgers, drinks, and french fries on paper plates. Everything prepared in advance, everything uniform."

Kroc wanted a taste of the McDonalds' success and hounded the brothers until they agreed to allow him to sell franchises. During the next six years, Kroc sold 200 McDonald franchises. In only twenty-two years, McDonald's became a billion-dollar company. The ingredients that led to the success of McDonald's over all others are simple. The menu is brief, containing only items whose consistent quality can be maintained in thousands of stores. There are strict standards for service, cleanliness, and store operations—and the standards are enforced. The company constantly researches its market (mostly families with children) to determine what customers want, and utilizes prolific and efficient advertising to carry its message to consumers.

CONSIDER THIS: The plan is simple: quality, consistency, cleanliness, and good value. Most people will agree with the plan, but only the winner will implement it with passion.

Parker Pens

"Our pens will write in any language."
— George S. Parker

George Parker kept his eyes open for new opportunities. Of course, he had to make a living in the meantime, so he taught telegraphy. One day in 1892, George finally found an idea worth pursuing. He had come up with a concept for a fountain pen design that would eliminate a bothersome leakage problem that had plagued pens for over fifty years. George knew that the market for his pen would be huge. Virtually every person in the entire world who wrote anything was a potential customer. As he began to have success distributing his pens in the United States, George encouraged his associates to expand into new markets with the message, "Our pens will write in any language!" To that end, George began exporting his pens in 1903.

George was a meticulous manufacturer. Even though he had a fine design, he insisted on spending plenty of time and money to make sure that the pen would write in all conditions. It had to write equally well when used left-handed, slanted forward, slanted backward, etc. George insisted on innovation but was never too eager to bring a product to market until he was sure it was the best. When ballpoint pens were introduced, George continued to research for another nine years before introducing the "T-Ball Jotter." Always keeping Parker pens at the top of the price lists, George acquired Eversharp in 1957 to address the lower price market. Today, Parker is one of the best-known American brands around the world.

CONSIDER THIS: Someone will be at the top of the heap, and it will probably be the company that pays the most attention to quality.

Famous Amos Cookies

*"It's important to start . . . start from right where
you are."*   — Wally Amos

Wally Amos is one of the most renowned black entrepreneurs in America. He calls himself the "Jackie Robinson of the theatrical business." It was Amos who "discovered" Simon and Garfunkel in a Manhattan club. Amos promoted talent at the William Morris Agency until he discovered something better. A friend dropped by one night with a batch of freshly baked chocolate chip cookies, and they were so tasty that Amos wanted to know how to make them himself. Simple—the recipe was on a bag of Nestle's chocolate chips. Amos's promoter mind went crazy. He had "discovered" something *big*. After months of making cookies for all his friends, and perfecting the recipe to make it his own, Amos was ready to let the world in on his new discovery.

It was opening day in Hollywood, California. Two thousand people had been sent special invitations. A red carpet decorated the sidewalk. Celebrities arrived in limousines. Music was playing and champagne was flowing. It was the grand debut of "Famous" Amos's first chocolate chip cookie store. Amos promoted his cookies nationwide, marketing them to exclusive department stores and specialty shops. Within five years, annual sales of Famous Amos cookies reached $5 million. Not everyone can afford a car phone, a Rolls Royce, a penthouse, diamonds, or jewelry. But almost everyone can afford a chocolate chip cookie.

CONSIDER THIS: What's out there waiting to be "discovered"? Look around. It may be the simplest, everyday thing that you can make the "best in the world."

Edison's Bright Idea

"Genius is 1 percent inspiration and 99 percent perspiration." — Thomas Edison

In 1878, when Thomas Edison announced that he would have a working small electric light "in a matter of weeks," gas stocks plummeted. Riding on his already legendary reputation, Edison raised money, organized the Edison Electric Light Company, and set out to invent the electric light. The trick was simply to find the correct element for the light filament. Thousands of materials were tested, but none lasted beyond a few seconds. After months of failure, Edison hired a physics expert named Francis Upton. With Upton's help, experimentation focused on a platinum filament, which showed some promise. It was now 1879. Work began early each morning, and Edison spent most of the day flitting from workbench to workbench observing the trials. At night he played songs at his pipe organ while he mulled over the day's findings in his mind. By mid-1879 it was clear that the platinum lamp would not work.

In October 1879, Upton and Edison's assistant Charles Bachelor began researching carbon. They devised a lamp with a short carbonized thread in a vacuum. Beginning on October 21, 1879, the carbonized lamp remained lit for 40 hours. The process had been messy, discouraging, and very non-romantic, but success was finally achieved. Edison believed the electric light could be produced. He placed his reputation on the line and endured more than a thousand failures before seeing that first successful lamp.

CONSIDER THIS: If you have a good idea, work toward its completion. The road may be difficult and discouraging, but the success will be sweet.

Dave Thomas

"Don't just study people who succeed, study people who handle success well." — Dave Thomas

Dave Thomas was adopted by a loving family, but his mother died when he was only five. His father remarried three times, and the family moved more than a dozen times before Dave reached his mid-teens. The only constant in his life was his grandmother, who gave him security and taught him the pleasure of hard work. Dave remembers first learning about restaurants because his father took him out to eat quite often. Since he liked to eat, Dave thought that owning a restaurant would be a great career. He took a job at a Hobby House restaurant, and when his father moved again, Dave stayed behind. At age fifteen, he was on his own.

During the Korean War, Dave joined the army and attended its Cook and Baker's School. After the war, he was given the opportunity to manage four Kentucky Fried Chicken restaurants. Dave learned the business well and in 1968 sold his KFC stock to begin his own chain of restaurants named after his daughter Wendy. His concept was to create a better hamburger—made from fresh meat, made to order, and served in a relaxed, family atmosphere. Wendy's grew rapidly until Thomas stepped out of the leadership in 1982. After several years of falling sales and declining quality, Thomas returned to the company as its "spokesman, in-house cheerleader, and roaming quality-control man." Once back under the founder's watchful eye, Wendy's rebounded and once again began to prosper.

CONSIDER THIS: Success is a long-term proposition. It requires constant attention to the guiding principles that made you successful to begin with.

Calvin Klein's
Fashionable Success

"The soul of this man is his clothes."
— William Shakespeare

At almost any clothing store in the world you can find racks filled with designer fashions—polo shirts with logos, jeans with designer names embroidered on back pockets. In fact, designer labels can be found on virtually every kind of apparel. This was not always the case; prior to the 1970s, designer fashions were found only in the most exclusive stores. But Calvin Klein changed all that. Calvin seemed to have a knack for fashion even as a child. Sometimes he would help his friends buy clothes. It was natural for Calvin to consider fashion as a career, and he studied at Manhattan's Fashion Institute of Technology in hopes of becoming a designer.

For six long years after graduation Calvin struggled with low-paying jobs around New York's fashion district. He believed that perhaps he was in the wrong industry, and he considered joining a family friend in the grocery business. Instead, his friend was so convinced of Calvin's talent that he provided $10,000 in seed money to enable the fledgling designer to start Calvin Klein Ltd. In 1968 Calvin began by designing women's coats. They were classy, simple, and elegant, and fitted right into the changing lifestyles of the era. Calvin seemed to have a knack for the tastes of the "post-hippy" generation. His comfortable, stylish, and relatively inexpensive clothes introduced the concept of designer fashion to an entire generation. By 1975 Klein had won three consecutive Coty awards and was inducted into the Coty Hall of Fame.

CONSIDER THIS: What are you good at doing? What do you enjoy doing? Is there any way you can do it for a living? Can you use that talent in the work you are doing today?

Steinway Quality

"Music is the universal language of mankind."
— Henry Wadsworth Longfellow

Heinrich Steinweg was born in the small German Hartz Mountain hamlet of Wolfshagen. Beginning in 1806, young Heinrich experienced a series of tragedies that wiped out most of his family. Orphaned, he joined the Prussian army and became a bugler. Despite having no formal training, Heinrich was an able musician, entertaining the troops on the zither and pianoforte. When he left the army, he became a church organist and began to build pianos in his kitchen at night. Although Heinrich worked in primitive facilities, people recognized the high quality of his work. But as his business prospered, revolution forced Heinrich and his family to move to America.

Settling in New York City, the family name was anglicized to Steinway. Heinrich and his three sons took jobs with different piano makers to learn the details of doing business in the United States. After three years of working for others, they started their own company, Steinway & Sons, producing one piano a week. The Steinway piano soon became known for its quality and clarity of sound. Steinway was more concerned with building the best rather than building the most, and Steinway pianos soon began to win awards. In 1872 Steinway Village, a Long Island mini-town that included employee housing, a school, library, and bathhouse, was opened. During tough economic times, companies offered Heinrich royalties to use the Steinway name on items such as radios. Since the Steinways could not control the quality of those products, they refused to compromise the integrity of their name. As a result, the Steinway name continues to be associated only with the finest musical instruments in the world.

CONSIDER THIS: A reputation built on quality must never be compromised.

Patton's Message of Mind Over Body

"Now, if you are going to win any battle, you have to do one thing. You have to make the mind run the body. Never let the body tell the mind what to do." — Gen. George S. Patton

In his book *Patton's Principles*, Porter Williamson recalls several of the general's pronouncements concerning the value of a healthy mind and body. Patton demanded that every soldier run a mile every day, twenty-five years before jogging became popular. He warned his officers to stay away from desks; they were to be out talking with the troops. Too much desk work, according to Patton, soured the brain. Patton taught that one must exercise beyond the point of exhaustion to gain superior strength and stamina. To overcome the weakness of one's body, the mind must play its part. Patton encouraged his troops to gain mental strength from daily readings of the Bible. When it was time for battle, he believed, the mind must be in charge of the body, since the body will always give up first.

Patton's troops were some of the most feared and respected of World War II. Many times, enemy soldiers would purposely arrange to surrender to Patton's units, since that was considered to be no disgrace. Patton demanded more physical fitness from those under his command than did any other leader. That emphasis on health gave his soldiers advantages over enemy troops that would become exhausted in battle. Today, we know that physical fitness is an important component of our own ability to face the "battles" of daily life. Exercise and diet directly influence our mental health and our ability to effectively carry out our activities.

CONSIDER THIS: Is your life controlled by aches, pains, and tiredness—or by a mental determination to reach your life goals?

Billy Sunday Speaks Plainly

"I have neither wit, nor words, nor worth, nor actions, nor utterance, nor the power of speech to stir men's blood: I only speak right on."

— Shakespeare

Billy Sunday was a premier baseball player. He was a man's man—tough, sweaty, and hard-drinking. One day in 1887, when Billy went out drinking with friends, he encountered a group of men and women from the Pacific Garden Mission playing gospel songs. They invited Billy and his friends to a meeting to hear alcoholics and prostitutes tell how their lives had been changed by faith in God. Something clicked inside Billy. In that moment, he turned to his friends and told them, "I'm through, I am going to Jesus Christ."

Billy not only went to Christ, he became an evangelist. When he came to New York in 1917, the city had never seen such a religious frenzy. A special tabernacle was built to seat 20,000, the structure being so large that it took four train carloads of sawdust to cover its floor. At the revival, Billy, who appealed mostly to men, preached to over 1.5 million people. "I am the rube of rubes," he declared. "The odor of the barnyard is on me yet. I have greased my hair with goose grease and blacked my boots with stove blacking. I have wiped my proboscis with a gunnysack towel, I have drunk coffee out of my saucer and have eaten with my knife." Billy would prop his feet up on the pulpit, say "done it" when he should have said "did it" and "I have saw" when he should have said "I have seen." At the end of each message, Billy would call for the people to "walk the sawdust trail" to salvation, and as a result, millions of lives were changed.

CONSIDER THIS: Are you speaking the language of your clients? More people will understand what you are talking about if you communicate with them on their own level.

Keep Your Eyes on Your Goal

*"Successful individuals have game plans and
purposes that are clearly defined to which they
constantly refer."*
— Denis Waitley in *Seeds of Greatness*

Have you ever walked near the edge of a cliff or on a small plank bridge over a crevice? Most people catch themselves looking down to see where they might fall. Feeding our fears of what might happen often makes that which we fear more likely to happen. Karl Wallenda thrilled millions of people during decades of high-wire walking. He walked tightropes that spanned stadiums, rivers, and buildings, and performed almost anywhere that a crowd could gather. He frequently said that, for him, living was walking a tightrope. Wire walking came naturally to the "Great Wallenda." Then one day Karl mentioned to his wife that he was concerned about falling. Before performing that day, he checked and re-checked the wire's tautness and its anchors. Never before had Karl shown such concern. Later, as he was performing an easy walk between two buildings without a safety net, Karl fell to his death. He had stopped concentrating on the walk and had begun to think about falling.

While training for sporting events, athletes often are taught how to visualize the desired outcome of a game, a jump, a dive, or a race. Thinking about a positive outcome gives the mind encouragement to make the body attain what the mind "sees." Have you noticed that when you tell small children *not* to do something, that is exactly what they do? We end up doing or obtaining those things we think about.

CONSIDER THIS: Are you concentrating on your goals or on the risks? Respect your risks, but once you have begun your journey, put all of your concentration, passion, and creative energies into the task at hand.

Dress Your Business for Success

"The clothes make the man." — Latin proverb

Much has been said about the concept of "dressing for success." What a business "wears" also makes a difference to customers and employees. For instance, when people enter the national headquarters of Frito-Lay, they will find a large bowl of hand-selected chips, carefully chosen to represent the best the company produces. A customer walking into Sewell Village Cadillac in Dallas will find the showroom filled with beautiful antiques. Trammell Crow, one of the largest real-estate developers in the United States, made a fortune constructing warehouse buildings that offered such amenities as first-class offices and manicured lawns with fresh flowers and shrubs. Part of the continued success of the Disney theme parks is their constant attention to authenticity and cleanliness. The McDonald's restaurant chain is very strict with its franchisees concerning the upkeep of their stores. A popular admonition to restaurant workers is, "If you have time to lean, you have time to clean."

It should not be surprising that these companies are among the top producers in their fields. Their attention to the details of public perception carries over to their attention to the other details of business. There are probably small "mom-and-pop" type stores you are familiar with that have a reputation for always being attractive and pleasant. Clear signs that a retail store is in trouble include items that are sloppily arranged on the shelves, a parking lot that is not swept, and clerks that can never be found. A company that pays attention to its public image dresses the entire organization for success.

CONSIDER THIS: How is your organization presented to the public, customer, and employee? Are you concentrating on getting the details right?

Getting a Foot in the Door

"I can tell where my own shoe pinches me."
— Don Quixote

Young Billy Scholl showed an interest in shoes from his childhood. He liked working with leather and made harnesses for the family farm's horses. He repaired and made shoes for twelve brothers and sisters. In response to his interests, Billy's parents apprenticed him to a local cobbler at the age of sixteen. One year later, he went to Chicago to work as a cobbler and shoe salesman. The number of foot ailments he encountered concerned Billy. The big city and the fast pace of modern times were rough on feet. Customers suffered from bunions, corns, and fallen arches. Billy saw a huge need, and decided to become the "foot doctor to the world." He enrolled in the Illinois Medical College, and by the time he had graduated in 1904, he had patented his first invention, an arch support called the Foot-Eazer.

Billy opened his own store and began producing arch supports for other shoe stores. To sell his wares, he would go to a shoe store and pull a skeleton of a human foot out of his bag. He would then proceed to explain the ailments of the foot to the proprietor and inevitably take an order for his product. For more than sixty years, Billy personally promoted his own products with flair and enthusiasm. He established a correspondence course for shoe clerks and hired consultants to criss-cross the country, giving lectures on foot-care products. Billy Scholl's enthusiastic dedication to good foot care and his endurance as an able spokesman has made his name a household word.

CONSIDER THIS: You are at your best when you are promoting something you really believe in—and when you promote it with enthusiasm, pizzazz, and knowledge.

Martin Luther King Jr.'s Dream

"I have a dream that one day . . . people will be judged more for the content of their character than the color of their skin."

— Dr. Martin Luther King Jr.

Americans love to dream about peace and prosperity. Some people dream only for themselves. Other people dream for us all. It is not surprising that a dreamer would come to the forefront of the civil rights movement in the 1960s. Dr. Martin Luther King Jr. was more than a gifted orator. His message of challenge and hope was fuller, more thought out, and more powerful than that of any other leader in the movement. He had a vision of the future in which all people would be given an equal chance for success and every person would be treated with dignity and respect. He painted a picture of the future based on his belief that God wanted all of His children to live together in peace and with honor for each other. However, not everyone appreciated his message.

Leaders are often loved deeply by some and hated intensely by others. As a result, leaders must pay a price for standing at the forefront of a cause. For his courage to stand against prejudice and hate, Dr. King was assassinated. Fortunately, dreams are more powerful than one person's life. Dreams based on truth, dignity, and righteousness somehow stand against those who would destroy them. As long as leaders have enough character to stand up against evil and to fight for honor, righteousness, and dignity, America will continue to grow closer to its dream of peace and prosperity for all of its citizens.

CONSIDER THIS: Open your eyes and determine where people are being treated unfairly. Be quick to respond. Use your influence to bring about equality and integrity among those with whom you deal.

Maugham Waits for Success

"A man will work and slave in obscurity for ten years and then become famous in ten minutes."
— Bob Ripley

W. Somerset Maugham graduated from medical college, but his heart was in writing fiction. Time and again, he tried to get jobs as a writer and failed. He went hungry. For eleven long years editor after editor ignored his writings. However, Maugham kept sending his manuscripts to whomever he could. Like a fisherman with many lines in the water, he held on, hoping for that "bite." One of Maugham's plays was on the desk of the manager of a London theater when the venue's current production failed. The manager needed to come up with something quickly to fill a time slot and fished around on his desk, ultimately finding Maugham's *Lady Fredrick*. The manager initially had not thought much of the play, and it had remained on his desk for a year. But since the show must go on, he decided to use Maugham's play to "fill the time."

Lady Fredrick was a smash! Instantly, every theater manager in London began clamoring for a Maugham play. Publishers wanted his works, and royalties came pouring in. Within a month, Maugham was the toast of high society and had obtained money, prestige, and fame. The rest is history. To "be in the right place at the right time," you or your work must be visible in the marketplace. Nothing sitting on the shelf can ever find success. It must be available, waiting for the public to try it, taste it, feel it. Good work will then be discovered and recognized for its quality.

CONSIDER THIS: Are your ideas being presented to the public? Is your product being tried and tested by those who would use it? Are you sitting on something that could be a success?

Mae Jemison Is First in Space

*"Hope is the thing with feathers that perches in
the soul."*   — Emily Dickinson

When *Star Trek* took to the small screen in the 1960s, it not
only introduced concepts of space exploration, it crossed a bar-
rier by involving minorities in major leadership roles on the
starship *Enterprise*. For young Mae Jemison, the role of Lieutenant Uhura was particularly exciting. As an African-American
girl interested in science and space, she found no role models
in the all-white and all-male astronauts going into space. Yet, in
the fictional world of *Star Trek*, she found a like mind. When
Mae graduated from high school, she entered Stanford and received degrees in chemical engineering and African-American
history. Following her undergraduate studies, she earned a medical degree from Cornell.

Mae's interests extend beyond the scientific. She served with
the Peace Corps in Africa, has learned three foreign languages
(Russian, Swahili, and Japanese), and is an accomplished amateur dancer. In 1985, Dr. Jemison interviewed at NASA and received encouragement from Robert McNair, one of the first
African-American astronauts. Mae was accepted as an astronaut
candidate in 1987 and in September 1992 became the first
African-American woman in space. Each day she began her
work shift quoting Lieutenant Uhura's words, "Hailing frequen-
cies open!" Since her stint aboard the space shuttle, Dr. Jemison
has often taken time from her busy work schedule to speak to
children and encourage them to follow their dreams.

CONSIDER THIS: America is a land of many opportunities,
but they are not given to you without cost. You often must
struggle, study hard, and overcome substantial obstacles to
realize your own American Dream.

If I Only Had a Brain

*"There's no place like home. There's no place
like home."*   — Dorothy

When *The Wonderful Wizard of Oz* was published in 1899, it
quickly became an American classic. One of the reasons for its
success is that so many people can relate to Dorothy's search
for her own American Dream. As depicted in the movie version, Dorothy sees her home in Kansas as a black and white
place—not offering her much of an exciting future. She looks
over the rainbow, wishing she could fly away to a land of wonder and opportunity. When a tornado sweeps her away to the
land of Oz, Dorothy meets three other friends who also have
their own problems. The lion is cowardly, the scarecrow thinks
he needs a brain, and the tin man desires a heart. Then they
hear that the mighty Wizard of Oz can provide a solution to
their problems.

During their journey to meet the Wizard, the lion over-
comes his fears, the scarecrow has ideas on how the travelers
can overcome roadblocks, and the tin man shows compassion.
Dorothy discovers that, for all the excitement in Oz, what she
really wants can be found at home. In many ways the story
shows us that we do not have to be transported to a wonderful
land by winning a lottery, being discovered as a movie star, or
suddenly inventing the equivalent of the light bulb. More
often, we find our dream by realizing that we have opportunities and riches where we are—with our families, friends, and
business associates.

CONSIDER THIS: Before seeking your dream in greener pas-
tures, look for the opportunities, talents, and wealth that may
already be yours in your own backyard.

Positive Thinking

"The mind grows by what it feeds on."
— J. G. Holland

Norman Vincent Peale is the founder of the "Positive Thinking" movement. His book *The Power of Positive Thinking* has sold millions of copies. The bases of Peale's theory are principles found in the Bible. First, you must believe in yourself; you must have a healthy respect for your own worth as a child of God. "I can do all things through Christ who strengthens me." Next, you must use your mind to tap into the power offered in the scripture. "You are given the mind of Christ." Then, you must be in touch with the power of prayer for guidance and inspiration. You must expect the best. "All things are possible to him who believes." Personal problems can limit your capabilities, so you must learn to rise above defeat, depression, and thinking that limits your potential.

Peale admits to being caught with his positive thinking down. When *Guideposts* magazine was in its infancy, it quickly ran out of capital, and Peale's board sat in a meeting ready to kill the project. Tessie Durlack, a member of the board, chided the other members for their lack of faith and vision. She had them pray "thanks" for new subscribers and for the ideas to make the magazine a bigger success than they had ever believed possible. The exciting change of attitude that took place saved *Guideposts*, which is now one of the most widely read publications in the world.

CONSIDER THIS: Positive thinking is a way to focus your mind on your goal, with the belief that you will obtain it. Do you believe? Do you reinforce that belief daily with some exercise of positive thinking?

Kresge's Change for the Better

"The old order changeth, yielding place to new."
Alfred, Lord Tennyson

Harry Cunningham went to work for the Kresge Company in 1928 as a stockroom trainee. Gradually, Harry was promoted to better jobs, and management noticed his good ideas. In 1957 he was appointed a vice president with an assignment to study the marketplace to determine the best plan for the company's future. Harry logged over 200,000 miles of travel and began to believe that discounting was the wave of the future. In 1959 Cunningham was made president of the Kresge Company but did not make the switch to discounting immediately. He instructed his executives to study the discount industry. Little by little, Kresge's management saw that discounting was holding a growing share of the retail market, and in March 1961 made the decision to move into discounting.

Forty K-Mart stores were opened by 1963, and the number swelled to more than a thousand stores by 1977. Hiring and training good management for those stores was difficult, and the company actively recruited at over 100 colleges and universities. Future management was trained in small discount stores named Jupiter. In 1976 K-Mart surpassed JCPenney as the nation's second-largest retailer. In a changing and competitive marketplace, K-Mart continues to find its share of success. It has responded to market challenges by emphasizing quality management, high-turnover merchandise, across-the-board discounting, and by clustering stores in a single market area to aid in advertising.

CONSIDER THIS: Organizations that refuse to adapt to the trends of society will vanish. Are you studying your competition to see how you will be able to adjust to the new order when it comes?

The World's Greatest Salesman

"If you throw enough spaghetti against the wall,
some if it is going to stick." — Joe Girard

Many people call themselves great salesmen, but Joe Girard has convincing evidence. He was listed in the *Guinness Book of World Records* for several years in a row as "The world's greatest salesman." As a Chevrolet salesman in Chicago, Joe racked up sales record after sales record. How did he do it? Joe's techniques are simple and straightforward and can be used in almost any market. He made himself known by giving away thousands of business cards each year. He even threw them into the stands at football games. Each customer was placed on Joe's list and received a greeting card every month, for New Year's, Valentine's, birthday, St. Patrick's Day, etc. Once a year Joe sent his list of "friends" a sales kit that included a packet of Joe's cards and a $25 reward offer to each friend who sent in a new customer. When Joe had free time at work, he was on the phone, cold-calling prospects and gathering names of new prospects.

Joe recognized the importance of each person. His "Law of 250" states that if a person is given a bad deal, he can adversely influence 250 other people. On the other hand, if that person is given a good deal, he can influence 250 other people to think highly of Joe Girard. If a customer had a problem with a car, Joe personally saw to it that the problem was resolved. The customer knew that he was buying more than the car, he was buying the services of someone who could and would step in to keep him satisfied with what he bought.

CONSIDER THIS: Are you working your list of customers, clients, or constituents? Are you keeping in touch, always saying "thanks" to them, and keeping them satisfied?

Powerful Mottos

"Without a vision the people perish."
— Proverbs 29:18

Many leaders have a "trademark," which is usually one or more sayings that concisely describe that person's or company's beliefs or management style. Harry Truman had his motto inscribed on a sign that sat on the presidential desk, "The Buck Stops Here." Ronald Reagan's desk had a sign saying "It Can Be Done." Tom Watson of IBM used signs that simply said "Think," and placed them in all of IBM's offices. Ray Kroc of McDonald's constantly talked about Q. S. C. & V. (Quality, Service, Cleanliness, and Value). Sysco, a Houston-based food wholesaler lives by the motto "Don't sell food, sell peace of mind." Carl Sewell preaches the concept of "customers for life" to stress superior service at his auto dealership.

Mottos usually do not mean anything unless management backs them up. Watson indoctrinated all new employees of IBM with an incredible amount of exposure to corporate beliefs. McDonald's will remove the franchise from any restaurant that does not fulfill Q. S. C. & V., as outlined in a detailed operating manual. Mottos serve the purpose of crystallizing a complicated issue. The two-finger "V" for victory sign in World War II, "Remember the Alamo," and "54-40 or Fight" were used to unite a people for a cause. Most people want something to believe in, something to give them a feeling of pride and belonging. Mottos can boil down a complicated issue to a short phrase or symbol that the masses can understand and rally around.

CONSIDER THIS: What motto do you live by? Do you have the opportunity to solidify your group or organization by adopting a saying or symbol that describes your goals?

Bill Lear Flies High

*"Every real accomplishment first begins as
a dream."* — Alan C. Elliott

William P. Lear loved Horatio Alger tales, stories that told of people who rose from obscurity and poverty to wealth and fame. Lear wanted to be an inventor; however, he had few resources to buy the tools and parts needed to realize his dream. He once told an interviewer that at age twelve he resolved "first to make enough money so I'd never be stopped from finishing anything." After studying engineering during a stint in the armed forces, Lear landed a job with an Illinois electronics firm. In the late 1920s he became a design engineer at Galvin Manufacturing Company (Motorola), a maker of radio chassis. It was there that Lear developed his first important invention, the automobile radio. He enjoyed sufficient success to acquire his own airplane. Aviation was still in its infancy, and Lear was sure that was a ripe area for his inventive powers. He soon found that navigating an airplane around the country was a very crude process—one simply followed known landmarks. To improve navigation, Lear invented the "Learoscope," an electronic device that allowed an aircraft to be navigated by the use of radio signals.

In 1939 Lear formed Lear, Inc., a producer of aircraft instruments, which was a highly successful enterprise. His next dream was to build a small general aviation jet, but his board of directors voted down the project as unfeasible. Lear sold his 23 percent interest in the company and formed a new enterprise, Lear Jet, Inc. His new jet took to the skies in 1963 and was an immediate success.

CONSIDER THIS: Have you taken the time to dream? Are you taking the initiative to follow your dreams?

Acres of Diamonds

"He most lives who thinks most, who feels the noblest, and who acts the best,"
— from "Acres of Diamonds"

Could one person giving one speech save a dying church, found a university, support a hospital, and change millions of lives? Yes! The man was Russell Conwell and his speech was titled "Acres of Diamonds." As a young traveling reporter in 1870, Conwell heard a folk tale as he traveled in a camel caravan along the Tigris River. The story told of a Persian farmer who was lured by the stories of riches in faraway places. The farmer deserted his fruitful lands in search of immense wealth. As the years passed, the farmer's youth and health disappeared, and he died far from his home, a disillusioned pauper. Soon after the farmer's death, acres of fabulous diamonds were discovered on the property he had abandoned.

That simple parable changed Conwell's life. He began relating the story to others, telling them, "Your diamonds are not in faraway mountains or in distant seas; they are in your own backyard if you will but dig for them." Other stories were added to the tale, and Conwell became a sought-after speaker. He believed what he preached, which led him into a life of helping others—including saving a dilapidated Massachusetts church, serving for forty-three years at Philadelphia's Grace Church, and founding Temple University and Samaritan (now Temple University) Hospital. Around the world, Conwell inspired audiences with his speech and raised money for his causes. By 1925, he had delivered the "Acres" speech more than 6,000 times.

CONSIDER THIS: People yearn for truths that will give them better and more satisfying lives. A message of inspiration, hope, and optimism never gets old. What messages are you sending to your employees, family, or customers?

Win Friends and Influence People

"Any fool can criticize, condemn, and complain—and most fools do." — Dale Carnegie

Dale Carnegie urged the YMCA to allow him to conduct public speaking courses. The organization refused to pay the normal $2 per night fee but allowed him to begin the courses on a commission basis. Within three years, Dale was making $30 a night in commissions. For over fifty years, the Dale Carnegie courses have been teaching the road to success. Lee Iacocca claims that it was the confidence he acquired from a Carnegie course that lifted him from being a mediocre manager to being a success.

Carnegie's practical advice is as relevant today as ever: Be interested in the other person, ask him questions about himself, and listen with interest. Avoid condemning people. Put yourself in their shoes, try to understand their perspective. You can't win an argument. Avoid arguments. Show respect for another person's opinion. If you are wrong, admit it and ask for forgiveness, quickly and with feeling. Never ask someone a question that you know will be answered "no." Ask "yes" questions. To get cooperation, make the other person feel like the new idea was his or hers. Give challenge and honor to those who would take on a task. If you must criticize, always envelop the criticism in praise. Talk about your mistakes first. Above all, let the other person save face. Praise people for every good thing they do, no matter how small. Make them live up to a reputation of excellence. Any person who can do all these things will find it easier to successfully work with people.

CONSIDER THIS: Be respectful of the other person, and always keep him or her in mind. Treat other people with the same respect with which you want to be treated.

Keeping in Touch with Your Customers

"A good listener is not only popular everywhere, but after a while he knows something."
— Wilson Milzer

Keeping in touch with customers is an essential part of every successful business. One industry that neglected to keep in touch with its workers and customers was the American automobile industry of the 1970s. In a 1983 analysis, a Stanford Sloan student from General Motors observed that people in Detroit had a different view of the automobile world than did the rest of the country. In Detroit, almost everyone was associated with the American automobile industry. As a result, they naturally bought and drove American cars. There were Chevys, Fords, and Chryslers in every parking lot. Automobile executives had their cars checked daily by the company mechanics, and any defect or problem was likely diagnosed and resolved before the end of the day.

At the same time in places like California, the American car was being passed over in favor of new imports which were less expensive and more reliable. While Toyotas and Datsuns were not common in Detroit, they were fast gaining foothold in other parts of the country. It wasn't until the 1980s that American car manufacturers began to respond visibly to the import threat by significantly improving the reliability of American automobiles. Since then, there has been a continued increase in quality and a realization on the part of U.S. automakers that the public will not automatically buy American cars, they will buy those cars that provide the quality, safety, and features the public wants.

CONSIDER THIS: What are you doing trying to run a business sitting behind a desk? Get up. Get out. Find out what's really going on.

Edwin Land's Better Photography Idea

"The stoical scheme of supplying our wants by lopping off our desires is like cutting off our feet when we want shoes." — Jonathan Swift

The age of photography provided a way to take pictures. You loaded your Brownie camera with film and snapped pictures of the new baby. You then processed the film in your own darkroom or took it to a developer, who had your pictures ready a week later. (We're talking quite a few years ago!) Edwin Land had a better idea. What if it were possible to take a picture and, within seconds, have the developed photograph in your hands? The marketplace was not clamoring for this capability. In fact, very few people probably even thought of the idea. Land developed the technology and then stimulated consumers' desires to "need" this convenience.

The Polaroid Land camera is a classic example of how a new technology can change our perception of our needs as consumers. It is serendipity. We didn't even think of that possibility before! All good ideas and products do not come just by reacting to consumer needs. Who would have thought of the microwave oven, 3M's "Post-it" notes, radio, the vacuum cleaner, digital watches, movies, or lasers? At the turn of the century, there were proposals to close the U.S. Patent Office because "everything has been invented!" If those people could see us now! There are still thousands, maybe millions of products and services that no one has thought of yet. When the new idea hits the market, everyone will say, "What a great idea, why didn't someone think of that sooner?"

CONSIDER THIS: Think beyond needs. Examine a new technology and consider how it might be applied in areas where no one has used it before.

Attitudes

"For they can conquer who believe they can."

— Virgil

We are what we think. Our mind is much more powerful than we know. It can cause us to be sick (it is a well-known fact that a vast amount of illness is caused by emotional stress), and it can bring us back to health (that is why placebos often work so well). Our mind can give us an attitude of failure or provide us with an attitude of success. Sports commentators often discuss the "mental" game that is taking place on the field of play. Talent and training will only get us so far. We must have the mental attitude that will push us into the winner's circle.

In his book *Secrets of Successful Selling*, John Murphy relates the story of the man who could make only $5,000 a year. No matter what situation the man was in, he believed he was a $5,000-a-year employee. When he was given a good sales territory, he made $5,000. In a bad territory, he made $5,000. In every place he was assigned, he made $5,000. He mentally believed that he was able to make only $5,000 a year—no more, no less—and he worked hard enough to prove himself right. Once, he made $5,000 early in the year and was sick for the rest of the year, although doctors could not determine why. Luckily, the salesman finally got the message that it was his limited belief in himself that was holding him back. He needed to raise his expectations and have a more positive dream of what he could accomplish. Once on track, he lived up to his new image of himself and proved to be a stellar salesman.

CONSIDER THIS: Are your attitudes, your limited opinion of yourself, and your abilities holding you back from really getting things done?

Eisenhower's Mentor

"You cannot teach a man anything; you can only help to find it within himself." — Galileo

Dwight Eisenhower was a mediocre student at West Point. During World War I, he missed seeing any action, although many of his classmates were in the thick of the fighting. After the war Eisenhower was transferred to Panama, where he wanted to work under Gen. Fox Connor, whom he admired. General Connor was a father figure and mentor to Eisenhower, and the relationship was a turning point in Eisenhower's life. He later reflected, "Life with General Connor was a sort of graduate school in military affairs and the humanities, leavened by a man who was experienced in his knowledge of men and their conduct. I can never adequately express my gratitude to this one gentleman. . . . In a lifetime of association with great and good men, he is the one more or less invisible figure to whom I owe an incalculable debt."

Unlike his previous lackluster performance at West Point, Eisenhower became a different kind of student when he was selected to take training at the General Staff School. The confidence he gained as a student of a great man made a huge difference in his self-confidence and determination to succeed. As a result, Eisenhower ranked first in his class in a tough, competitive school. The rest is history, as Eisenhower became one of the most important leaders of the twentieth century. Without his experience of learning from a mentor, one cannot speculate if Eisenhower ever would have "found" that capability within himself.

CONSIDER THIS: Who is it around you that you can learn from? Have you submitted yourself to a mentor? Are you being a mentor to someone else?.

Wrigley Didn't Overlook the Little Things

"When business is good it pays to advertise; when business is bad you've got to advertise."

— Anonymous

Bill Wrigley was a problem child. He was thrown out of school and was always "up to no good." At the age of thirteen he was taken out of school and put to work stirring pots of boiling soap at his father's factory. His father later decided to try the boy as a salesman and sent him to the small towns of New England. Bill soon demonstrated that he could sell. He readily made friends on the road and made it a point "to be always polite, always patient, and never to argue." At the age of twenty, in 1891, Bill struck out on his own. He moved to Chicago and became a sales representative for a baking powder company. As an incentive to those buying his product, he included two sticks of chewing gum with every package. It was just a sales gimmick, but he kept getting requests for more gum. The requests increased to the point that Wrigley was selling more gum than powder, and he eventually dropped all other products and concentrated on promoting the gum.

By 1910, Wrigley's Spearmint was the top-selling gum in the country, and his Juicy Fruit gum was not far behind. In 1915 Wrigley sent free sticks of gum to 1.5 million telephone subscribers. Later he repeated the mail-out to 7 million people. Wrigley poured more marketing money into advertising his gum than any other single product advertiser of the day. Despite the fact that a pack of gum sold for only five cents, Wrigley amassed a fortune and used it to create a giant financial empire.

CONSIDER THIS: Look for clues about what you are doing now that could turn into big business if you gave it the chance.

Million Dollar Phrases

"You'll wonder where the yellow went when you brush your teeth with Pepsodent."

— Pepsodent advertising slogan

Why are some companies more memorable than others? Why do some products climb to the top of the pack, while similar products of the same quality lag behind? One of the factors that makes a company successful is its "ownership" of a specific position in the public's mind. Often, that position can be described in a catch phrase that is almost universally associated with the company or product. For example, when you hear "The Real Thing," you think of Coca-Cola. When you hear "Absolutely, positively overnight," you think of Federal Express. Even a common phrase such as "pizza delivery" has meaning—many people think of Domino's Pizza because of its original thirty-minute delivery guarantee. Which rental car company tries harder? What washer repairman is lonely? Who flies the friendly skies? Where's the beef?

These phrases are worth millions of dollars because they are easily and effectively locked into the consumer's mind. Marketers may try for decades to capture the consumer's attention with cute, funny, or feature-laced advertising, but it seems that these phrases are elusive. It's amazing that companies sometimes abandon their million-dollar phrases, such as "Plop, plop, fizz, fizz. Oh, what a relief it is," "See the USA in your Chevrolet," and others. For most companies, another memorable phrase will never be as effective.

CONSIDER THIS: What catchy phrase describes a major benefit or feature of your product? Do you have one that sets your product apart from the rest? If not, search for one. If you have one, recognize it as a treasure, and abandon it at your own risk.

The Risks of Leadership

"When we think we lead, we most are led."
— Lord Byron in *The Two Foscari*

In emergency situations some people rise to the occasion. They think fast, bark orders, and get people to follow their lead. However, most other people would simply rather be followers. To find out why, Dean Frost, Fred Fiedler, and Jeff Anderson studied leadership in the military to determine the role of risk-taking in effective leadership. Bravery and courage are not generally thought of when defining leadership qualities in business; however, there are parallels. In the armed forces, those in command who are willing to take personal risks by exposing themselves to danger in combat gain high esteem among the troops. In business, the "theater of combat" may be at the corporate office, where bosses fight on behalf of their employees.

The Israeli military, generally considered to be among the best in the world, requires its commanders to be the point men of an attack, where the danger is greatest. American Gen. George S. Patton knew the value of having a leader in the thick of the action. During his World War II campaigns in North Africa and Europe, Patton's jeep often could be seen moving toward the fighting. Many times he joined his troops at the very point of attack. Patton understood that the soldiers under his command would interpret such action as a vote of confidence in them and thus would maintain good morale.

CONSIDER THIS: Are you seen as a leader who goes to bat for your "troops"? When things are rough, do you take the heat yourself? If you desire to be a leader, then expose yourself to risks that will help build confidence and morale in those working for you.

The Band-Aid

"To accept good advice is but to increase one's own ability."
— Johann Wolfgang von Goethe

Even when hundreds or thousands of people hear a good idea, it is the rare individual who does something about it. Robert Johnson was a co-owner of the Seabury & Johnson company when he attended a meeting during which Joseph Lister describe the science of bacteriology and made a plea for sanitary conditions in hospitals. The year was 1876, and most of those in attendance listened with skepticism. It was hard to imagine those little "bugs" causing problems. However, Johnson was convinced that Lister was on to something, and he talked his brothers Edward and James into developing products that would help make hospitals more sanitary.

In 1886 the brothers formed their own company, Johnson & Johnson, and began promoting their sterilized gauze. By 1910 the company needed forty buildings to produce a growing line of medical products. One day Earle E. Dickson, a cotton buyer in the company's purchasing department, showed a co-worker a self-stick bandage he had developed and was using at home. Earle had put a dab of sterile cotton and gauze on a strip of surgical tape to create a bandage that he could use to take care of his family's cuts and scrapes. He placed a crinoline fabric on the sticky parts of the bandage until it was needed. James Johnson saw one of the bandages and immediately recognized its potential in the marketplace. The invention was dubbed the "Band-Aid," and it soon became one of the world's most recognized trademarks.

CONSIDER THIS: Listen to the ideas of those around you. New ideas are often the basis of new products and perhaps new companies.

Peter Jennings

"If a man bites a dog, this is news."

— John Bogart

Although Peter Jennings' father (who was a distinguished broadcast journalist for the Canadian Broadcasting Corporation) may have helped him get his first broadcasting job, Peter still had to prove that he could be a first-class journalist. His early chance came at CBC, where he hosted a half-hour radio show for children. Peter showed promise and dedication, and was soon allowed to host several public affairs programs. Eventually, he became a special events commentator and the host of *Vue*, a late-night talk show. In 1964 Peter's coverage of the Democratic National Convention in Atlantic City impressed ABC News President Elmer Lower. Lower immediately offered Peter a job as an ABC correspondent, but he turned it down. Three months later, Peter woke up in a cold sweat one night and thought, "What have I done?" He wrote Lower back and got the job.

In 1965, in an effort to boost their national broadcast ratings, ABC made Jennings the anchor of their nightly newscast. Although he did a good job, he did not have the qualifications to compete with Cronkite and Huntley and Brinkley. Jennings returned to reporting in 1968 and established himself as one of the foremost foreign correspondents. His in-depth analysis of the news gained him award after award. In 1983 Jennings was named sole anchor for the *ABC Nightly News*. As he looks back on his career, Jennings admits that it was the role model of his father that pushed him to continue, to strive to be the best. "I'm still trying to live up to my father's standards."

CONSIDER THIS: Pick a mentor with the kinds of attributes you desire. An example of excellence can give you the motivation to do and become your best.

Face Your Troubles Squarely

*"Three things give hardy strength: sleeping on
hairy mattresses, breathing cold air, and eating
dry food."* — Welsh proverb

Theodore Roosevelt was a weakling. Does that surprise you?
As a child, Roosevelt was thin, in poor health, timid, and afraid
of getting hurt. The Roosevelt family took trips to find places
more amenable to young "Teddy's" ailments. When he became
a teenager, Teddy decided to conquer his frailty. After traveling
to parts of America and Europe, it was apparent that a simple
change of climate would not cure the adolescent's health problems. Teddy decided to immerse himself in physical activity.

His formula was to do things he was afraid of doing, so he
became a cowboy in the Dakotas. In that campaign to improve
his strength and courage, Teddy at one time or another broke
his wrist, his arm, his nose, his ribs, and his shoulder. After entering Harvard, he took up boxing. Although Teddy was often
"beat to a pulp," he became an adequate fighter and even fought
in a championship match (he lost). In the Spanish-American
War, Teddy was a lieutenant colonel in the "Rough Riders,"
where he became a hero for his exploits at the battle of San
Juan Hill. It was because of his "Rough Rider" image that Roosevelt became a popular military and political figure, and was
elected governor of New York in 1898. He was elected vice
president of the United States in 1900, and after President
McKinley died in 1901, Roosevelt became president.

CONSIDER THIS: Struggle often provides us with our most
productive times of growth. The caterpillar gains strength in its
struggle to tear out of its cocoon. Without the struggle, it does
not have the strength to fly. Can we step back while we are in
the midst of a struggle and see how it will give us strength and
insight for the future?

Ole Evinrude

"Everything that is new or uncommon raises a pleasure in the imagination, because it fills the soul with an agreeable surprise." — Joseph Addison

One hot, lazy August afternoon, Bess Cary, Ole Evinrude, and friends picnicked on an island two miles from shore. The sweltering heat made Bess think about one thing: ice cream. Ole was deeply in love and would do anything for Bess. Jumping into the rowboat, he made it to shore quickly. On the way back, however, the breeze was against him, and the ice cream was melting fast. When Ole finally made it back and he and his friends were drinking the melted ice cream, Ole's mind focused on something else. The big Norwegian had owned a company that made small gasoline engines, but the enterprise had failed. He had also helped Harley and Davidson develop an air-cooled engine. Now, Ole began to consider ways to build a small engine to propel a rowboat.

Bess and Ole were married in 1906, and Ole worked on his project. In 1909 he built his first outboard motor. Bess thought it looked like a coffee grinder, but when Ole took it down to the river, he amazed the deckhands by skimming around the water at five miles per hour. Confident in his design, Ole made a few cosmetic changes, and built engine number two. This time he loaned it to a friend, who promptly ordered ten and paid in cash. Bess and Ole went into business, with Bess handling the correspondence. She analyzed the market and wrote an advertisement that began "DON'T ROW, use the Evinrude Detachable Row Boat Motor." With Ole in the shop, and Bess in the office, the Evinrude outboard motor became a success.

CONSIDER THIS: How often has a product been made that takes away drudgery? That is the kind of machines Americans want.

Sewell's Customers for Life

"Keeping your word is worth more than all the empathy, smiles, and chocolates on your pillow in the world." — Carl Sewell

A customer entering a Sewell automobile dealership may be impressed by the atmosphere of the showroom—antique furniture, fresh flowers, and soothing music. However, it takes more than good looks to entice and keep the car-buying public. Sewell's goal is not only to make a sale, but to create a "Customer for Life." To rise above the crowd, Sewell has developed a reputation for taking care of more details than any other dealership—including keeping promises to fix problems the first time, never exceeding an estimated price, and providing exceptional customer service where "yes" is always the answer. When a customer calls for help, a Sewell employee rushes to the rescue in a specially equipped Suburban—making a key, fixing a flat, providing a jump-start, or providing whatever the customer requires to get back on the road.

Carl Sewell Sr. learned selling from his family's first "dealership," which was actually a livery stable and movie theater. When the Sewell family began selling Model T's, the cars arrived in boxes. The final assembly was done at the dealership, and customers were taught how to drive. Like many other families with successful businesses, the Sewells adopted the motto "Treat people like you want to be treated." It has served them well. Today, Carl Jr.'s relentless and systematic demand for his employees to meet the highest standards in service, sales, and friendliness has made his dealerships among the most successful and emulated in the country.

CONSIDER THIS: Quality is difficult to obtain and it will never develop by chance. Superior service requires a powerful commitment to a systematic plan of constant and long-term improvement.

Pockets of Genius

"Two heads are better than one."
— John Hegwood

Many important advancements and movements throughout history can be traced to groups of individuals who gathered together to form a fellowship in which new ideas and discoveries were melded together to produce a new great idea that changed the world. These groups have been religious (Jesus and the disciples), political (the framers of the Constitution), literary (the British writer's group called the "inklings" that included C. S. Lewis, J. R. R. Tolkien, and others), and scientific (the Manhattan Project).

In the mid-1970s, in an area between San Francisco and San Jose, California, a small group known as the Homebrew Computer Club was organized. The bearded and blue-jeaned members were some of the best computer "hackers" and engineers of the day. Most worked in the emerging high-tech companies in what has come to be known as Silicon Valley. Within the group, secrets of the trade were openly discussed, and fellow members gave advice to anyone who attended their meetings. Notable among the members of the Homebrew Computer Club was Steve Leininger, who went to work for Tandy Radio Shack and developed the TRS-80 Model I computer. Two other Steves also were members of the club. They developed a computer board called the Apple I and showed it to the group. Through encouragement and contacts, Steve Wozniak and Steven Jobs improved their board into a full-fledged microcomputer and dubbed it the Apple II computer.

CONSIDER THIS: Discovery is seldom made in isolation. Progress usually comes after many people have contributed. Who do you have to talk over ideas with to get input, criticism, and encouragement?

Chicken from Pilgrim's

"When you can do the common things of life in an uncommon way you will command the attention of the world." — George Washington Carver

Bo Pilgrim appears on a television advertisement wearing a pilgrim's hat and gives a deadpan description of the wonderful new ways in which chicken can be prepared. Bo and brother Aubrey started "messin' with chickens" in 1946 in their hometown of Pittsburg, Texas. At first they operated a small farm supply store but soon opened a chicken processing plant. After Aubrey died in 1966, Bo incorporated into Pilgrim's Pride. For years Bo stayed in the background, quietly building his company into a major chicken concern. By 1980, it was the twenty-second-largest chicken processor in the nation. Then, in 1982, a new ad campaign began. Bo had developed a way of deboning a chicken from the inside, and the result was a completely boneless chicken.

In the commercial, Bo tells the television audience that the creation of the boneless chicken was a "mind-boggling experience." He ranks the achievement "right up there with marriage and my first bicycle." Bo became a celebrity almost overnight, and he now spends much of his time as a spokesperson for Pilgrim's Pride. He is a favorite speaker at colleges, charity events, and chicken-cooking contests. He even makes appearances with the Famous Chicken at baseball games. Bo's humor belies his business acumen, as evidenced by the fact that his company has grown to become the fifth-largest chicken processor in America. His ads have won several awards, and the bottom line is that people remember his brand name.

CONSIDER THIS: A lot of advertising goes in one ear and out the other. Gimmicks may not be artistic, but getting people to hear you above the noise is all-important.

Marion Laboratories

"Those who apply themselves unswervingly to a task are amply rewarded."
— Ewing M. Kauffman

Ewing M. Kauffman had been described as "too friendly, too eager to accept challenges." This poor Missouri farm boy decided from the start that when he was faced with a task, he had better give it his all. In 1908, at the age of eleven, Ewing was giving his all in every sport when he was struck with a severe illness that left him with a faulty heart valve. The doctor prescribed a year in bed, flat on his back. He could not leave his bed for any reason and could not even sit up. For a year, Ewing did not violate his doctor's orders. However, he did not waste the time. He began devouring books at the rate of 100 per month. He read the entire Bible several times. He not only read adventures such as Tom Sawyer, he also learned about astronomy, mathematics, and medicine. All of the positive input from his reading had a major impact on Ewing's future.

After his recovery, Kauffman finished school and spent two years in junior college. He excelled in the navy and later as a salesman with a Kansas pharmaceutical company. When he began drawing commissions higher than the president's salary, his commission was cut, and Kauffman quit and formed his own business, Marion Laboratories. Kauffman packaged vitamin pills at night and sold them during the day. As he recruited employees, he promised them a bright future for the company. Once Marion passed $100 million in sales, those who went with him reaped huge rewards.

CONSIDER THIS: Use every opportunity to read, study, and learn. Put your knowledge to work for you, and allow those that help you to share in your success.

Ted Turner's Superstation

"Be sure you're right, then go ahead."
— Davy Crockett

Ted Turner created the most sensational television "network" in recent communications history. His opinion of the competition: "The networks produce materialistic, stupid-American, anti-family, anti-government programming; instead of offering information on saving money or family budgeting, they emphasize violence and crime and promote a live-for-today-and-let-the-devil-take-tomorrow attitude." In his own words, Turner desired to promote "uplifting programs, with enough variety to appeal to all members of the family."

If Turner did not have the success to back up those statements, many would have ignored him as a do-gooder or idealist. In reality, he has taken television by storm. It began in 1970 with his purchase of an Atlanta UHF station. In 1976 the station went nationwide as the first "superstation," WTBS. Using the SATCOM satellite, Turner found a way to transmit programming from his then-tiny station via cable systems to the entire nation. He launched the first twenty-four-hour news network, CNN, in 1980. Then he began CNN2 (now Headline News) as CNN's short-format sister service, and in the following years other stations were added to his empire. Turner claims that his success is the result of hard work, enthusiasm, and not becoming discouraged. Against formidable odds, Turner forged ahead, not always winning, but always coming back with new ideas.

CONSIDER THIS: Do you have good ideas, but never take them to fruition? If you believe in your idea, and if you know you are right, then forge ahead with dogged determination to make your idea work.

Merck's Research

"Do few things, but do them well."
— St. Francis of Assisi

Finding a new drug is often like taking your chances on a roll of the dice: you mix up several compounds and see if any of them do anything good. That's how most of the drugs manufactured today got their start. It seems crude, and it is. Under the leadership of CEO John Horan, Merck & Co. decided to do something about the situation. In the early 1980s Merck began looking for effective drugs by pouring millions of dollars into basic research. The research was meant to discover how life worked, and the company believed that if that could be understood, perhaps its scientists would be smarter in formulating drugs. Merck refused to diversify as other drug companies have done. Focusing 100 percent of its energies on the discovery of drugs has had enormous consequences. Research scientists find the corporate atmosphere at Merck to be an academic heaven, where they are permitted to use the latest equipment in their research, publish, confer with colleagues, and participate in creating products that will help the world.

In 1982 a third of Merck's sales were in older, established drugs. By 1987, however, because of new introductions created through Merck's innovative research, old drugs represented less than 10 percent of the company's sales. The new drugs produced as a result of Merck's commitment to research are overpowering the pharmaceutical industry and garnering notice on Wall Street. For its success, Merck has the honor of becoming one of *Fortune* magazine's most admired companies.

CONSIDER THIS: Diversification's lure is to minimize risk. However, diversification can destroy your primary focus. Keep your eyes focused on your main business, and stay away from enticing sidelines that can sap your energy.

Coming Back After Failure

"The only man who never makes a mistake is the man who never does anything."

— Theodore Roosevelt

Many people hide their failures. After one or two failures they may be so ashamed that they will quit trying to do anything difficult. Successful people usually fail, too. They often leave a trail of "could have been successes" on their journey to real success. To some, failure is a stopping point, but for those with the character to persevere, failure represents a chance to gain knowledge that can be applied to their next attempt. Babe Ruth failed many times at home plate, recording more strikeouts than home runs, yet he is remembered as the "Sultan of Swat," one of baseball's greatest batters. The British army suffered a staggering defeat at Dunkirk but went on to win the war. Abraham Lincoln was born to a poor family and started life in a dirt-floor log cabin on the outskirts of pioneer America. He failed in business, was defeated more than once while running for Congress, lost his sweetheart, suffered a nervous breakdown, lost two bids for the Senate, and was defeated in a run for the vice presidency before being elected president of the United States in 1860.

Many people suffer a defeat and then lower their expectations or abandon their dreams. Leaders must help others learn to fail without fear. They must teach by example that it is right and good to dream, seek, fail, and try again. In his book *Bringing Out the Best in People*, Alan Loy McGinnis says, "If leaders can teach people how to handle failure creatively, it may be the most important contribution they can make."

CONSIDER THIS: Don't be disheartened if your life has been riddled with temporary failures. Success favors those who persist.

Edson deCastro of Data General

"Don't be afraid to take a big step when one is indicated." — David Lloyd George

Edson deCastro was an ordinary but bright student in Plainfield, New Jersey, during the 1950s. He graduated from high school, decided on an engineering career, and went to school at the University of Lowell. After graduation and a stint in the National Guard, he went to work for Digital Equipment (DEC), briefly attended the Harvard Business School, and then returned to DEC. At DEC, he participated in the early development of six-bit computers and was instrumental in the development of DEC's popular PDP8 computer. When IBM introduced its System 360 as an eight-bit machine, deCastro believed that computers based on eight-bit multiples would be the future standard. However, after much discussion, DEC decided to stay with the old six-bit standard.

DeCastro saw that decision as an opportunity and left DEC in 1968 to begin Data General. In 1969 Data General introduced a sixteen-bit computer. To establish a particular niche in the highly competitive computer field, the company aggressively marketed its computers to those who needed a small powerful computer at low prices. While other computer companies were marketing service, Data General marketed performance, specifically targeting people who already knew computers and applications well. In the decade from 1968 to 1978, Data General's profit margins were second only to IBM's, and its employee base swelled to more than 10,000.

CONSIDER THIS: Pay attention to changes in technology. New advances often open doors to develop new products and new companies. Jump on the bandwagon early and beat the competition.

McManus's Ten Commandments of Business

"When we do the best that we can, we never know what miracle is wrought in our life, or in the life of another." — Helen Keller

James McManus prepared for business at the University of Wisconsin (B.B.A. '55) and Northwestern (M.B.A. '56) before gaining experience at Procter and Gamble and at Glendinning. In 1971 he started the successful Marketing Corporation of America. MCA analyzes consumer behavior and sells its knowledge and ideas to some of the nation's largest corporations. One such idea was that Ralston Purina distribute, through veterinarians, Puppy Care Kits containing food samples and a pet-care booklet. It proved so successful that Purina was able to start charging the vets for the kits.

In a speech for University of Wisconsin-Madison business alumni, McManus outlined his "ten commandments of business":

1. "With whom you go" is more important than where.
2. Execution is critical, how you do what you do.
3. Pay attention to the product before the profits, or "Make sure the product works."
4. You have to spend money to make money.
5. It is important to plow back some of your profits into research and development.
6. Don't be afraid to fail. That's how you learn.
7. Provide your future employees with an environment that stresses individual accountability and rewards.
8. Share the rewards. Power and profits for the people!
9. Be the best that you can be.
10. Have fun!

CONSIDER THIS: The basics of business are to do your best and to treat other people with respect. Develop your own rules for success and stick to them.

Winchester's Second Effort

"Take calculated risks. That is quite different from being rash." — Gen. George S. Patton

For most orphans born in Boston in 1810, there would be no shining future. However, Oliver Winchester pulled himself out of poverty with hard work. His enthusiasm, honesty, and determination allowed him to work his way into the ownership of a small Baltimore clothing store. Although his store was quite successful, Winchester was not satisfied. He enjoyed the journey toward success too much to be content once he had achieved it. In 1847 Winchester decided to sell his store and move on to more profitable ventures. His ambition took him to New York, where he believed there was a bigger market and more opportunity. Using his expertise in the clothing industry, he patented a new shirtmaking method and made handsome royalties from its use.

Not content with that success, Winchester used the profits from his invention to buy an interest in a rifle manufacturing business. He acquired the patents of Hotchkiss, Browning, and other weapons builders to develop his rifle into a state-of-the-art device. In 1860 Winchester introduced the Henry repeating rifle, which was used extensively during the Civil War and in 1866 was renamed the Winchester. That weapon became the settler's and cowboy's rifle of choice in opening up the American West. Through his firearms company, Winchester finally found the industry that intrigued him enough to satisfy his ambition to succeed.

CONSIDER THIS: Do you have too much energy to be satisfied with just an initial success? Use one success to finance your next adventure, and continue the journey toward your dream.

Howard Corbin's Trousers

*"Thinking is like living and dying. Each of us has
to do it for himself."* — Josiah Royce

At the age of twenty-one, Lt. Howard J. Corbin left the air
force to enroll in New York's Columbia Business School.
Howard had been bombardier/navigator aboard a B-25 during
World War II, flying out of North Africa and Italy. In the service, he got used to his trimly cut officer's uniform. In the civilian market, pants were baggy and, to Corbin, presented a
sloppy appearance. During his college years, Corbin worked
with his brother and father, who operated a small pants factory
in Brooklyn, to design and tailor a line of "natural shoulder"
pants and jackets. The style was soon called the Ivy League
look. Corbin figured that many other ex-GIs would be interested in that kind of look, and by the time Corbin was completing his B.S. degree in 1947, he was producing his line of Ivy
League clothing. He must have been right about what men
wanted, because within a few years, his fashion caught on
throughout the nation.

Corbin's family business developed a reputation that enabled
it to sell its trousers and suits under the labels of the best clothiers in the world. Once the company's reputation was firmly established in men's clothing, Corbin introduced a line of
women's apparel in 1982. Even after Howard Corbin retired, he
continued to help other entrepreneurs find their American
Dream by serving as an executive-in-residence at Columbia
University.

CONSIDER THIS: Trust your own tastes. If they are different
from what the market is promoting, maybe there are others out
there who share your concepts. Can you use this to develop
new ideas for products?

How Kodak Got Its Name

"Man's distinction is his determination to think for himself." — Adm. Hyman G. Rickover

The Eastman Kodak company calls its name one of its most valuable assets. How did the Kodak name come into being? According to George Eastman, the company's founder, he purposely invented the unique name out of thin air. In a 1920s article from *System Magazine*, Eastman is quoted as saying, "I devised the name myself . . . the letter *K* had been a favorite with me. It seemed a strong, incisive sort of letter. . . . It became a question of trying out a number of combinations of letters that made words starting and ending with *K*." The word *Kodak* was devised after a considerable search for a word that would be short, unique, easy to spell, and meet requirements of the trademark law. Eastman wrote, "There is, you know, commercial value in having a peculiar name; it cannot be imitated or counterfeited."

Kodak was first registered as a trademark in 1888. The first Kodak camera sold for $25 and came loaded with film for 100 exposures. Owners would return the entire camera for processing, and for $10 it was filled with a new roll of film. The pictures were of good quality, and the easy-to-use camera brought photography to the masses. Since that time, the Kodak name has served the company well. Because "Kodak" had no meaning of its own, it could only be associated with the company. It was also almost impossible to misspell. Now registered in ninety countries, the Kodak name has become a trademark that is unique and distinctive.

CONSIDER THIS: A unique and distinctive name or symbol helps your company establish recognition. What distinctive traits do people see in you—and remember you by?

With a Name Like Smucker's

*"Small opportunities are often the beginning of
great enterprises."* — Demosthenes

Jerome Smucker was born in 1858. By the late nineteenth century, he and his wife, Ella, had developed a good business, making apple cider in Orrville, Ohio. During the off-season, Smucker transformed his mill and made apple butter for the local farmers, who supplied their own apples. Jerome also made his own apple butter using a recipe developed by his family. Everyone in the family helped in the business. The apple butter was first sold door-to-door for twenty-five cents per half-gallon crock. By 1900, word of the apple butter had spread, and Smucker began selling the crocks to local grocery stores.

The apple butter business became a major part of Smucker's production, and by 1920 the company had added a line of jams and jellies. Smucker's quality quickly became known, and soon the enterprise was the largest independent producer of preserves in the country. Jerome had four children, and one of them, Willard, took over the reins of the company when Jerome died in 1948. Willard's son, Paul, was named CEO in 1970. Under the family leadership, the company continued to prosper. It introduced new ways of shipping fruit in steel drums rather than the older wooden barrels. It also became the first preserves maker to use essence recovery, a technique whereby fruit essence is captured during cooking and then returned before bottling. Although the Smuckers still make apple butter, their most popular products today are strawberry preserves and grape jelly. Today, Smucker's is one of the most recognized names in the jelly industry.

CONSIDER THIS: Keep an eye out for those side opportunities that may turn into a gold mine.

Hewitt Hires Chemistry

"An industrial family should be united in purpose, as well governed, contented, and peaceful, and the members as courteous to one another as a domestic family." — C. W. Post

In 1940 insurance salesman Ted Hewitt began thinking about starting a business. He made precise plans about the business structure, the kinds of people he would hire, and the business principles he would instill in the new company. That basic structure and philosophy defined by its founder still provide the company with direction and identity today. Hewitt Associates, a management consulting firm specializing in employee benefits, has been rated as one of the best 100 companies to work for in America. It has a low (5 percent a year) turnover, and many of the associates become partners.

One secret of Hewitt's success is its hiring practices. Because the firm is very picky, only five applicants in every 100 are offered positions. The process used to choose employees is critical. The company looks for people who are bright, hardworking, and ambitious, but it avoids individuals who are so ambitious that they might try to succeed at the expense of the company. Associates must be team players, possessing the right chemistry to learn to consult within the model used throughout the company. Few titles are used, and the only real promotion is to be made a partner. Even then, everyone is treated the same, from secretaries to senior partners. The bottom line is that Hewitt Associates is one of the top consulting firms in America.

CONSIDER THIS: Each business must take special care in putting together a family of employees who create a fabric of cooperation and support in meeting the corporate goals. Create a family that will help each other reach for their dreams.

Graham at Baxter Travenol

"A reputation for good judgment, for fair dealing,
for truth, and for rectitude, is itself a fortune."
— Henry Ward Beecher

William B. Graham is perhaps the most successful business leader in America. When Graham took over leadership of Baxter Travenol Laboratories in 1953, sales were just over a million dollars. During his years as chief executive officer of Baxter Travenol Laboratories, the medical enterprise's earnings grew cumulatively in excess of 20 percent per year for twenty-five years, a record no other Fortune 500 company can match. What made Graham so wildly successful for such an extended period of time?

Graham believed in risk-taking. For example, in the mid-1950s he gambled with a kidney dialysis machine that had already been a commercial failure for its Dutch inventor, Willem Kolff. Graham saw the machine as a pioneer effort, and it took seven years before the machine really made a significant impact in the medical community. Graham took his risks in limited but promising fields, where the hope for expansion was good. That policy has resulted in a stream of innovative, medically oriented products that have become standards in the healthcare industry throughout the world. Graham's management style has always been open, and his company's employee benefits are among the best in the nation. Graham's blend of high standards, folksy ways, and caring for people have paid dividends to everyone involved.

CONSIDER THIS: High standards and care for the individual employee can exist side by side. In fact, one is essential for the other. High morale always seems to be an antecedent to productivity and innovation.

Quality Is Ewes' Best Advertisement

"Don't do anything haphazardly, don't scratch the surface, don't give a job part-time attention; give it your best." — Clinton Davidson

Progressive Farmer magazine often reports on new ideas from America's heartland. One such story was about entrepreneur Robin Giles. Robin raised sheep in west Texas. However, in the 1980s prices began to decline, and losses mounted to $10 to $15 per head. "I realized that if we were going to continue in the sheep business, we'd have to find a way to make it profitable," Robin recalls. Sitting around one day, Robin and his wife, Carol, devised a plan. They had been selling lamb to friends in the area and thought that others might be interested in their high-quality meat.

The Gileses contacted restaurants, hotels, country clubs, and every potential customer they could think of, but they did not receive the volume of orders that could generate the kind of income they needed. Then, Robin and Carol decided to focus on selling directly to the people they already knew. After the couple let it be known that they wanted to expand their operation, their few customers began singing the praises of the Gileses' fresh cuts of lamb. Over the next few years, Robin and Carol's customer base grew to over 400. The Gileses knew that quality and personal attention was their reason for success. They sold only the highest-rated meat, and they guaranteed everything they sold. "Our customers don't like fat," Robin says. The Gileses' reputation for producing high-quality meat provided another bonus as their breeding stock came into strong demand among other sheep breeders.

CONSIDER THIS: Quality sells products, keeps customers, and is one of the best advertisements for new customers—for small family businesses as well as for large corporations.

George Washington

"The test of the progress of mankind will be their appreciation of the character of Washington."
— Lord Brougham

The ideals of American character and integrity were originally established by the examples set by our Founding Fathers. We have truly become children of their beliefs and the principles they honored. George Washington is perhaps the most eminent example. Even during his lifetime, Washington symbolized the quality of character that Americans look up to today. Daniel Webster said that America owed a considerable debt to the Old World, and that the debt has been paid through the character of Washington: "If our American institutions had done nothing else, that alone would entitle them to respect." Even the fabricated cherry-tree story by Mason Locke Weems—"I can't tell a lie, Pa; I cut it down with my hatchet"—is testament to the respect Washington's integrity commands. There has perhaps never been an American who has been more revered in his lifetime.

Washington was a true living hero. He could have been king. Yet it was the example Washington set as our nation's first president that gave America its respect, stability, and unique flavor of democracy. Henry Lee called Washington "First in war, first in peace, and first in the hearts of his countrymen." Other heroes have used their popularity to benefit their own kingdoms. Washington used his popularity to establish a code of conduct in which the welfare of the people came first. Because of Washington's example, later American leaders have had a superior model to try to match.

CONSIDER THIS: It is important for the leader to set a strong example of character and integrity. No rules or commandments will speak louder than a leader's actions.

Levi Strauss Invents Bluejeans

"Study how to do the most good, and let the pay take care of itself." — Lyman Abbott

In 1853 Levi Strauss was invited by his brother-in-law David Stern to help start a dry goods store in San Francisco during the gold rush. Levi packed goods onto a ship that sailed 17,000 miles from New York to California. During the trip he sold most of his goods to the passengers. In fact, the only item he had left was canvas material used to make tents. Upon his arrival in California, Levi was told, "You shoulda brought pants." All the prospectors were wearing out their pants almost faster than they could dig. Levi immediately went to a tailor and had the man make pants from the remaining canvas in stock. Word spread about the sturdiness of Levi's pants, and his inventory was soon sold out.

Levi then was able to get some heavy cloth from France called "serge de Nimes," which was Americanized to "denim." The original cloth was brown, but Levi dyed it indigo to make the color deep purple. Since the weight of their gold often ripped the prospectors' pockets, Levi began riveting the pockets to the pants to give them added strength. Levi and tailor Jacob Davis patented the innovation in 1873. Levi's business flourished, and he became a wealthy man. Until his death in 1902, Levi Strauss spent much of his wealth helping others, including the California School for the Deaf. He also provided scholarships to the University of California. Because Strauss was a bachelor when he died, he willed a considerable portion of his estate to orphanages and benevolent associations. Today, relatives descended from Strauss's brother-in-law own the apparel company.

CONSIDER THIS: Look at the resources you have and determine what needs you can meet.

Phillip Caldwell at Ford

"It is good to rule and polish our brains against those of others." — Michael DeMontaigne

Phillip Caldwell took over as chief executive officer of Ford Motor Company during a bleak period in 1979. The oil crisis and the growing importation of foreign cars had stunned the American automobile market. Ford's costs were skyrocketing, and its cars were rated "poor" in quality and design. Caldwell remembers that it was tempting to cut all expenses to save what little was left, but adds, "That would have given away our future . . . we didn't even give it serious consideration." Instead, Caldwell and other leaders at Ford went on an unprecedented spending spree, pouring more than $13 billion worldwide into new products, processes, machinery, and equipment, and spending another $9 billion on research and engineering development. Company management agreed that "quality was our primary objective," says Caldwell.

Everyone at Ford seemed to get the message. By 1984, Ford had reduced its operating costs, introduced higher-quality cars, and posted a record profit of $2.9 billion—one of the largest turnarounds in American corporate history. Caldwell gives much credit to Ford's employees, who originated many of the ideas that set the company back on the right course. There was a great change in attitude. Workers felt they were being heard and that their talents were being put to good use. Management and workers alike wanted to produce high-quality products—it was a matter of pride. Caldwell opened the doors of communication, and everyone, from assembly-line personnel to top management, listened to each other. That is what makes business successful.

CONSIDER THIS: Do you make it profitable for employees and management to communicate? Does everyone have the same goal of making your organization the best that it can be?

The Invention of the Telephone

"Attempt the end, and never stand in doubt;
nothing's so hard but search will find it out."
— Robert Herrick

Alexander Graham Bell was the son of a speech teacher from Scotland. In fact, both his father and grandfather made careers of teaching people how to speak correctly and also developed a method for teaching the deaf to speak. Tuberculosis in the family triggered the Bells' move from England to Canada, and an offer to present teaching methods for the deaf in Boston brought young Alexander to the United States. During his study of speech, he read a German article (Alexander could barely read German) and mistakenly thought it said that vowel sounds could be produced by electricity and tuning forks. That misconception led Alexander to begin experimenting with electricity.

At first he tried to develop a multiple telegraph and took out a patent on an invention that never worked. While experimenting, he realized that vibrations made by the voice could be picked up and changed into electrical pulses. His assistant, Thomas Watson, helped in the breakthrough by connecting some vibrating reeds too tightly. When a wire was plucked, Alexander heard the sound emanating from another reed attached to the wire. He realized that something important was happening and studied the situation for several days, making various changes. On March 7, 1876, Alexander was working on the device and spilled some acid on his pants. "Mr. Watson, come here, I want you!" he shouted. Watson, who was in another room, heard the message transmitted over the wire. The apparatus was the first working telephone.

CONSIDER THIS: There is no telling what can be accomplished once you think it is possible.

Tom Landry Learns Football

"Coaching: To get people to do what they don't want to do in order to achieve what they want to achieve." — Tom Landry

In the small town of Mission, Texas, during the Great Depression, a scrappy boy by the name of Tommy Landry began learning about the game of football. There were no organized leagues for kids, so Tommy and his friends would stage their own games on a field near his house. They played thousands of football games, often stopping only when their moms demanded that they come home for supper. Tommy played center and quarterback, coached, and organized the games. But he needed more than a small-town sandlot league to set him on the track to becoming one of America's greatest sports legends. He needed a coach.

When young Tom entered Mission High School, he was fortunate to become a member of Bill Martin's junior-varsity team. Tom thrived on the competition provided by football. The fanaticism of Friday night football in Texas, combined with the increasing success of the Mission team under Coach Martin, ignited a blaze of enthusiasm throughout the entire community. During Mission's 1941 championship season, Tom experienced what he still remembers as his most memorable and sweetest victories. After World War II, Tom become a gridiron star at the University of Texas, then went on to play and coach in the National Football League. His astoundingly successful reign as coach of the Dallas Cowboys from 1960 through 1988, which led to his enshrinement in the Pro Football Hall of Fame, possibly never would have occurred had it not been for the experience he gained under Coach Martin as a youngster in Mission, Texas.

CONSIDER THIS: Raw talent plus effective coaching equals success. Seek and hire the most talented people possible, then train them to be their best.

Jay Leno's Big Break

*"Laffing is the sensation ov Pheeling good all over,
and showing it principally in one spot."*
— Josh Billing

Jay Leno was headed for a career of flipping burgers. He brought home poor grades and was known as the class clown. Even when slicing potatoes into fries at a McDonald's, he earned a reputation as a "cut-up." Jay remembers hating homework until his English teacher, Mrs. Hawkes, encouraged him to write down some of his funny stories as a creative writing assignment. Suddenly, Jay was spending hours writing and rewriting his stories. When he read them in class, he got laughs, and that encouraged him to create more funny stories.

Jay spent plenty of time in detention. Luckily, the overseeing teacher, Mr. Walsh, liked his stories. One day he asked Jay, "Why don't you go into show business?" That was a new concept for Jay—and it was the beginning of a dream. He got his first break as the French Fry Cut-Up in a McDonald's talent show and won $150. While in college, Jay began learning the comedy craft by performing in non-paying, low-paying, and often sleazy joints. After spending years in New England, he decided to try his luck in California. Jay played comedy clubs and began to land small roles on TV sitcoms and in movies. To a comedian, a successful appearance on *The Tonight Show* is the ultimate break. It eluded Jay until one night when Steve Martin dropped by the club where he was performing. Martin liked what he saw and talked to the people at *The Tonight Show*, and Jay got his chance on March 2, 1977. His first *Tonight Show* performance drew big laughs and a "wink" from Johnny Carson, and Jay was on his way to stardom.

CONSIDER THIS: Big breaks come to those whose hard work and talents prepare them for their "moment of judgment."

The Plastics Revolution

"Every addition to true knowledge is an addition to human power." — Horace Mann

Recent technological inventions and discoveries have caused an explosion of businesses and products that are changing our everyday lives. In a similar way, plastics were the technological marvel of a previous era. Although Celluloid, the first plastic, was invented in England around 1850, it was an American who recognized plastic's commercial potential. In 1868 an ivory shortage prompted a New England manufacturer of billiard balls to offer a $10,000 prize for a suitable substitute. John Wesley Hyatt purchased the British patent for Celluloid, presented it as an ivory substitute, and won the prize.

With his winnings, Hyatt not only produced billiard balls, he began to discover other uses for the new material. In 1872 the Celluloid name was trademarked. Some of the first successful Celluloid products were "wipe-clean" shirtfronts, cuffs, collars, and combs. Other uses that followed include dental plates and children's toys. In 1889 Kodak introduced Celluloid photography film, and Thomas Edison used strips of the film to create motion pictures. In 1906 a Belgian-American named Leo Baekeland created, trademarked, and promoted another type of plastic as a rubber substitute named Bakelite. Other polymer-based products appearing in the years following include rayon, polyvinyl chloride (used in plastic pipes), plastic tableware, Plexiglas and Teflon. During World War II, plastics provided a wealth of substitutes for materials that were in short supply. After the war, the research that had begun into new uses of plastics exploded into an industry that is still growing today.

CONSIDER THIS: One invention can lead to the development of an entirely new industry. Keep your eye on the cutting edge—that's where new products and companies are born.

A Little Something Extra

"And if any one forces you to go one mile, go with him two miles." — Jesus Christ

Like the extra day that is tacked onto leap year, we all take notice of a little something extra we get for our money. Everyone is familiar with the prize in Cracker Jacks. But would Cracker Jacks be around today if the company had not thought of that innovative extra? Children will always pick out the cereal that has something extra inside. In a service business, that something extra might be a call-back after a job is finished to see if the customer is satisfied. It is IBM's policy to make call-backs to customers within twenty-four hours. To an employee, the little something extra may be a bonus or recognition for a helpful idea. Encouragement costs nothing, yet many managers hold onto it as if it were gold. In fact, it only becomes gold when it is given away. The same thing can be said of friendliness to a customer.

Many people use the phrase "go the extra mile," which comes from a portion of the Sermon on the Mount in which Jesus tells his followers that if a soldier requires that they carry his equipment for one mile, they should carry it for two. People expect to get what they pay for, and they seldom take notice when they get only that. When someone goes the extra mile in giving the customer more than is required, the customer remembers that good feeling, develops loyalty, and tells others about it. Doing business or serving others is no more complicated than treating people with respect, kindness, and concern for their satisfaction. Go the extra mile in everything you do.

CONSIDER THIS: When someone receives something from you, do they feel that they got their money's worth—and more?

Otis Elevators

*"With ordinary talent and extraordinary
perseverance, all things are attainable."*
— Thomas Buxton

In the mid-1850s elevators were too dangerous to be used for anything but freight. If the rope snapped, a rider would certainly risk life and limb. It was this problem that Elisha G. Otis solved in 1854. Otis had a knack for things mechanical. By age fifteen, he was already an engineer at a bedstead factory. In 1852 Otis was sent to Yonkers to supervise the construction of a new factory, and it was there that he developed several new enhancements to the elevators as they were being designed and installed. Otis' elevators were equipped with a simple spring device that would trigger if the cable broke and prevent the elevator from falling. The invention was patented, and *Scientific American* called the device "excellent." Otis built a similar elevator at another factory, and while he was installing that one, he received a request for another.

Otis was encouraged by the interest in his elevator and formed the E. G. Otis Company in 1853. Then, orders virtually stopped. Companies were simply unwilling to build an elevator for public use. To address this fear, Otis decided to prove his safety device's usefulness by building an elevator and demonstrating it to the crowds at a New York fair. Although he was successful, orders still came slowly. It was not until 1857 that Otis finally built his first elevator specifically for passenger use. Although he died in 1861, Otis's sons took the company into prosperity, and by the turn of the century, Otis elevators were a key element in the appearance of skyscrapers.

CONSIDER THIS: Success may take time, even when you have the right idea. Keep trying. Prove your concept. Stick to your beliefs.

John H. Johnson

"Nothing beats a failure but a try."
— John Johnson's mother

John Johnson stands as an example to persons of all races that people can overcome poverty if they refuse to buckle under to failure. Born into poverty in Arkansas City, Arkansas, Johnson lost his father when he was only six years old. When he reached high school age, there was no school available for African Americans to attend. His mother saved enough money during the depression to send John to school in Chicago, and once there, he became editor of the institution's newspaper and yearbook. He later took a job at an insurance company and was assigned the task of searching newspapers and magazines for stories relevant to the African-American community. That experience convinced John of the need for an African-American publication. His mother allowed him to pawn her furniture to start up the *Negro Digest*. In 1945 John founded *Ebony* magazine, and although it sold well, virtually no one would advertise in the fledgling periodical.

His mother kept telling him, "Failure is not in your vocabulary!" and John continued to diplomatically approach potential advertisers. Before talking to Eugene McDonald, the president of Zenith, John researched McDonald's life fully and discovered that he greatly admired African-American explorer Matthew Henson. McDonald was impressed with John's interest in him and in the way he handled himself. After Zenith agreed to advertise in *Ebony*, other companies followed suit. Today, in addition to owning Johnson Publishing, John Johnson sits on the boards of some of the most influential corporations in America.

CONSIDER THIS: The best way to interest other people in you is to show a genuine interest in them.

Colonel Sanders

*"Genius, that power which dazzles humans, is oft
but perseverance in disguise."* — H. W. Austin

Before beginning his famous franchise, Col. Harland Sanders
worked as a streetcar conductor, a railroad fireman, a justice of
the peace, an insurance salesman, and held other occupations.
In 1930, at the age of forty, he was operating a service station
in Corbin, Kentucky, when he decided to offer food to his customers. At first, he served them right off the dining table in his
living quarters. His food was popular, and he eventually opened
a restaurant across the street from the station. Over a period of
years, Sanders developed the secret combination of eleven
herbs and spices that went into his chicken recipe. But when a
new interstate highway bypassed his town, Sanders sold his
business and began collecting Social Security. That could have
been the end of the story, but the colonel decided that he was
not ready for the retired life.

At the age of sixty-six, Sanders took to the road in an old
station wagon. Every time he saw a restaurant, he stopped,
knocked on the door, and prepared a batch of his special recipe
chicken. Restaurant owners made handshake deals to use the
recipe and pay Sanders a nickel for every chicken they sold.
After the Kentucky Fried Chicken recipe was introduced, most
of the restaurants found that their customers couldn't get
enough of the "finger lickin' good" chicken. Success blossomed
and KFC restaurants were franchised throughout the United
States and around the globe. In a poll taken in the late 1970s,
Colonel Sanders was listed as one of the five most recognized
persons in the entire world.

CONSIDER THIS: It's never too late to begin, but once you
begin, it often takes enthusiasm, perseverance, and patience to
realize success.

Earl Tupper's Party Plan

"The most successful men have used seeming failures as stepping-stones to better things."
— Grenville Kleiser

While he was still in his teens, Earl Tupper began a small business selling fruits and vegetables to his neighbors. He was good at it and learned quickly about the finer points of salesmanship. This was a big asset to Tupper when, years later, he began a new business. That enterprise, started in 1945, was a line of plastic containers that he dubbed Tupperware. At first, Tupper used the conventional method of marketing his products through retail stores. But after five years of mediocre sales, he began to envision a new plan of action. Recalling his earlier days, when he sold produce directly to housewives, Tupper decided to try this same direct approach in selling Tupperware.

It was 1950 when Tupper began selling his plastic containers directly to the people who would use them most. He invited people into homes and demonstrated the product. Sales were good, better than they had been in retail stores, and it was clear that this approach had considerable promise. However, it was also clear that Tupper could not sell enough product by himself, so he arranged for housewives to become Tupperware dealers. They could hold "parties" at friends' houses, and each hostess would receive a gift. The housewives would have a part-time income, while maintaining their freedom to take their children to school and do the other household chores. By 1954, Tupperware had a network of over 9,000 dealers across the United States. Sales eventually spread to Europe, and today Tupperware is found in kitchen cabinets around the world.

CONSIDER THIS: A product alone is not enough. You must devise a plan to sell your product, sometimes with a unique method, to your customers.

Bill Gates

"Only the paranoid survive."
— Intel CEO Andrew Grove

Bill Gates is the Edison and Ford for our times. He became a success not just by being in the right place at the right time, but by being prepared, intelligent, committed, and lucky. As a young student he and Paul Allen, his future partner, began playing around with computers on a clunky teletype terminal and got jobs finding bugs in computer programs. Bill helped write a scheduling program for his school and included instructions that put him into classes with the girls of his choice.

While attending Harvard, Bill became even more committed to computing and saw a technical revolution coming. He and Allen created a BASIC language interpreter for the first wave of microcomputers. However, Bill's company was just one among thousands fighting for a share of the microcomputer market. He hired the brightest minds he could find, and his Microsoft firm competed well and established itself as a "language" company. Microsoft's big break came when IBM was searching for a company to help it write an operating system for the new IBM personal computer. IBM initially went to another company that was already marketing the leading micro-operating system, called C/PM. The other company was reluctant to sign IBM's non-disclosure agreement, so the company continued its search. When IBM approached Microsoft, Bill saw the potential and grabbed the deal. The resulting PC-DOS and MS-DOS operating systems established Microsoft's dominance in the software market and were the foundations for Windows and many other popular application programs.

CONSIDER THIS: If you want to be lucky, be smart and be prepared. Hire the brightest people you can afford, and fight to take advantage of every opportunity.

Practice in the Mind

"Imagination is more important than knowledge."
— Albert Einstein

Concentration is one thing that Americans often seem to lack. We are frequently too busy to think about any one thing for too long. However, research and practical examples have shown that concentration can play a major role in training our minds for success. Air Force Col. George Hall endured five and one-half years as a prisoner of war in North Vietnam. Many of those days were spent in solitary confinement, leaving him with plenty of time for concentration. To pass the time, Colonel Hall "played" a round of golf each day. As he paced back and forth in his small cell, he remembered his best shots and how the ball had landed in just the right spot. Every detail of his imaginary game was real to him, from the Titleist balls to the blue tees that he placed in the grass still wet from the morning dew. The smell of the fresh grass replaced the musty smell of the prison, and for a while, the colonel was having the time of his life.

Day after day, Hall mentally played and replayed every golf course he had ever been on. He climbed up the hills, looked out onto the fairways, and studied the greens. In his imagination, he played a good game of golf. Col. George Hall finally made it back to the United States at the end of the war. One month after his arrival, he played in the New Orleans Open and was paired with touring pro Orville Moody. Hall shot a sizzling round of seventy-six. His years of "practice" had not been in vain.

CONSIDER THIS: We become what we "practice" in our minds. If we imagine failure, it will come. If we imagine success, it will come. Are your thoughts leading you toward your goals?

Anne Sullivan and Helen Keller

"We can do anything we want to do if we stick with it long enough." — Helen Keller

When Helen Keller suffered an illness that made her blind and deaf, she gradually adopted animal instincts in order to survive. That is how teacher Anne Sullivan found Helen when she arrived in Tuscumbia, Alabama, to teach the child. What transpired next was a clear example of tough love, leadership, and discipline. Sullivan literally had to fight Helen and attempted to communicate with her through the sensation of touch, the only real sense the youngster still recognized. Week after week, Anne pressed her hand into Helen's, making symbols with the positions of her fingers against Helen's palm. She was spelling out words, but to Helen, it made no sense. When Helen finally understood the relationship between the word "water" and the patterns pressed on her palm, Helen remembered, "I was caught up in the first joy I had known since my illness."

Anne was tough on her pupil. "As soon as I knew right from wrong," Helen wrote, "she put me to bed whenever I committed a misdeed." The story of Anne and Helen has become an American wonder, as the physically challenged girl eventually grew up to be one of the brightest minds of her time. Helen became a communicator and a symbol of the power that people have to rise above difficult circumstances, but she did not (could not) do it on her own. Anne Sullivan demanded that her pupil learn beyond all expectations and gave her love and fulfillment in return.

CONSIDER THIS: Whom are you teaching and encouraging? How are you making them stretch beyond their expectations? What persons are waiting for you to encourage them into discovering their own genius?

Voit Bounces Back

*"Persistent people begin their success when others
end in failure."* — Edward Eggleston

In a discussion of successful business people, it is rare to find someone who made it big the first time around. It is much more common for success to play hard to get and to come only after one makes several attempts. Many achievers experience several failures and some small successes before attaining lasting success. William Voit is an example of that pattern. Voit worked as a salesman for several rubber companies during the 1910s and early 1920s. In 1924 he decided to start his own operation and began producing camelback, a material that was used in the tire recapping process. Voit expanded his business by introducing an inflatable multicolored rubber ball, which immediately became popular on California beaches. In what could be called a preview of today's state of affairs, his ball was knocked out of the market by cheaper products manufactured in Japan. The stock market crash of 1929 also spelled trouble for Voit's business.

In 1932 Voit developed a plan for a comeback. He introduced a series of rubber athletic balls that were superior to the leather balls that dominated the market. His product line soon included basketballs, footballs, soccer balls, and volleyballs. By the time of William Voit's death in 1946, Voit athletic balls were standard equipment at many American high schools, colleges, and universities. Voit drew on his experience with failure to help him avoid past mistakes and create a lasting success.

CONSIDER THIS: Like a good running back, when one lane is blocked, look for another and plow ahead.

Charles Schwab

"I have yet to find a man, however exalted his station, who did not do better work and put forth greater effort under a spirit of approval, than under a spirit of criticism." — Charles Schwab

Charles Schwab was one of the first persons in history to collect an annual salary of $1 million. How could anyone be worth that much money? The person who paid Schwab that unprecedented salary was none other than industrialist Andrew Carnegie. Although Carnegie had made his fortune in steel manufacturing, he knew little about the steelmaking process. Carnegie possessed the business acumen, but for the daily operation of this plant, he had to rely on the ability of Charles Schwab.

Schwab possessed a talent that is as valuable today as it was many years ago. Anyone with the same talent as Schwab could deserve the same kind of compensation. Schwab himself revealed that his salary was deserved because he had the ability to deal with people effectively. His secret was simple: First, he aroused enthusiasm in people; second, he developed the best in a person through genuine appreciation and encouragement; and third, Schwab never criticized anyone. He was aptly described as being "anxious to praise but loath to find fault." Carnegie appreciated Schwab's secret. On his tombstone, he continued to praise his associates with the inscription, "Here lies one who knew how to get around him men who were cleverer than himself."

CONSIDER THIS: No one works well under the spirit of criticism. However, most people will rise to meet the task if they know their work is genuinely appreciated.

Managerial Freedom Scale

"The successful businessman is training an understudy if he is as wise as he is successful."
— Ray L. Smith

Like most employees, managers want to make their boss happy. They don't want to step out of line but often don't know where that line is drawn. Managers working under a cloud of anxiety will not perform as well as they should. They will often bother their boss with minor details in order to save themselves from doing something wrong. Bosses need to free managers from this complication. William Oncken Jr., author of *Managing Management Time*, created a "management freedom scale" to help managers understand how to make decisions. The five-point scale lists the most common ways in which managers approach the decision-making process:

1. WAIT until being told.
2. ASK what to do.
3. Recommend, then ACT.
4. ACT, but advise at once.
5. ACT on your own, routine reporting only.

Option one should never be allowed. In ordinary situations, managers should not pester their boss by asking what they are supposed to do. Managers are supposed to think for themselves. Managers should be told they must operate under options three, four, or five. This frees the boss from having to make unnecessary decisions and frees the manager to devise methods of leadership that work well with his or her personality.

CONSIDER THIS: If a person does not know what is expected, he cannot effectively make progress in an organization. Tell your employees what you expect of them.

Herman Miller

"The deepest principle in human nature is the craving to be appreciated." — William James

Herman Miller, Inc. produces fine office furniture and systems. Working for a company that makes desks and chairs could be just another job, if it had not been for the death of an employee named Herman Rummelt in 1927. Company founder D. J. DePree went to visit the man's widow and discovered that Rummelt had excelled at handicrafts, with beautiful examples throughout the house. He also was a World War I hero and had written poetry. "I walked away from that house that morning rather shaken up," DePree recalled. "God was dealing with me about this whole thing, the attitude toward working people . . . I had looked on him as a man who was good at fixing machinery and motors." That day, DePree decided that his company would make an effort to consider each employee as a person. He believed that there was a relationship between the way employees were treated and the quality of their work.

As a result of DePree's experience, the direction of his company's management changed. Innovations were instituted, among them the Scanlon Information Meeting, which brought together employees once a month to discuss performance. Today, more than 40 percent of Herman Miller employees own stock in the company, and the firm contributes to a childcare referral service, adoption aid, and productivity bonuses. One of its manufacturing plants is described in the *AIA Journal* as "A Splendid Workplace." Even the bottom line has benefitted, and Herman Miller today is a highly profitable enterprise that maintains its commitment both to its owners and its employees.

CONSIDER THIS: Sincerely care about your workers, and they will care for you.

Adolph's Meat Tenderizer

*"Observation is more than seeing; it is knowing
what you see and comprehending its significance."*
— Charles Gow

Like Ray Kroc with McDonald's and Col. Harland Sanders with his family chicken recipe, there are many good ideas waiting in the wings for the right person to sell the concept in a big way. The next major business success story may well be about that person who keeps his or her eyes (and taste buds) open to the right idea. Adolph Rempp owned steak houses in Los Angeles and Santa Barbara, California, during and after World War II. They were popular restaurants not only for their delicious steak but also for their low prices. Rempp had discovered a way to use an extract of papaya as a meat tenderizer. Using the concoction, he could transform inexpensive cuts of meat into tender steaks that could pass for much higher-priced selections. One evening after the war, two hungry veterans named Larry Deusch and Lloyd Rigler visited one of Rempp's steak houses.

Deusch and Rigler liked the steaks but were curious how such an inexpensive cut of meat could be made to taste so good. They did a little research and found out about the tenderization process used by Rempp. After some persuasion, Deusch and Rigler contracted with Rempp to market the extract to local grocery outlets. The product, named Adolph's Meat Tenderizer and introduced in 1949, proved to be a success in the Los Angeles market and was soon introduced throughout the United States.

CONSIDER THIS: If you find something you like, other people will probably like it as well.

Screaming Eureka

"Science does not know its debt to imagination."
— Ralph Waldo Emerson

Jim Edmonds of Phillips Petroleum remembers the discovery as "a genuine screaming eureka." Edmonds was attempting to devise an inexpensive way to make a "super plastic," something that in 1962 involved a very complicated process. "I wasn't even supposed to be working on it," he recalls. "It was just something I did because I thought the darned thing might work." The result of Edmonds's research was a new product that became the base material for Phillips Petroleum's Ryton business line. There are some common traits among companies that produce breakthrough inventions. First, their employees are typically curious, hard workers, knowledgeable, and lucky. Second, the culture of such organizations supports the quirks of "inventorships."

Inventions are often the result of some tangent to an original objective. The potential inventor may be struck by an idea from something totally off the subject. Often, management may not see a need to pursue a new idea, which leads many inventors to bend or break the rules a bit to do some research on the side. Some progressive companies actually build in funds and time for off-the-wall projects. Once an idea is firmly conceived, it may take some selling, which means the inventor must then become the idea's champion. If management does not squeeze the life out of the inventor, it may find its next billion-dollar product simmering in a test tube from an unsponsored project.

CONSIDER THIS: Progress occurs more often by accident than by direct planning. Are you looking for accidental opportunities?

Reach for the Stars

> *"Give the world the best you have and the best will come back to you."* — Madeleine Bridges

The Leo Burnett agency is one of the world's best-known advertising concerns. Until his death in 1971, founder Leo Burnett inspired his company with his personal motto, "Reach for the Stars." Minimizing the value of advertising awards, Leo concentrated on selling products. After all, what good is advertising if it doesn't sell the product? Thus, the Burnett agency's primary criterion for superior advertising is not awards but sales. To achieve that goal, the firm tries to become an adjunct marketing department for its clients, "holding their hands," meeting with them on a regular basis, and essentially becoming a member of the client's family. After the Burnett agency gets to know its client well, it devises an advertising campaign that will sell products.

Leo was known for being hardheaded, argumentative, and difficult to get along with when he thought a client's ideas were bad. He generally won those arguments, and his clients were the winners at the bank. Leo's results speak for themselves. When United Airlines was suffering from an image as being a big, uncaring company, Leo brought out the "friendly skies" campaign. When Maytag wanted its washing machines to be known as reliable products, the lonely Maytag repairman was the answer. McDonald's "American slice of life" campaign and such familiar "spokespersons" as the Jolly Green Giant, Charlie the Tuna, and the Pillsbury Doughboy are but a sampling of the creative and effective strategies that can result from a thorough knowledge of the client.

CONSIDER THIS: It is not always the awards from peers that make a business great. What really counts is the reason you got into business to begin with.

Wal-Mart Buys American

"There are efforts and there are results. And it is the strength of the effort that usually determines the size of the result." — E. F. Girard

Sam Walton began his retail career as a management trainee for JCPenney. After a tour in the army, he opened a Ben Franklin store. Along with his brother, Sam opened more Ben Franklins until 1962, when he ventured into discount merchandising with his first Wal-Mart store. Sam focused mostly on small towns, and under his powerful leadership, the number of Wal-Mart stores grew quickly. Part of Wal-Mart's image and appeal has been its American character. It is a hometown place, with friendly people and a clean image. In 1985 Sam embarked on an ambitious campaign to buck the trend of buying imported merchandise and to institute a program that would encourage American manufacturers to produce more competitive goods.

To encourage domestic manufacturers, Wal-Mart provided long-term commitments and guaranteed orders to American firms. Calling the rising importation of goods a "threat to our free enterprise system," Wal-Mart's program provided several small companies with orders that allowed them to expand their operations and hire more workers. One shirt manufacturer moved some of its operations from offshore back to the United States to participate in Wal-Mart's program. The campaign not only provided Wal-Mart with quality merchandise, it resulted in a host of positive articles about the retailer in newspapers all over the country.

CONSIDER THIS: Imports will always be with us. The answer to preserving the American system of free enterprise is to meet the challenges with innovation, intelligence, and hard work.

Wynton Marsalis

*"Invest yourself in everything you do. There's fun
in being serious."* — Wynton Marsalis

Most people have a talent, but few are serious enough to develop their talent into excellence. For those who do develop their talent, it is often because someone prepared them and pushed them toward making a commitment. Ellis and Dolores Marsalis were parents determined to prepare their children for success. Since Ellis was a jazz pianist, the children were exposed to music at a very early age. Four of the six Marsalis sons pursued professional musical careers, and all were raised to take education seriously, go to church on Sunday, and join the Boy Scouts.

Although Wynton, the second-eldest, was learning to play the trumpet, he liked to play Little League baseball better. Then, one day as he was listening to his father's albums, he came across the song "Cousin Mary" as played by John Coltrane. The music filled Wynton with wonder and he felt a warm sensation throughout his body. He tried to play the melody himself but couldn't come close. He went to his mother and told her that he "couldn't fool around with baseball anymore." Wynton had found the love of his life and dedicated himself to becoming the best trumpet player his talent would allow. He studied under the best musicians, played in jazz bands, and attended prestigious music schools. His first album sold 100,000 copies, and in 1983 Wynton won Grammy Awards for both a jazz and a classical album. Today, Wynton carries the message of excellence to students, encouraging them to set high goals and to work hard to reach them.

CONSIDER THIS: Talent alone will not give you success. You must dedicate yourself to excellence, work hard, study the masters, and set your sights high.

Hallmark Cards

*"Every day is a new day, with new possibilities
and unlimited opportunity."* — Ernest Reeves

Ask people in and around Kansas City, Missouri, what is special about their community, and one of the things they probably will mention is Hallmark Cards. Few companies have such warmth associated with them as does Hallmark. Greeting cards as we know them began to appear some 150 years ago, when the Penny Postage Act of 1840 put the cost of mailing letters within reach of almost everyone. Hallmark got its start when eighteen-year-old Joyce Clyde Hall came to Kansas City in 1910. He and his brothers had owned a small gift store in Nebraska, and Hall came to Kansas City seeking a better market. His brother Rollie soon joined him, and the store was known as Hall Brothers, Inc.

Joyce carried postcards in his store and soon recognized the beginnings of the greeting card industry. Hall Brothers, which became Hallmark in 1954, now has the largest art department in the world. Its creative staff of over 600 people produces more that 10 million greeting cards each year. Joyce led the company until 1966, when his son Donald became president. Under their leadership, Hallmark has carefully manufactured high-quality greeting cards designed and produced by some of America's top artists, writers, and printers. It can take up to 3,000 people and 300 controlled steps to produce and market each card design, and 18,000 different designs are produced each year. The Hall family has created a company that is proud to be known as one of the best 100 companies to work for in America.

CONSIDER THIS: Do you see the beginning of an infant industry in your midst? If not, look. If so, how are you going to take advantage of it?

Jack Welch at GE

"There is an infinite potential for savings. The human mind is always able to find a better way to do things." — Jack Welch

When Jack Welch became General Electric's youngest chairman at age forty-five in 1981, he took charge of a company that had been one of America's largest and most successful. Welch's view of the future had no room for the status quo, however. He saw rapid worldwide technological change, slower economic growth, and intense global competition for available business. If GE was to survive, massive changes were needed. Welch's strategy called for each of the company's key businesses to be number one or two in market share, and for the company to increase its participation in fast-growing service and technology businesses. Businesses that couldn't be leaders in their field were sold, while those that could be leaders received billions of dollars in investments and complementary acquisitions.

To increase agility, Welch removed an entire level of management between the company's diverse businesses and the headquarters staff. Though the move saved $40 million, GE's chief executive officer says the real payoff was "the sudden release of talent and energy that poured out after all the dampers, valves, and baffles had been removed." Over several years, Welch made GE 100,000 workers slimmer than the company he took charge of in 1981. The results have been impressive. Welch has been able to continually grow this "mature" company at an impressive rate. "Maturity is a state of mind," says Welch. If a company wants to act young and competitive, it can do so when its leadership maintains an energetic and innovative a state of mind.

CONSIDER THIS: How can you prevent a giant from getting fat to begin with? If your organization is fat and lethargic, then you need to give it some innovative medicine.

The Beliefs of Borg-Warner

"A man should have the courage and conviction to do what is right, and what is for the interest of his principles, no matter whether he represents a corporation or an individual."

— Philip Armour

Many times the "beliefs" of a company are promotional hype developed by a marketing agency to put the best face (and often a false face) on the enterprise. Other companies really do operate from a set of beliefs that guides corporate decisions. In 1981 James Bere, chairman of Borg-Warner, began a process that involved more than 100 managers in an effort to define the basic business principles that governed the corporation. The results are summarized in five major statements:

1. Dignity of the individual: Each person is unique and has pride, needs, values, and innate personal worth.
2. Responsibility of the common good: To create superior good, to provide meaningful jobs, to honor life, and to improve the world.
3. The endless quest for excellence: To continue to improve and to surpass that which has already been achieved.
4. Continuous renewal: Adapt to change, discard that which is no longer true, and seek vision for the future.
5. The commonwealth of the company and the people: To maintain freedom while building strength, recognizing the need for faith in political, economic and spiritual heritage; pride in work; and the conviction that power is strongest when shared.

CONSIDER THIS: Beliefs are the foundation of any great movement. But beliefs are a hollow nothing unless they are backed up by a strong commitment to make them work.

Pete Musser and Safeguard

"Diligence is the matter of good fortune."
— Miguel de Cervantes

Safeguard Business System manufactures a rather mundane product, a folding double check-writing system for small businesses that sells for about $150 each. Safeguard Chairman Warren (Pete) Musser saw the product as a hard way to make much money. When Musser entered the business world in 1954, he wanted to be involved in something glamorous, like the cable television business. He started such a firm but lacked the cash to make it successful. In 1963 he launched a small business that made check-writing machines. As an add-on, the company offered the small folding notebook. While this business plodded along, Musser heard Wall Street's call to diversify and went on a buying spree that took the company into auto parts and marketing.

When the economy turned sour, most of the new businesses Musser had acquired began drowning in red ink. It was only after several years of trying to prop up his empire that Musser again focused his attention on the folding notebook, whose sales were supporting everything else. Safeguard distributors who sold the notebook system were independent contractors, and by offering them all the repeat business on any sales as long as they remained distributors, Musser's company was able to build a substantial sales force. Once a critical mass of customers was using the check-writing system, it became well known to accountants and banks, who presold many customers. Musser's slow, mundane business was much like the fabled tortoise who plodded along slowly but surely until he had defeated the hare.

CONSIDER THIS: Is it glamour you are looking for, or a business that can bring in a good, steady profit?

Chrysler's Decision

"Be true to your highest conviction."
— William Ellery Channing

Walter Percy Chrysler was born in 1875 in Wamego, Kansas. His father was an engineer with the Union Pacific Railroad, and young Walter took an interest in the big machines. He became an apprentice machinist and traveled the railroads, building a reputation as an extraordinary mechanic. An auto enthusiast as well, Walter bought a 1908 Locomobile for $5,000, even though he was only making $4,200 as a machinist with the Chicago and Great Western Railroad. He fell in love with the automobile and was soon offered the opportunity to become works manager for Buick. The railroad offered him $12,000 a year to stay with them, but Chrysler took a $6,000 salary with the automaker.

At Buick, Chrysler introduced a series of innovations and within a few years was made president of the division. Soon, however, his ideas clashed with those of GM President W. C. Durant, and Chrysler resigned. In 1921, he was offered the position of president at the ailing Willys Overland Company and the Maxwell Motor Company. While Chrysler got those companies on their feet, he was designing a new automobile with innovations the industry had never seen. In 1924 he introduced the Chrysler, and it wasn't long before even the company bore the name of Walter Chrysler. Chrysler soon acquired Dodge Brothers and began the Plymouth and DeSoto lines. By the time he retired in 1935, Walter Chrysler's company was the second-largest producer of automobiles in America.

CONSIDER THIS: Salary should not be the only factor to consider when looking for a job. Choose work that provides the best long-term advantage for your desired career.

Walter Wheeler at Pitney-Bowes

"Six essential qualities that are the key to success: sincerity, personal integrity, humility, courtesy, wisdom, charity." — Dr. William Menninger

Many historians find Walter Wheeler to be a study in contrasts. He admittedly was a hard-nosed executive who was determined to promote his company, yet he instituted some of the most farsighted programs to benefit employees and the public of any company during his era. Wheeler was educated at Harvard and came to work at Pitney-Bowes when that company made a stamp-canceling machine. By age twenty-seven, he was taking a leadership role in the company and in 1920 spearheaded the project to convince the government that a postage meter was a good idea. When the machine was approved, seven other manufacturers were also given the right to produce a machine. However, because of the efficiency of its workforce, Pitney-Bowes became the low-cost producer and claimed the majority of the market.

One of the reasons the company's workforce was so productive were annual jobholder meetings that brought some 250 workers face to face with the president and top executives to discuss labor and management issues. This strong emphasis on worker-management communication provided Pitney-Bowes's employees with some of the best working conditions and benefits packages in the nation and provided company management with a highly motivated workforce. Walter Wheeler devoted fifty-five years of his life to Pitney-Bowes, and it was his strong belief that making the company responsive to human needs made it one of the most profitable businesses in its industry.

CONSIDER THIS: Human needs count. In the long run, a company can't generate exceptional profits without the enthusiastic support of its workers.

Fritos Corn Chips

"The only way to get anywhere is to start from where you are." — William Lee

Charles Doolin owned an ice cream business in San Antonio, Texas, but during the depression, a price war erupted and he was unable to make a profit. Doolin looked around for other products to make and discarded countless ideas as unfeasible. One idea he discarded was the possibility of making some new product out of the Mexican tortilla, because they went stale too quickly. Doolin also took notice of the popular potato chip snack, but dismissed that idea since he wanted something unique. Then, one day while buying lunch, he saw and purchased a bag of a new corn chips snack called Fritos.

Doolin liked the new snack and tracked down the manufacturer—a native Mexican who offered to sell his entire operation for $100 so he could move back to Mexico. Doolin couldn't afford the price and had to borrow part of the money from his mother. She helped him set up the production machinery in her own kitchen and, using a crude converted potato ricer, they were soon turning out ten pounds of Fritos an hour. As word of the product spread, sales rose to as much as $10 per day. To meet the demand, Doolin developed a new, more efficient method of production. Eager to expand his successful operation, Doolin went on numerous sales trips. On some of those trips, he took a temporary job as a cook in the cities he was visiting, since he couldn't afford to pay himself a salary. The company grew slowly at first and then faster after the end of World War II. By the 1950s, Fritos was a household name and one of the nation's most popular snack foods.

CONSIDER THIS: Consider carefully what you might add as a new product. Discard those that aren't sufficiently promising, and dedicate yourself fully when you find a potential star.

Hugh Downs

"When you're afraid, keep your mind on what you have to do. And if you have been thoroughly prepared, you will not be afraid."

— Dale Carnegie

Watching Hugh Downs on television, one would figure that the longtime host of the *Today Show, Concentration,* and *20/20* has it all together. Not necessarily so. Hugh's climb to stardom was part courage, part luck, and (surely) part talent. As a youngster, he was not naturally outgoing and shunned social activities and sports. He decided to become an artist, but at age thirteen Hugh discovered that other people saw colors and he was 90 percent color blind. He would have to find another interest. Hugh was intrigued by the family radio and listened for hours while other children were outside playing. After high school, he won a speaking contest and a scholarship to college. But after one year, the Great Depression forced him to return home.

Jobs were scarce, but Downs wanted to help his family. One day as he was walking home, carrying a gallon of milk, he stopped by the offices of WLOK radio and asked for a job as an announcer. The station manager liked his voice and offered him the job! That break soon led the young Downs to Chicago as an announcer for NBC, and then to national fame. Downs remembers being quite scared of the microphone and the camera in his early days. His solution to the problem: "Go out and scare yourself." Downs forced himself to face his fear of speaking and, as a result, became one of the most polished and relaxed television personalities on the air.

CONSIDER THIS: Fear can prevent us from making the best use of our talents. We must face fear head-on and put ourselves into situations in which we can overcome it.

Napoleon Hill

*"If we abide by the principles taught by the Bible,
our country will go on prospering."*
— Daniel Webster

Virtually every salesman has read (and probably reread) Napoleon Hill's classic motivational book *Think and Grow Rich*. This book has become the basis for many other self-help and motivational books. Its message is simple, and people who follow it are sure to see results. Hill's primary emphasis is on your personal belief in who you are and what you can accomplish. The messages are simple but profound: Don't quit too soon. Follow your dreams. If other people think it is impossible, it must be worth doing. There is no such thing as bad luck. Belief makes a person both poor and rich—take your choice.

These simple messages provide a strong foundation on which individuals may anchor their lives. Many of the people profiled in the book you are now reading have adopted simple yet profound principles such as those found in Hill's book or in the Bible, or espoused by such inspirational leaders such as Lincoln, Washington, and Emerson. Beliefs built on these principles can muster hope when depression overwhelms. Without a foundation of belief, most people succumb to the inevitable failures in life. Something must be there to hold a person up when things go wrong. Like the pig who built his house of bricks, those who have built their beliefs on something solid will survive the big bad wolves of defeat, failure, and rejection. A person who has a weak character foundation will find it difficult, if not impossible, to build one under himself while the rest of his world is falling down.

CONSIDER THIS: What is your foundation? When things go wrong, where will you turn? What will you do? Where will you go? Make sure you are preparing now for tough times to come.

Being a Millionaire

"It is no use to wait for your ship to come in unless you have sent one out." — Belgian proverb

Amazing as it may seem, there are over a million millionaires in the United States today. The wide-eyed dream of children, and the more serious dream of college graduates, is to be a member of that elite club—even if a million dollars isn't what it used to be. Surveys and opinion polls of young Americans today show that becoming well off is often a major life goal. Even with its high-sounding mystique, millionaire status no longer requires that a person be a corporate magnate or a Hollywood idol. Today's millionaires own the local dry-cleaning establishment or make automobile antennas in a small factory. According to studies, most millionaires made their money "the old-fashioned way"—they lived below their income and saved the rest of their money.

According to professor Thomas Stanley of Georgia State University, 80 percent of all millionaires today are self-made. The average millionaire works about twelve hours a day and runs an ordinary business but usually gives it a new twist. Dave Drum took advantage of the camping craze and began Kampgrounds of America. Valerie Freeman, a former teacher of business administration, founded the Wordtemps temporary personnel service. Jimmy Verttos, the son of a Greek immigrant, rented a fruit stand that he eventually parlayed into a large food store. These people took ordinary ideas, worked hard at making them successful, and turned their hard work into hard-earned dollars.

CONSIDER THIS: Prosperity is still usually based on how hard and how long you are willing to work.

Rita Moreno

"A smooth sea never made a good sailor."
— Oren Arnold

Rita Moreno was born Rosa Alverio in a small town in Puerto Rico. After her parents divorced, she moved with her mother to New York, where they lived in a tenement in the Washington Heights section of Manhattan. Rosa took dancing lessons and was soon able to supplement the family's income by performing. She often imitated popular entertainer Carmen Miranda at parties, bar mitzvahs, and weddings. Rosa seemed to be a natural at performing and landed parts in various children's plays and then in the Broadway production of *Skydrift*, which lasted only seven performances. By the mid-1940s, Rosa had changed her name to Rita Moreno, taking the last name of her stepfather, and was dubbing the voices of Elizabeth Taylor and other stars for films being prepared for distribution in Spanish-speaking countries.

Rita broke into the movies at MGM with *So Young, So Bad*. Other films followed, but she was stereotyped as the sultry Latin temptress. Seeing her career going nowhere drove Rita into depression. Finally, a story in *Life* magazine brought her back into the public spotlight, and she was finally given some fresh roles. Rita was able to fight off the bad times, and with her career revitalized, captured the four most important entertainment awards in America—an Oscar, a Tony, a Grammy, and two Emmys—a feat that landed her in the *Guinness Book of World Records*.

CONSIDER THIS: Sometimes the awards go to those who can stick it out through the bad times and who can do their best when the good times come along.

Armstrong World Industries, Inc.

"I attribute my success to always requiring myself to do my level best, if only driving a tack straight." — Russell Conwell

In 1860 Thomas Armstrong worked for a Pittsburgh glass company, but he ran a small business on the side that made cork stoppers for bottles. Armstrong's slogan for that company was a twist on the motto "Let the buyer beware." His more positive slogan was "Let the buyer have faith." He expanded his business by using the cork remnants as an ingredient for linoleum, which at the time was a commodity with virtually no known brand names. Armstrong felt he could produce a superior product and introduced a brand of linoleum under the Armstrong name.

In 1917 Armstrong began a campaign of informative ads in the *Saturday Evening Post* that offered the reader helpful ideas as well as information about his product. Although some of his associates thought the ads were too non-commercial, they proved to be effective and were popular with readers. The ads developed for the Armstrong name a strong sense of quality and also helped build strong product loyalty. The Armstrong name became so associated with floor coverings that in 1960, when a survey about carpeting was conducted, Armstrong ranked fourth in consumer preference, even though the company had never, up to that point, produced carpets. Today, Armstrong offers a wide variety of floor coverings, building products, furniture, and specialty products.

CONSIDER THIS: The company name and its association with quality are an important part of developing sales and product loyalty.

Kellogg's Cereals

"Advertising is to business what steam is to machinery, the great propelling power."

— Thomas Macaulay

Will Kellogg never finished high school, but he went to Dallas in 1879 and worked as a broom salesman, helping to turn an ailing business around. He later returned to Battle Creek, Michigan, and worked with his brother John at the family-owned health sanitarium. There, he and John developed a wheat flakes breakfast cereal. The idea was sound, and the Battle Creek entrepreneurs produced forty-two brands of the flakes. John refused to allow Will to spend much money on the project, and the market became dominated by producers such as Charles Post. Will saw the marketing possibilities of several products developed at the sanitarium. In 1905 Charles Balin, a patient, offered Will the financing to begin his own company to produce a new idea, corn flakes.

Production began modestly at about thirty-three cases of cereal a day. Then Will began to advertise. He placed an ad that encouraged people to convince their grocer to buy a case of the corn flakes, offering boxes of the cereal to the person who secured such a sale. The plan worked, and by 1909, the company was selling over a million cases of corn flakes a year. Kellogg sensed the value of advertising and spent over $2 million in 1911 to promote his products. During the depression, Kellogg doubled his advertising budget, and sales continued to grow. Today, Kellogg's is one of leading breakfast-cereal brands in the world.

CONSIDER THIS: When others are afraid to advertise, that is a prime time for you to gain market share through new advertising.

Marshall Field

"Follow the river and you will get to the sea."

— Unknown

Marshall Field was born in 1834 in Conway, Massachusetts. As a teenager, Marshall became a clerk in a dry goods store in Pittsfield but left at the age of twenty-two to go west. Landing in Chicago in 1856, Marshall found a job as a clerk and saved his money by sleeping in the store. His first year's salary amounted to $400, of which he saved $200. Within five years, he was general manager of Cooley, Farwell and Company, and later became a partner. By 1867, Marshall was the major partner and head of the business. In 1881, with the other partners in retirement, the company became Marshall Field and Company. The firm sustained severe losses in the Chicago fire of 1871, the Panic of 1873, and another fire in 1877, but it continued making a profit.

Field adopted the successful merchandising methods of Stewart in New York and Wanamaker in Philadelphia. Prices were clearly marked for each item. Field sold quality goods and built a reputation on honesty and "the golden rule." He was also adept at finding and hiring managers with excellent capabilities. Field bought goods around the world and often paid cash in order to underbid other stores. Until his death in 1907, Marshall Field used considerable sums of his money to fund buildings for schools, the Columbian Museum at the Chicago World's Fair (now the Field Museum), and a library in his hometown.

CONSIDER THIS: Find out what works for others and use the same idea, perhaps improving on it with your own touch and hard work.

Knox Gelatin

"Let us endeavor to live, so that when we die, even the undertaker will be sorry." — Mark Twain

Rose Markward married Charles Knox in 1893. The couple bought a small gelatin business in Johnstown, New York, and Rose tested gelatin recipes in her kitchen at home. The ambitious couple also acquired several other businesses, including a newspaper, a hardware store, and even a power company. However, when Charles died, Rose sold all of the companies except the gelatin business. She was very interested in finding new ways of using gelatin, and she set up an experimental kitchen in which to conduct research. Rose's enthusiasm to make something from gelatin showed as the company's profit line tripled from 1908 to 1925, with sales topping the $1 million mark.

Besides being involved in the business operation, Rose became active in the Johnstown community. She founded the Federation of Women's Clubs for Civic Improvement and in 1949 was named America's Foremost Woman Industrialist by *Collier's* magazine. Rose continued as president of the company until she was ninety years old. She died in 1950 at age ninety-three. Rose Knox was a determined soul who took the business she loved and devoted all her energy to making it a success. In a 1937 interview in *Time*, she stated, "I just used common sense—a man would call it horse sense—in running my business. But from the first, I determined to run it in what I called a woman's way."

CONSIDER THIS: Your business, career, or job is an extension of your personality. In order to achieve success, your personality and occupation must meld together like a team.

Eddie Bauer

*"Ideas must work through the brains and arms
of good and brave men, or they are no better
than dreams."*   — Emerson

Eddie Bauer was an experienced hunter and fisherman, but one fishing trip almost cost him his life. It was in 1928 and his partner had gone to the car while Eddie stayed to pack 100 pounds of fish. A sudden cold front came through, and Eddie found himself becoming sleepy and disoriented. His partner saved him, but the experience gave Eddie an idea. His family had emigrated from Russia, and he remembered stories of Russian soldiers who wore down-filled jackets to survive the freezing temperatures of Manchuria during the Russo-Japanese war of 1904. Eddie designed a down jacket for himself and began making a few for his hunter friends. The idea was so successful that Eddie patented it.

When World War II arrived, Eddie contracted with the United States government to make goose-down-insulated sleeping bags, flight suits, and high-altitude bags. Thinking of his future, Eddie made sure that his name was on each item he made. After the war, his products had instant recognition to thousands of former servicemen. The end of the war brought an end to Eddie's war contracts and almost meant the end of his business. But Eddie survived by developing mail-order sales. Offering a "100 percent, unconditional, money-back, lifetime satisfaction guarantee," Eddie Bauer was considered a friend by nearly every outdoor sportsman who ever used his quality products.

CONSIDER THIS: Opportunity may get you started, but you will have to keep finding new opportunities to replace the old ones that pass.

Success Is Hard Work

*A young man was walking down the streets of
New York when he stopped a lady and asked,
"How do I get to Carnegie Hall?" The woman
answered, "Practice, practice, practice."*

— Anonymous

What makes one person successful while another can make only modest gains? Often we see only the successful person's innate talents as the answer. We often think that if someone is not blessed with talent, there is no amount of hard work that can make a difference. However, studies have shown that this is not correct; there is more to success than talent. In fact, the reason for most success is often good old-fashioned hard work. In his book *Developing Talent in Your Children*, Benjamin Bloom reported the results of a five-year study that was undertaken to discover what made some people extraordinary successful. The study consisted of detailed research into the lives of 120 of the nation's top artists, athletes, and scholars.

Bloom was surprised to find that natural abilities played only a small part in the development of those individuals. As children, they were often mediocre musicians, baseball players, or math students, but Bloom found that they possessed a powerful drive to succeed. They practiced the piano hours every day, rose at 5:30 every morning to swim, or spent hours alone working on science projects. Parental support was also a key factor. The parents of the successful individuals had exposed their children to great ideas and influential persons, and many had made sacrifices to ensure that their offspring received necessary training.

CONSIDER THIS: Opportunity for success often comes as the result of hard work. Are you preparing yourself for opportunity?

Ziegfeld Follies

"Curtain! Fast music! Lights! Ready for the last finale! Great! The show looks good . . ."
— Florenz Ziegfeld's dying words

Florenz Ziegfeld thrilled Broadway audiences for more than twenty-five years with his spectacular shows and extravagant Ziegfeld Girls. He was called the "Glorifier of the American Girl," and under Ziegfeld's direction, hundreds of ordinary showgirls were transformed into dazzling stars of the stage. Every starlet of the day wanted to be a part of the renowned Ziegfeld Follies.

What made those dancers different from so many others? What made them perform better than dancers in other stage productions? Ziegfeld made his performers feel special. He paid his showgirls up to five times the going rate, and all were given the best and most glamorous costumes to wear. Even the linings of their dresses were made of the finest silk. Many times after a performance, the showgirls would receive a telegram of congratulations or a large bouquet of American Beauty roses. Ziegfeld believed that for his performers to be beautiful, they must feel beautiful. His enthusiasm and excitement spilled over to the players in his shows. His obsession with extravagance thrilled audiences for decades and made the Ziegfeld Follies the most remembered shows of the era. Even on his death bed, Florenz Ziegfeld was busily planning his next big event.

CONSIDER THIS: People try hard to perform at the level that is expected of them, when they know their performance is appreciated. Are your standards high? Do you let people know that you think they are very, very special?

Role Models

"A man is no greater than his dream, his ideal, his hope, and his plan."   — Doctor Fern

Whether we are aware of it or not, the character we have developed in our own life is a copy of other people's behavior. We learn how to live life by observing other people. Our own actions are a synthesis of what we have learned by watching the actions of others. If we do not consciously select our role models, we will have little control over who we become. But our character will still be fashioned from our perception of others. If we choose our models carefully, we can be master of our life's potential. Role models can have a tremendous influence on our life. During childhood, our role models are generally our parents or siblings. Later, we develop other interests and may adopt role models that are associated with our desired profession. Role models give us insight into how others have overcome failures and how they persisted in pursuing their goals.

In *The Scientific Study of Political Leadership*, G. D. Paige examines how many of the most noted leaders of our time modeled themselves after other great leaders. Mao Tse-tung constantly read about Washington, Napoleon, Catherine of Russia, Peter the Great, Gladstone, Lincoln, and others. Woodrow Wilson wrote a biography of Washington. John F. Kennedy wrote of those he admired in *Profiles in Courage*. Napoleon read and reread Plutarch's *Parallel Lives*, and Winston Churchill researched the life of his ancestor Malborough.

CONSIDER THIS: Purposefully select your role models. Read biographies of people you admire. This can give you the self-confidence that you can achieve your goals.

Small Wins Can Mean Big Success

"For every disciplined effort there is a multiple reward."
— Jim Pohn

Sometimes we expect our American Dream to come true in the form of a million-dollar lottery win or an unexpected inheritance. But if we wait for that big event to occur, it is likely that we will never see our ship come in. Success generally arrives after a series of small steps, or "wins," says Tom Peters in *Organizational Dynamics*. It is only on rare occasions that success comes suddenly and unexpectedly. Success usually comes one step at a time, and some of those steps can be so small that they may not be readily evident. NASA's goal to put a man on the moon by 1969 did not happen as the result of a single space shot. It was the culmination of countless thousands of small advances in space technology, many failures, and a series of successes.

Wins come from spending a lot of time working toward a goal and persisting when others would give up. Participation by other people is usually necessary, and you must reward those individuals with appreciation and recognition. Many times success only comes after a tremendous number of attempts, so you must try many options. When an idea doesn't work out well, learn from the error and try another path. You must be a positive spokesman for the task, explaining progress to those participating so they will know something important is being accomplished. Each element may be small, but small wins are what lead to a big finish.

CONSIDER THIS: Expect good things to take time. Because the best tends to take time, many people give up too soon. Keep going and make those little steps of progress toward your goals.

Steven Spielberg

"To him that is determined it remains only to act."
— Italian proverb

What and how we think has a lot to do with how much we can accomplish. If we believe we will succeed, our chances of success are great. If we cannot see ourselves as being successful, we will likely never experience our dreams. William James was a noted American psychologist. He wanted to discover the human factors that gave certain people the ability to succeed. One of the principles that James uncovered was the "As if" technique. Using "As if" means to act as if that which you desire is already in hand.

By the time he was thirteen years old, Steven Spielberg knew he wanted to be a movie director. When he was seventeen, he visited Universal Studios as a tourist. It was too much for him. He sneaked away from the tour and into the sound stage where a real movie was being made. Finding the head of the editorial department, young Steven talked to him about making films. The next day, Steven put on a suit, borrowed his father's briefcase, and walked onto the studio lot as if he belonged. He found an abandoned trailer and painted "Steven Spielberg, Director" on the door. He spent his summer "working" on the lot and learning everything he could about the movie-making business. In time, Spielberg became a studio regular, produced a short film, and was eventually offered a seven-year contract. Today, he is one of the world's most renowned film directors.

CONSIDER THIS: Know what you want to be. Dream your goals. Learn everything you can about what you want to become. Associate with those who can take you where you want to go. Step out with confidence and begin working.

American by Choice

"Be honest, work hard, and don't be afraid to take a chance." — Sam Ziady's father

America has long benefitted from the energy and ideas brought by immigrant dreamers with pioneering spirits and can-do attitudes. One such dreamer was Sam Ziady from Beirut, Lebanon. In 1950, when he was nineteen, Sam's father gave him enough money to begin studies at South Carolina's Columbia Bible College. To continue his studies, Sam sold Bibles and dictionaries door-to-door during the summer. As he worked his way though college and then a master's program at the University of South Carolina, he expanded his business by hiring other students. When Chase Manhattan offered Sam an executive position, he was on the verge of realizing his dream of a banking career.

"Why do you want to work for Chase Manhattan Bank for $7,200?" asked his father when Sam returned to Beirut for a visit. "Security," said Sam. "How much did you make last summer with your door-to-door business?" asked his father. "Seventeen thousand dollars," said Sam. "Why do you need security? You have a master's degree, you are young, and you speak three languages," said his father, who encouraged Sam to expand his success in book selling. Sam took his father's advice, returned to America, and started the National Book Company. When he became a U.S. citizen, he changed his name to Sam Moore. His book business grew, and in 1968 Sam bought the American division of Thomas Nelson Publishers, one of the world's oldest publishing companies. His biography is called *American By Choice* because, he says, "Only in America would a Lebanese immigrant have the opportunity to become one of the nation's leading publishers."

CONSIDER THIS: You are what you are by choice. To achieve success, you must choose your dreams carefully and work smart and hard to bring them to fruition.

William Danforth at Purina

*"When we do the best that we can, we never know
what miracle is wrought in our life, or in the life
of another."* — Helen Keller

William H. Danforth was such a sickly child that a teacher once dared him to become "the healthiest boy in the class." Danforth responded by daring himself not only to become physically fit, but also to excel in all areas of his life. He graduated from Washington University in 1892 and got a seasonal job in the brick business. Observing that "animals must eat year-round," he and a partner began selling formula feeds for animals. Instead of packaging his feeds in plain bags like his competitors, Danforth recognized the value of a distinctive trademark. He based the distinctive red-and-white checkerboard pattern that became synonymous with his Purina company on a family in his hometown that had always dressed in checkered clothing.

Danforth devoted much of his life to the development of young people. He organized the American Youth Foundation in 1924 for the purpose of training young people in Christian leadership principles. His book, *I Dare You*, has gone through thirty printings and has been used to inspire both youngsters and business executives to lead balanced physical, mental, social, and religious lives. Danforth and his wife established the Danforth Foundation in 1927 as a national educational philanthropy. Although he died in 1955, the message of the man who led Purina for sixty years remains relevant today: "Aspire nobly, adventure daringly, serve humbly."

CONSIDER THIS: What we get out of life has everything to do with how we respond to the call upon ourselves to be the best that we can be, while helping others to become the best that they can be.

Jolt Cola

"To be a success in business, be daring, be first, be different."   — Henry Marchant

Some people make their living looking for trends and then following them. Others see the same trends and realize that there may be a niche available for something a little different. C. J. Rapp was a beverage distributor in New York when he noticed that "every day they were taking something out of soft drinks." Companies were advertising their products as "sugar free," "no caffeine," "low salt," "no-this," and "no-that." Rapp saw the opportunity to bring back a full-bodied soft drink reminiscent of "the good old days."

Rapp quit his job, raised $100,000, and introduced Jolt Cola, which contained all the sugar and twice the caffeine of regular colas. His lightning-bolt logo and posters featuring wide-eyed Jolt drinkers took the soft-drink industry by surprise. Jolt began receiving media attention, which was essential to make the product stand out from Coca-Cola, Pepsi, and other soft drinks that were spending millions of dollars on advertising. Stories about Jolt appeared in magazine after magazine. The beverage even made the cover of a popular computer-programmer's magazine and may be destined to become the cola of preference for those late-night hackers who need something to keep them awake. Following its debut in New York, Jolt Cola was soon available in several eastern states and was then marketed throughout the country. After the element of surprise had worn off, Rapp found that people actually liked his drink, and he is confident that his product has found a lasting niche in the soft-drink market.

CONSIDER THIS: If everyone is looking one way, maybe it's worth looking the other way to see what is being left behind.

Ella Fitzgerald

"Buried seeds may grow but buried talents never."
— Roger Babson

Ella Fitzgerald was born in 1918 in Newport News, Virginia. Her parents died when she was very young, and she eventually attended school in an orphanage in Yonkers, New York. Ella loved to sing and dance, and thought she was pretty good. At the age of fifteen, Ella decided to put her talent to the test and entered an amateur contest at Harlem's Apollo Theater. At first, she wanted to enter both the singing and dancing contests, but she was too nervous to dance and decided that singing would have to be enough. That proved to be the case as jazz drummer Chick Webb heard Ella perform and hired her on the spot.

Ella's natural talent was polished during the time she spent as a vocalist with Webb's band. Together they wrote the hit song "A Tisket A Tasket," based on the old nursery rhyme. Ella's melodious rendition of the song vaulted her to stardom. When Chick Webb died the following year, Ella took over the dance orchestra and became its soloist. Her initial hit recording was followed by many others, among them such classics as "Into Each Life Some Rain Must Fall" and "He's My Guy." Ella's friendly demeanor and upbeat style won the hearts of millions, and she became known as America's "First Lady of Song." The little orphan who decided to take a chance has sold more than 25 million records and is recognized around the world not only for her distinctive musical style but as a product spokesperson.

CONSIDER THIS: Many people have talent but are too nervous or too self-conscious to let that talent come to the forefront. Talent in the hands of a master can be shaped into a gift for the entire world, if we will take the first step to use what we have.

Ueberroth Responds to the Cause

"People can do, but don't do, without motives to keep going."
— David Laird

Peter Ueberroth had a massive job ahead of him. The XXIII Olympic Games were to be held during an era of terrorism, skyrocketing budgets, and boycotts. To Ueberroth, it was precisely those problems that made the plan for the Los Angeles games even more exciting. In a *Time* magazine article, Robert Ajemian wrote that Ueberroth "has a way of turning whatever he touches into a cause. To be involved in difficult problems with difficult goals lifts him up." To sell his Olympic cause, Ueberroth inspired his workers again and again with stories of climbing up "a majestic mountain."

When one employee asked for a raise, Ueberroth (a volunteer himself) responded, "You shouldn't be working here if you don't understand what we are trying to do." He was saying, "Either buy into this great idea or get out." Great causes have no place for slackers. By motivating and inspiring the entire team of Olympic workers, Ueberroth managed to pull off the Los Angeles Games with little disruption and in the unheard-of financial position with money left over. People responded to the impossible. Ueberroth motivated them with encouragement, helping them visualize in their minds the great thing they were about to accomplish. Everyone wants to be a part of the team that wins, and Ueberroth inspired his team all the way to the gold medal.

CONSIDER THIS: It is no secret, people from the beginning of time have given themselves, even their lives, for a cause when the leader could articulate a great purpose and inspire the soul.

Elmer Andersen of H. B. Fuller

"All of us encounter, at least once in our life,
some individual who utters words that make us
think forever." — Benjamin Disraeli

When Elmer Andersen took over the H. B. Fuller company, it was on the verge of selling out to its competitor. Although it had survived for fifty years in the adhesive business, the company had only a small portion of the market, and its leadership was getting old and tired. Andersen was a thirty-three-year-old sales manager when he took the helm at H. B. Fuller. He had a dream that the company one day would be great, and toward that end, Andersen instituted broad incentive plans for salesmen, executives, and employees. Fifty years later, H. B. Fuller was a Fortune 500 company with over $425 million in sales.

One visionary leader had pulled the company from smallness to greatness. On the occasion of H. B. Fuller's 100th anniversary, Andersen reflected on the influences in his life. He recalled his Christian parents, who had died when he was just fourteen but had instilled in him the joy of work. He also recalled a grade school teacher who taught him to keep his mind open because "some day an even greater truth may come." Andersen also cited another instructor who had introduced him to the Robert Browning quotation "A man's reach should exceed his grasp or what is heaven for." These and other influences led Anderson to develop H. B. Fuller into a business whose goals were "to do as well as it could in providing services to its customers and to share the fruits of its rewards with its employees."

CONSIDER THIS: A leader must care about people, must have vision, and must desire to share with others the gifts of insight.

APRIL 13   **Enthusiasm Makes the Difference**

"A man can succeed at almost anything for which he has unlimited enthusiasm."

— Charles Schwab

Enthusiasm is rarely taught as a course in college or included in an MBA curriculum. Yet most businesspeople will agree that enthusiasm is a critical factor in the success of most enterprises. Why it escapes discussion in the classroom is probably a function of our culture. Since it cannot be accurately measured, enthusiasm is not a good topic for scientific research. Cynics see enthusiasm as something that only motivational speakers preach to make money. Yet, biographies of people who have made a difference in the world almost unanimously reveal a single-mindedness, a determination, and an enthusiasm to make an idea work.

In his book *Enthusiasm Makes the Difference*, Norman Vincent Peale tells of the Scottish physicist who helped make worldwide broadcasting possible and won a Nobel Prize. The secret of the physicist's amazing achievement? According to Peale, "It was enthusiasm. I rate enthusiasm even above professional skill." Without enthusiasm, one would hardly be motivated to endure the endless toil and self-discipline that is required to make something great happen. Enthusiasm is a powerful force that keeps people moving toward their goal.

CONSIDER THIS: Business is more than the figures printed in a financial statement or technological advances. Business depends on some factors that escape measurement—an underlying flow of enthusiasm that makes everything come together and work.

Clarence Birdseye

*"Take time to deliberate, but when the time for
action arrives, stop thinking and go in."*
— Andrew Jackson

Clarence Birdseye was sure he would make something of himself. He was the son of a New York Supreme Court judge and the grandson of a successful inventor. However, by the age of forty, Clarence had not yet managed to find a successful career. In 1923 he began evaluating his talents and knowledge in the hope of discovering something he could do well. The idea he settled on was inspired by a practice he had seen some ten years earlier in Labrador. The Eskimos there placed their freshly caught fish on the sub-zero snow and froze them instantly. Months later, when the fish were cooked, they still tasted fresh.

Birdseye did some extensive research and discovered that the reason the Eskimos' fish tasted fresh after lengthy storage was that they had been frozen so quickly. He consulted nutritionists and was told, "You've got a great idea." Birdseye worked on a technique to freeze fish quickly and by 1924 had perfected a device called a "belt froster." He received preliminary financial backing and built a freezer forty feet long. The enterprise he formed became known as General Foods Company. Although the quick-freezing idea had considerable merit and made sense for long-term food storage, Clarence Birdseye spent many years experimenting with various marketing approaches before frozen foods became commonplace in grocery stores.

CONSIDER THIS: Have you ever stopped to think what ideas you have had in the past may be worth a second look?

Silly Putty

*"He that waits upon fortune is never sure of
a dinner."* — Benjamin Franklin

Japan's invasion of rubber-producing countries at the beginning of World War II cut off the world's supply of natural rubber. America responded with research as companies began working to create synthetic rubber. One promising idea involved the "rubberization" of silicon. It was felt that, since silicon is derived from sand, rubber made from silicon would be cheap and abundant. Researchers experimented with a number of compounds in their quest to produce synthetic rubber. One of those experiments involved combining mineral oil with boric oxide. The result was a "bouncing putty," which became a hit among scientists. Its fame circled the globe as a number of researchers tried to find a good use for the material; however, it primarily became an unusual conversation piece at cocktail parties.

In 1949 the bouncing putty appeared at a party attended by catalog toy retailer Ruth Falgatter. Ruth showed the new plaything to her catalog designer, Peter Hodgson, who put it in Falgatter's next catalog on the same page as a spaghetti-making machine. The bouncing putty outsold everything in the catalog except Crayola crayons. When Falgatter decided not to include the new toy in her next catalog, Hodgson took it as his own product. He named it "Silly Putty," copyrighted the name, packed it in colorful plastic eggs, and slowly convinced retailers to carry it. When an article about Silly Putty appeared in a New York magazine, it became an overnight sensation. Within three days of the article's appearance, Hodgson received orders for over 750,000 Silly Putty eggs.

CONSIDER THIS: Keep your eyes open. Find a popular new product and make it your own. Market it with enthusiasm until it catches on. Then, be prepared for success.

Oprah Winfrey

"I have been driven many times to my knees by the overwhelming conviction that I had nowhere else to go." — Abraham Lincoln

Oprah Winfrey's experiences as a child may account for her compassion for those in need and for her sensitive understanding of life's struggles. Born in a small Mississippi town in 1954, Oprah found little stability in her early homelife. She moved back and forth between separated parents and her grandmother, and eventually rebelled against life. However, even in the midst of uncertainty, Oprah found strength in faith, education, and the performing arts. While still in high school, she was hired by a local radio station to read the news. As a sophomore at Tennessee State University, she was picked as a reporter for a local television station. From there, Oprah became co-anchor of a news program in Baltimore and in 1984 was given a chance to revive a dying half-hour talk show called *A.M. Chicago*. Her emotional and honest style soon made the show a hit, and when its ratings surpassed the popular *Donahue Show*, it was renamed *The Oprah Winfrey Show* and expanded to one hour.

In 1985 Oprah appeared in the film *The Color Purple*, was nominated for an Academy Award, and was well on her way to stardom. Even with all her success, she remembers her spiritual roots. Her grandmother taught Oprah the importance of Bible study and prayer, and those lessons continue to be important in her life today. True to the message of the Bible, Oprah Winfrey shares her wealth with others, speaks up for those who are downtrodden, and challenges those who continue to live in bigotry.

CONSIDER THIS: Even when your beginnings are rough, you will do well to look forward to the future and to leave the troubles of the past behind.

Frederick Weyerhaeuser

"Necessity is the mother of invention."   — Plato

The life of Frederick Weyerhaeuser is an example of how American Dreams can come true. Immigrants from Germany, Weyerhaeuser's family had heard of the opportunities in America and had left the village that had been the ancestral home for 300 years. Arriving in Pennsylvania at age eighteen, Frederick found work as a brewer's assistant, a farmhand, and then as a laborer at a sawmill. He was a good worker and was rewarded. "My wages were raised from time to time," he recalled later. "The secret of this lay simply in my readiness to work. I never counted the hours or knocked off until I had finished what I had in hand." Within a few years Frederick joined with his brother-in-law to run his own sawmill in Rock Island, Illinois.

During a severe economic depression, Weyerhaeuser had to resort to barter, trading lumber for eggs, meat, and grain, and then trading the food to men bringing logs down the river. At that time, northern Wisconsin and Minnesota were covered with forests, and the trees were being discarded as people cleared the land. Weyerhaeuser had the foresight to see that the timber was not worthless and that other parts of the country would soon need it for their growing cities. He bought all of the timberland he could afford, taking on lumbermen as partners. Weyerhaeuser gained the confidence and respect of many in the lumber trade. He spoke the language of the lumberjacks, was known for his honesty in business, and made decisions with "intelligent courage." Weyerhaeuser became the wealthiest American of his time.

CONSIDER THIS: What resource are people overlooking that will someday be worth much more than it is worth today?

Ken Cooper's Aerobics

*"Exercise is the chief source of improvement in
our faculties."* — Hugh Blair

During his thirteen years of service in the United States
Air Force, Dr. Kenneth Cooper developed a method for keeping score of aerobic exercise and published the book *Aerobics* in
1968. Cooper's book and his evangelistic promotion of aerobics
were major contributors to the emergence of the jogging
boom. As a result of the increased emphasis on exercise
throughout the country, Americans experienced a 14 percent
reduction in heart disease during the 1970s. Cooper's message
has been carried around the world. "Have you done your
Cooper today?" is a frequently asked question in Brazil, and
around the globe in Japan, a new 750-acre Cooper's Aerobic
Center has been constructed.

Aerobics has caught on because it saves lives and helps
people manage stress. With the cost of health care soaring,
wellness programs save businesses money and also save employees' lives. While the drudgery of work has vanished for
many people, the mental stresses of modern life can exact a
heavy toll on the body. Exercise relieves stress, helps to eliminate depression, and builds stamina. By now, it should be apparent to everyone that jogging and exercise are not simply
fads. They have become a familiar part of many people's daily
routines, particularly those who want to make the best of their
lives.

CONSIDER THIS: What good is it to become wealthy, successful, or famous when you cannot enjoy life because of depression, or if you die early because of poor health? Good
health must be a high priority in your life.

John F. Queeny and Monsanto

*"Determination and gumption will carry a
man far."*   — E. F. Girard

John F. Queeny worked hard to see his dreams pay off. After the Chicago fire of 1871, Queeny dropped out of the sixth grade to earn money for his family. He got a job as an office boy in a pharmaceutical firm and slowly worked his way up to buyer. In 1896 he married Olga Mendez Monsanto and moved to St. Louis to become a buyer for Meyer Brothers Drug Company. Queeny saved his money and in 1899 opened a sulfur refinery on the side. It promptly burned down, costing him $6,000. It took Queeny two more years to save $1,500 in hopes of beginning a chemical shop. As a drug buyer, he was aware of the growing popularity of saccharin, which was purchased from Germany. Needing $5,000 to launch his enterprise, Queeny convinced a saccharine buyer to loan him $3,500 and give him a contract to purchase a five-year supply of saccharin.

In 1901 Queeny opened his new company, naming it Monsanto. Since chemists were hard to come by, especially those who knew how to make saccharin, Queeny imported three Ph.D. chemists from Switzerland. Due to a tight budget, most of the factory was outfitted with used equipment. It was a month before the first small batch of saccharin was made, and when Queeny tasted it, and it was not sweet. Something was wrong! However, he had promised a victory dinner, and when Queeny arrived at the restaurant, the waiter tasted the substance. "This is so sweet!" he exclaimed. Realizing that their taste buds had been deadened by constant exposure to the saccharin dust, Queeny and his chemists leapt to their feet and did a victory dance around the table.

CONSIDER THIS: What you want may not come out right the first time. Those who make it are those who keep trying.

The Phillips 66 Name

"Attention is the stuff that memory is made of, and memory is accumulated genius." — J. R. Lowell

Most companies want to have a catchy name and a trademark people will notice. However, some trademarks come about in strange ways. Take Phillips 66, for example. Over the years, Phillips Petroleum has been deluged with inquiries about its choice of "66." Some believed that one of the company's founders was sixty-six years old (he was really forty-four). Another fable alleges that co-founders Frank and L. E. Phillips had just $66 in their pockets when they first struck oil. One lady even protested that the "66" referred to the number of books in the Bible, which in her opinion was "bad taste commercialism."

With all of the erroneous stories floating around, surely there must be a logical reason the company chose "66." The truth is that Phillips *was* seeking a trademark for its first gasoline, which was to go on sale November 19, 1927. Like all businesses, the company wanted something catchy and descriptive, something that would arouse curiosity. Some of the scientists suggested "66" because that was the specific gravity of the new fuel. However, this was rejected since future gasolines might have different specific gravities. Then someone mentioned that Phillips' first refinery was located on Highway 66. But that seemed to limit the gasoline to a regional area. On the evening of the meeting to select a trademark, a Phillips official hurrying to arrive on time exclaimed to the driver of his speeding vehicle, "This car goes like sixty on our new gas!" "Sixty, nothing," answered the driver, "we're doing sixty-six!" "Where did this happen?" he was asked at the meeting. "On Highway 66." That settled it. The trademark became "Phillips 66."

CONSIDER THIS: If you're looking for a catchy phrase, see what catches on.

Bette Nesmith's Liquid Paper

"Adopt the pace of nature; her secret is patience."
— Emerson

Bette Nesmith, like many other secretaries in 1951, had a problem. When she made a mistake at the typewriter, it was difficult to erase. She had been a free-lance artist, and it occurred to her that artists never erase, they simply paint over any mistakes. With that in mind, Bette tested a variety of concoctions in her kitchen until she devised a paint-like substance that she initially called "Mistake Out." Bette convinced the secretaries around her to begin using it, and an office supply dealer encouraged her to manufacture the paint. She was willing to do so and tried to find partners or someone else to provide financing, but everyone turned the idea down. Finally, Bette decided she would have to produce the paint on her own.

At first, she hired a college student to help sell the product, but the first year's sales amounted to only $1,142.71 and Bette's expenses were $1,217.35. As a single parent, Bette found it hard to juggle her new enterprise and a full-time secretarial position, so she took a part-time job in order to spend more time promoting her paint. She hired a chemist to develop a faster-drying formula and soon took the improved product on the road, demonstrating it to office supply dealers throughout the United States. After giving her sales presentation, Bette would leave behind twelve sample bottles. Eventually, her hard work paid off, and orders began to increase. The Liquid Paper Corporation continued to grow and was sold in 1979 for $47.5 million.

CONSIDER THIS: Even if an idea is good, it still may take the evangelism of a fanatic and the patience of Job before it will finally catch on.

Leaders as Learners

*"Successful men, in all callings, never stop
acquiring specialized knowledge related to their
major purpose, business, or profession."*
— Napoleon Hill

In the book *Leaders*, authors Warren Bennis and Burt Nanus report on a comprehensive study of ninety American leaders. When they were asked to identify the qualities of leadership, the leaders never mentioned charisma, time management, or the way they dressed. What they frequently mentioned were persistence, continual learning, taking risks, and being consistent, committed, and challenged. Some leaders were avid book readers. Most learned from the people around them, the people who worked for them, and most importantly, their customers or clients. They all believed it was important to grow mentally, to be open to new ideas, and to explore new areas of thought.

With such a vast amount of information available in America today, acquiring knowledge, in the words of one leader, is much like "taking a sip of water from a fire hose." It is important for leaders to be selective in the knowledge they acquire. They must learn to filter out useless information while paying attention to the things that really matter, such as information that would prove valuable to their own organizations. Leaders acknowledge their own uncertainty about questions so they can be addressed. They examine failure to learn from it. They look at the future to see how it will affect them. Most importantly, they nurture their interpersonal skills so that they will be good listeners, for without listening, they would never learn.

CONSIDER THIS: What new areas of thought are you exploring? What is your source of learning? Are your interpersonal skills such that you can learn from those around you?

Neiman-Marcus

"There is never a good sale for Neiman-Marcus unless it's a good buy for the customer."

— Stanley Marcus

From the minute its doors opened in September 1907, Neiman-Marcus was a different kind of store. Herman Marcus, along with Carrie and Al Neiman, had a vision for a unique kind of specialty store. At a time when most fine dresses had to be purchased in New York or Paris, a few companies were beginning to produce "ready-made" clothes. Neiman and Marcus saw the emerging boom and based their store on a select line of women's ready-made "outerwear." Early ads proclaimed: "We have . . . garments that stand alone as to character and fit," "We will be known as a store of Quality and Superior Value," and "We shall be hypercritical in our selections."

Their desire to satisfy customers spawned numerous stories of "golden rule" service that have become part of the Neiman-Marcus legend. For example, employees are encouraged to tell customers when a purchase is not becoming or appropriate. They are encouraged to satisfy even the most unusual customer request—such as one from a man who wanted two ducklings delivered to his nephew before Easter. Or, the customer whose wife and child were coming through Dallas during World War II and needed housing and transportation. Or, the customer in New York who wanted to be taken directly to the fashion houses in order to select an appropriate dress. Why do it? When people experience Neiman-Marcus service, they become loyal customers. When they tell their friends, their friends become new customers . . . and so the company grows.

CONSIDER THIS: Give your constituents more than they expect, then they will become loyal customers and walking advertisements for your business.

Desktop Publishing

"What is required is sight and insight. Then you might add one more: excite." — Robert Frost

Few entrepreneurs have the wherewithal to start companies that could compete with firms the size of Boeing or General Motors. However, there are times when new technologies open markets that can be captured by the company ready to fill the void. Such was the case with the computing industry in the late 1970s and early 1980s. Apple Computers grew from a small garage workshop to compete with IBM, while fledgling companies such as Microsoft provided innovative software that drove the new industry. One potentially lucrative new market made possible by advances in personal computing was desktop publishing, a term coined by Aldus Corporation's Paul Brainerd. Desktop publishing enables the operator of a personal computer, using special software, to create sophisticated layouts that formerly could be produced only by expensive publishing equipment.

Aldus was formed by former employees of Atex, Inc., a manufacturer of publishing systems for newspapers. Brainerd and four other executives saw an opportunity to create a publishing system that would work with microcomputers. In order to form an alliance with a major computer maker, they convinced the people at Apple Computers that desktop publishing would be viable. When Apple introduced its Macintosh personal computer, a capability that set it apart from other computers was Aldus's desktop publishing software, called PageMaker. Since almost every business had a need for brochures, newsletters, pamphlets, and reports, the market was ripe. Aldus sold over 50,000 copies of PageMaker in it first eighteen months of production.

CONSIDER THIS: What innovations in technology are opening up possibilities for new products? How can you capitalize on these product possibilities?

Disneyland

*"The idea of Disneyland is a simple one. It will be
a place for people to find happiness and fun."*
— Walt Disney

Walt Disney began thinking of creating his own park when he took his young daughters to local amusement parks. He would sit on a bench and watch his girls ride the carousel round and round. Other parents and grandparents did the same, but they didn't seem to be enjoying themselves. The parks were dirty and run by workers with cigarettes hanging out of their mouths. Disney thought, what if a park were clean and fun for children, parents, and grandparents alike?

Originally, Disney considered opening a small Mickey Mouse Park at the Disney Studios. The more he thought about it, the more his dream grew, but he lacked financing. Then, when Disney was given the opportunity to create his own television show, he had a brilliant idea. "That's how we'll finance the park!" he declared. Disney convinced ABC to become a key investor in his park and used the TV show to promote it. Every Sunday, America watched Disney's dream grow. Known as Disneyland, the park started as an orange grove and became a wonderland. It was clear that Disneyland would be different from all other parks. Buildings were planned with exquisite detail. Rides were unique, imaginative, and entertaining. Disney carefully orchestrated every aspect of the visitor's experience, from hand-clapping music to patriotic shows and flower-filled gardens. Disney's dream continues today, and his parks are admired throughout the world.

CONSIDER THIS: Even an idea that has been around for hundreds of years can be improved. Develop your dream to its fullest potential, and you will stand alone at the top.

John Wooden

"You don't make your character in a crisis, you exhibit it." — Oren Arnold

John Wooden was the basketball coach at UCLA for twenty-seven years. He never had a losing season. Wooden's teams won seven consecutive national championships, and UCLA posted an eighty-eight-game winning streak that spanned four seasons. Surprisingly, he never talked to his players about winning. Wooden's formula for success was to emphasize constant improvement and performance. He avoided getting his teams "up," because he knew that would eventually bring a valley. Instead, he was never satisfied with past performances; they could always be improved. Improvement meant rigorous preparation toward new goals. "I believe that failure to prepare is preparing to fail," Wooden told his players. But the coach never prepared his teams to play a particular opponent; he prepared his teams to play anyone, at any time.

Wooden preached that success was not outscoring the opponent, it was being able to hold your chin up after the game and know that you have given your best effort. Of course, if you have done your best, the score will usually be to your liking, when you are deserving. Wooden was more concerned about his players' character than ability. A person with good character will respond to adversity by learning and overcoming. Wooden believed that good players will be honest, consistent, and work together as a team, and if those players also have ability, they will become true champions.

CONSIDER THIS: Should winning, or profits, be an ultimate goal? Or are they the expected by-product of doing something better than anyone else? Which concept will produce the most long-term success?

**Procter and Gamble's
Ivory Soap**

"Opportunities are seldom labeled."

— John Shedd

Procter and Gamble's founders thought that their original products—candles and twenty-four kinds of soap—were good enough. Harley Procter, son of one of the founders and head of marketing, was anxious to promote a white soap to counter European castile soaps. James Gamble, son of the other founder, had developed such a soap, but it was designated only as White Soap. One Sunday, Harley listened as the minister read from the Forty-fifth Psalm: "All thy garments smell of myrrh, and aloes, and cassia, out of ivory palaces, whereby they have made me glad." The next day, he designated the soap "Ivory." Harley could not get approval for advertising funds, but he proceeded to gather materials that could be used to promote the soap.

Chemical analyses compared the European soap to Ivory. While some soaps contained fillers, Ivory was found to be 99 and 44/100 percent pure. Also, Harley received a letter from a retailer who asked for more of the "soap that floats." After checking, it was found that an error in a stirring machine had caused the white soap to have an additional mixture of air. Since the customer liked the idea, Procter and Gamble adjusted the production of Ivory so it would float. When the company finally approve advertising funds, Harley included those two features in the promotion of Ivory soap. While other soaps claimed to be "pure," Ivory's 99 and 44/100 percent statistic seemed to be more official and set it apart from its competitors. Advertising for Ivory has kept this original image for over 100 years.

CONSIDER THIS: If your product has some unique or memorable feature, point it out, play it up in your advertising. That's the kind of thing people remember.

Price Clubs

"At a great bargain, make a pause."
— Unknown

Sol Price practiced law for seventeen years before launching the FedMart Corporation, a successful "one-stop" mass merchandise and supermarket chain. A West German retailer purchased the company, fired Sol, and promptly went broke. Calling it a low point in his life, Sol began envisioning a warehouse-like store that would cater to small businesses. He raised $2.5 million and opened the first warehouse in a former airplane parts factory in San Diego. The first year Sol lost $750,000 on $16 million sales. To broaden his customer base, he began selling memberships to government employees, credit union members, bank employees, and the like. Originally, each wholesale member had to pay a $25 fee and could designate two other "buyers" for $10 each. The warehouse added more "retail" items, from appliances to fresh baked goods.

Once the concept caught on, news about the operation was spread by word of mouth. Prices generally run about 8 percent above cost, whereas regular retail stores have a 30 percent to 50 percent markup. Sol Price claims the secret of his success is simple: "We sell things as cheaply as we can." Stores are in non-prime locations, and no credit cards are taken. Price says that selective membership and the membership fees help to reduce shoplifting and bad checks. Even the stores' hours of operation are limited to save labor costs. The entire company makes an effort to set the appropriate mood, as corporate offices are Spartan and the annual report is plain, with no pictures.

CONSIDER THIS: Even in discounting, the secret to success is having people who care about providing top-quality service and merchandise, and making sure that customers get what they want.

Winnebago

*"A habit of labor in the people is as essential to the
health and rigor of their minds and bodies as it is
conducive to the welfare of the state."*
— Alexander Hamilton

As modern technology reduced the number of workers
needed to run a farm, the citizens of Forest City, Iowa, watched
in dismay as the town's young people began moving to the big
city to find employment. To counteract the trend, the chamber
of commerce decided to develop a new industry for the town.
One of those playing an active part was John K. Hanson, a
prominent local businessman. With John's help, and interest in
travel trailers, a factory was set up to manufacture the then-pop-
ular "Aljo" trailer. The company was successful and provided the
jobs the community wanted. When a managerial shakeup led to
the start-up of a second trailer manufacturer in town, the first
company cut production and threatened to close.

With the community's investment in danger, and with the
end of the Aljo agreement, Hanson and a committee of local
leaders agreed to manage the new factory for a year. Knowing
that the new company (eventually named Winnebago Inc.)
needed credibility, Hanson began applying his knowledge of
the furniture business to help the factory build better and
lighter trailers. He also took an active role in the national trailer
manufacturers' organizations. Drawing on his automobile
dealer experience, Hanson organized dealer shows and promotions, and offered such incentives to trailer buyers as free delivery anywhere in the U.S. By the end of the 1960s, Winnebago
was established as a premier trailer manufacturer.

CONSIDER THIS: Community needs can be a catalyst for the
capitalization of a new industry. By helping to entice or launch
an industry, everyone can benefit.

Jantzen Swimwear

*"To know is nothing at all, to imagine
is everything."*   — Anatole France

John and Roy Zehntbauer started a small knitting company in Portland, Oregon, in 1910 and soon invited their friend Carl Jantzen to join them. While tinkering with the knitting machinery, Jantzen developed a rib-stitching idea that produced a fabric with excellent stretching qualities. Originally considered for use in sweaters, it was used to produce a pair of trunks for a friend who was a member of the Portland Rowing Club. The rower returned to report that the trunks were the best-fitting he had ever worn, and he ordered a full suit for swimming. The swimming suit was also well received, but it was too heavy when wet. Zehntbauer and Jantzen experimented and soon developed a fabric that provided the proper comfort and lightness.

In 1916 the company introduced its bathing suit. To promote the item in the firm's 1920 Line List Catalogue, a drawing was made of a diving girl in a red suit. When people came asking for the picture and young men began putting it on their car windows, Zehntbauer and Jantzen decided to capitalize on the popular symbol. Renaming their company Jantzen Knitting Mills, they promoted the now famous diving girl in their advertising. With their bathing suits becoming more popular, the manufacturers abandoned their other knit lines. By 1922, they stopped using the term "bathing" suits, and in 1924 promoted the slogan, "The suit that changed bathing to swimming." From these beginnings, the founders went on to build Jantzen into one of the nation's most innovative and successful swimwear companies.

CONSIDER THIS: Even a good product needs a promotional idea that will catch the eye of the public, and become in itself a "spokesman" for the product.

Longtime Rock and Roll

*"Ambition's a good thing if you've got it headed in
the right direction."* — Josh White

Many people think the Rock-ola jukebox name is a combination of "rock and roll." In fact, the name comes from David C. Rockola, who began building jukeboxes in 1930. He had been in the business of making mechanical scales when he decided to move into a larger growth industry. With the record industry booming, and jukeboxes appearing in every cafe across America, Rockola believed the coin-operated music business was here to stay. Although the business has had its ups and downs, recent years have seen an upsurge in interest in jukeboxes. By adapting his machines to keep pace with changing consumer tastes and advances in electronic wizardry, Rockola kept his business viable while others failed. David's oldest son, Donald, was elected president of the company in 1975, and David's wife has been an officer and corporate secretary for over fifty years. David continued to take an active role in daily operations even after his ninetieth birthday.

While other major music companies have merged or moved their manufacturing operations offshore, Rockola maintains its longtime reputation of giving its customers what they want— from futuristic machines with bubble tops and light shows to a nostalgic 1950s model that allows customers to select records using a telephone dial. Throughout the years, Rockola has concentrated on reliability. David was tenacious and strict, and understood that when rapid growth levels off, only those companies that give customers the best value will continue to survive. This has been Rockola's secret to success: to maintain quality and adapt to changing market tastes.

CONSIDER THIS: Keep your focus. Once you find something you do very well, stick with it.

Stephen Cannell Overcomes Dyslexia

"Everyone has handicaps. Don't give in to your handicaps."
— A. P. Gouthey

We often see the final product of someone's work and immediately come to the conclusion, "The person who created this has it all together." We may never think that a particular work of art was a labor of love, that it was conceived and created by someone we would call too handicapped to do such a thing. Stephen J. Cannell was convinced that he was a loser by the time he was eleven. Raised in an upper-middle-class family, he attended private schools but flunked classes almost every year and had to repeat three grades. Stephen had a condition known as dyslexia, and often saw words and numbers transposed. He had trouble reading, writing, and doing math. Many thought it impossible that Stephen would ever be able to perform anything but the most elementary jobs.

But Stephen somehow found the gumption and fortitude to make it through college. He then went to work for his father's design company in California. Even though he had trouble putting things on paper, he had a dream of writing for a living. Encouraged by his wife to pursue his dream, Stephen began to write for television. Although he admits that he was "scared to death," Stephen persevered and finally penned his first successful series, *The Rockford Files*. Following that were *Baretta*, *Baa Baa Black Sheep*, and others. Now an internationally known producer/writer, Stephen J. Cannell has shown that he is also an overcomer. He stands as an example to those who would not let handicaps stand in their way of success.

CONSIDER THIS: When we overcome a personal weakness (or challenge or handicap), we often end up with greater skills in that area than those who never had to struggle.

Truett Cathy Is Closed on Sunday

"And on the seventh day God ended his
work which he had made; and he rested on the
seventh day." — Genesis 1:31

When Truett Cathy left military service, he started the Dwarf House restaurant in Atlanta, Georgia. Since he lived next door to his restaurant, Truett worked virtually all day, every day—but he did not open on Sunday. Having become a Christian at the age of twelve, Truett felt that he could not be robbed of his day of rest. "If it takes seven days to make a living," he often said, "I ought to be doing something else."

The Dwarf House was successful, and Truett enjoyed experimenting with new dishes to serve his patrons. Some were well received, and some were not; however, there was one new idea that stood out above all the rest. It was called the Chick-fil-A, a specially prepared breast of chicken sandwich. Since it was so popular, Truett decided to try his sandwich in a fast-food location at a local mall. He opened his first Chick-fil-A store in Atlanta, and it was every bit as successful as he had hoped it would be. By the 1990s there were over 750 Chick-fil-A restaurants in the U.S., all still observing Truett's original "closed on Sunday" rule and many making better profits than seven-day restaurants next door. The Chick-Fil-A business is based on two principles: Glorify God in financial soundness, and have a positive influence on employees and customers. Teenage employees of Chick-fil-A stores are given college scholarships, and many have been given the opportunity to own their own business.

CONSIDER THIS: Stick to your principles, even if they go counter to popular wisdom.

Carol Channing's Big Break

*"Opportunities should never be lost, because they
can hardly be regained."*   — William Penn

Young people hear it all the time: "Without experience, I can't hire you." But how does one acquire the needed experience? To many people, getting that first real job means camping on the employer's doorstep until they are given a chance. It means thinking up ways to get attention or doing anything that will make you appear to be a good risk. Carol Channing was a drama major at Bennington College, and her ambition was to be onstage. During a winter break, each student was encouraged to go out into the "real" world to seek a job in his or her major. Carol hoofed it to New York and went straight to the William Morris Agency, one of the most prestigious talent agencies in the world. With a client list that boasted such renowned stars as Katharine Hepburn, the company had no use for a college student, especially one with no real experience. The agency would not even give Carol a chance.

But Carol refused to give up and camped out in the waiting room, just like an act waiting to jump at any possible booking. She was sitting between two actors when the secretary came in and said, "You!" and motioned with her finger. Who did the secretary want? Carol knew it had to be one of the others in the room, but she jumped up first, and marched into the president's office like she knew what she was doing. She sang one tune but drew no response. She tried another, and the agent got up to escort her out. Gamely, Carol launched into yet another song. "Wait, my grandmother used to sing me that song," the agent said, and with that, Carol was hired.

CONSIDER THIS: Be in the right place at the right time, and forge right in when opportunity knocks.

Facing a Crisis

*"When you face death, it puts everything into a
totally different light."*   — Paula Hill

Everyone who knew Paula Hill looked to her as an example
of success. She was a vibrant trainer, director of the Business
Leadership Center at Southern Methodist University, and a
successful wife and mother. But at the peak of her success,
Paula's world came crashing down. First, her ideal marriage was
shaken and dissolved. Then, as she began to recover from the
painful divorce, Paula discovered a suspicious lump in her
breast. Doctors assured her that the cyst was probably benign
but said further tests needed to be performed. When she received the call at her office telling her that she had cancer,
Paula screamed at the top of her lungs, "There must be some
mistake! This can't be me!" Following a mastectomy, she under-
went five months of unpleasant and depressing chemotherapy.

Paula had always been the one to help other people, but now
that she faced the possibility of death, she needed help herself.
She learned to accept the kindness, prayers, and comfort of others. Fortunately, Paula had many church friends, colleagues, and a
loving Christian family who volunteered to be with her through
the crisis. But in spite of the help she received from those around
her, Paula at times felt alone and abandoned, and called out to
God. "I thought I had faith," she said. "But I learned that faith is
when you step out and have nothing else to hold onto except the
Lord." Paula made a full recovery and continued her role in the
Business Leadership Center and in corporate consulting, helping
other people to succeed in business—but now with a new perspective about what it means to live a successful life.

CONSIDER THIS: The strength of your character will be
tested, sometimes by fire. Do you have the support of friends
and family, and a faith that can carry you through the trial?

Harry S Truman

"The buck stops here." — Harry S Truman

At the outbreak of World War I, young Harry Truman wanted to stand up and be counted. However, since he was virtually blind in one eye, he had to memorize the eye chart to pass the physical exam. Once in the army, he excelled and rose quickly to the rank of captain. His toughest assignment was commanding of one of the most unruly artillery batteries in France. As he faced the men for the first time, Harry was shaking in his boots. The soldiers made bets among themselves about how long their new captain would last.

Soon after taking command, Truman's battery was sent into battle. The troops pounded a German position with the intention of quickly moving before fire could be returned. Things started to go awry when the horses needed to move the artillery pieces arrived late. The weather was stormy and the gun carriages became stuck in the mud. Before Truman's unit could retreat, the Germans opened fire. With shells falling all about, the Americans began to run for their lives. Truman stood his ground and yelled at the top of his lungs, calling them back to their posts. He quickly reorganized his men and marched them to safety. None of his troops were lost in the action, and Truman won their allegiance for the duration of the war. This critical event in his life helped Truman define himself and his leadership capabilities. After the war, and after failing in business, Truman entered politics, rising from local commissioner to U.S. senator, to vice president of the United States. Upon the death of Franklin D. Roosevelt in 1945, Truman became our nation's thirty-third president.

CONSIDER THIS: If you want people to follow and respect you, take a stand for integrity when others are seeking the easy way out.

John D. Rockefeller

"The removal of human friction is 90 percent of the problem of handling people."

— Dr. Paul Parker

W hen trying to resolve strife, the direct approach is often best, as working through third parties can take the personality out of any negotiation. Listening to individuals who have problems, talking directly to those who are hurting, and seeing for one's self what is really happening can quell the storms of mistrust and anger. John D. Rockefeller knew he had a fight on his hands. For two years, Colorado miners had staged a bitter and violent strike. With no resolution to the conflict in sight, Rockefeller decided he had to approach the miners directly. After he had done his homework on the strike, Rockefeller was prepared to make the best of a bad situation and went to Colorado to see, talk to—and listen to—the disgruntled workers.

At a meeting with a group of miners that could easily have become a lynch mob, Rockefeller began by saying, "This is a red-letter day in my life . . . I am proud to be here, and I shall remember this gathering as long as I live." He continued, mentioning that he had visited all of the mining camps, visited the miners' homes, met their wives and children, and felt that he and the miners were meeting in a "spirit of friendship." Making friends with the "enemy," enabled the opposing sides to begin to see eye to eye, and they soon moved toward a solution to their problems.

CONSIDER THIS: People who have ill feelings about each other will seldom reach agreement on anything. Friends, on the other hand, will make a strong effort to reconcile differences.

Vernon Jordan

"Laws grind the poor, and rich men rule the law."
— Oliver Goldsmith in *The Traveller*

Advice is critical when important decisions are to be made, but no one can make your decisions except you. No one else can have that responsibility. Sometimes you see a vision greater than any one else can imagine. Sometimes you have to go against the odds. Vernon Jordan fought against odds and the advice of others to become one of America's best known and effective civil-rights lawyers. Jordan's vision to move up in life came from his humble beginnings. He remembers his grandfather, a lifetime sharecropper, having the dream of someday using an indoor bathroom before he died. Jordan was brought up in a housing project. He often helped his mother cater meals at the Lawyers Club of Atlanta. There, Jordan listened to the speeches by the members and their guests, and began to see the legal profession as a way to break out of his poverty and to help others.

Jordan decided to become a lawyer, and the plan he devised for his life became a strong motivating force. Jordan's high school counselor advised him not to attend DePauw University, but since that is where Jordan felt he would receive the best education, he went there anyway. A college counselor advised against entering a public speaking contest, but Jordan won first place in the competition. Vernon Jordan later received a law degree from Howard University and upon graduation began a fruitful career as an advocate of the poor and oppressed.

CONSIDER THIS: If you have a dream, it can be a great motivator that will help you overcome formidable odds.

The Mother of Mother's Day

"No person was ever honored for what he received. Honor has been the reward for what he gave."
— Calvin Coolidge

Anna Jarvis was never a mother herself. The daughter of a Methodist minister, she became a schoolteacher, worked as an advertising executive with an insurance agency in Philadelphia, and spent fifteen years of her life caring for her ailing mother. Anna never married. After her mother died in 1905, Anna wanted to find a way to honor her mother's memory. She recalled the days after the Civil War, when her Virginia community held a yearly picnic on Mother's Friendship Day to help heal the emotional wounds of those who had lost sons and to honor all the mothers who had given of their families in the war effort. With this in mind, Anna thought there ought to be a day to honor all mothers.

Obtaining a patent copyright for "Mother's Day," Anna next explained her idea to public officials in state and federal government. She even approached President Woodrow Wilson with a persuasive argument for making the day a national celebration. Anna's years of persistence paid off when Wilson signed a proclamation in 1914 declaring Mother's Day a national observance. Once the celebration was deemed official, Anna worked to keep Mother's Day from becoming too commercialized and to ensure that honoring mothers remained the prime emphasis of the day. Her efforts spread throughout the world, and when Anna died in 1948, forty-three carnations were placed on her grave to signify the forty-three nations that had adopted "her" day.

CONSIDER THIS: Who is it that you should honor? Do you feel strongly enough about a cause to give your time and energy to make it happen?

Black and Decker

"No idea is worth anything unless you have the guts to back it up." — Al Decker

S. Duncan Black and Alonzo Decker joined together in 1910 to start the Black & Decker Company. Black sold his prized Maxwell car for $600 and Decker borrowed $600 to launch the enterprise. At first they built a milk bottle-capping machine, a candy-dipping machine, and other devices. In 1916 their most successful machine was introduced, a hand-held portable drill with a pistol-grip trigger switch. To promote their drill and other tools to industry, Black and Decker built a showroom on wheels and traveled throughout the country. In 1929 they equipped a Travel-Air monoplane as an airborne showroom. In 1930, when they attempted to enter the consumer market with a washing machine, they priced it too high for the economically depressed era, and the venture was abandoned.

During Word War II, the company built a wide range of portable industrial tools. After the war, the two principals noticed a small newspaper article describing how workers were stealing electric tools from their respective companies. Black and Decker felt the time was right to make another attempt to tap the consumer market, but this time they carefully planned to introduce a home-duty drill with a popular price. Black & Decker's production expertise enabled the firm to market an electric drill for only $16.95, a price that was as low or lower than that offered by most competitors. Building on that success, Black & Decker introduced a wide variety of successful, low-priced, high-quality do-it-yourself tools. After almost thirty years on the market, the successor to the $16.95 drill retailed for less than $10 in 1973.

CONSIDER THIS: Often the key to expansion is to do what you do best, but perhaps expand the same idea to a fresh market.

Bill Veeck's Home Runs

"The power of listening: it borders on the bizarre."
— Tom Peters in *A Passion for Excellence*

Bill Veeck left a lasting impression on baseball. As the owner of several clubs, he introduced such new ideas as the exploding scoreboard, placing players' names on uniforms, after-game fireworks, bat night, fan appreciation night, and a host of other special ballpark promotions. Veeck knew how to draw a crowd. In 1948, his Cleveland Indians attracted 2.6 million fans, an attendance mark that stood for more than a dozen years. Who could forget the night that the inventive Veeck sent three-foot-seven-inch Eddie Gaedel to the plate to bat for the St. Louis Browns in 1951? Eddie wore the number 1/8 on his uniform and drew a walk.

Veeck was interested in learning. He learned from the people around him, from the players and fans as well as the business types. Veeck read five or six books every week of his adult life. Baseball was not his only interest; Veeck was an expert on tropical fish and cultivated rare strains of flowers. He knew virtually everything there was to know about dogs and horses. People remember Veeck as a "people person." He never used obscenities; he had the door to his office removed so that anyone could see him anytime. Often, during games, Veeck would take off his shirt and sit in the bleachers with the fans. He always wanted to know what they thought and what ideas they had. Bill Veeck paid attention to what the fans wanted and then gave it to them.

CONSIDER THIS: Do you stay in touch with the "fans," your customers? Do you really know what they want? Isn't it time you found out?

Jim Treybig

"Man seeks his inward unity, but his real progress on the path depends on his capacity to refrain from distorting reality in accordance with his desires."
— Goethe

During the 1960s and 1970s, computers began to shrink as new and smaller electronic components were developed. Jim Treybig took note of that quickly changing industry and studied it in detail to find a niche where he could develop his own company. The area he chose was on-line transaction processing (OLTP), a relatively new field with applications in such diverse businesses as airline reservations and monitoring devices that require highly reliable non-stop computing. In 1974, the year Treybig was determined to begin his new venture, RCA got out of the computer business and IBM was at its pinnacle of success. It was hard to sell the need for a new computer company.

However, Palo Alto, California, in 1974 proved to be the right place and the right time for Treybig to pursue his dream of a fail-safe computing system. He received some initial backing from the venture capital firm of Kleiner-Perkins and began to recruit the technical expertise he required from his former employer, Hewlett-Packard. With a core group of five men, Treybig developed a business plan that included details on system design and architecture, financing, a people-oriented business atmosphere, and teamwork. After almost non-stop planning and brainstorming, Tandem Computers was incorporated in November 1974 and shipped its first NonStop computer in May 1976.

CONSIDER THIS: Great events usually don't just happen. They begin as someone's dream, and they usually require a lot of work and heartache before they become reality.

The Chip that Jack Built

*"We expected to reduce the cost of electronics, but I
don't think anybody was thinking in terms of
factors of a million"* — Jack Kilby

Today, an electronic chip the size of a fingernail can contain millions of circuits. It can serve as the heart of a personal computer, keep your wristwatch accurate, determine the correct fuel mixture for your car's engine, keep a satellite in orbit, and perform thousands of other tasks. However, in the 1950s, any of these tasks would have required a computing machine larger than a house. The postwar era was a transition period for electronics. The theory behind electronic computing was developed during World War II, but the technology of the day was too cumbersome and expensive. This resulted in a problem called "the tyranny of numbers." There was too much calculating to do and not enough horsepower to do it!

In this environment, a young engineer named Jack Kilby, decided to "fool around" with the problem. He understood that complicated circuits required the interconnection of transistors, diodes, rectifiers, and capacitors, each of which was made from a different substance. However, Jack reasoned that if all of those components could be fashioned from of a single substance, such as a semiconductor, the resulting circuitry would be smaller, cheaper to manufacture, and more reliable. In September 1958 Jack built and demonstrated a strange contraption made of semiconductor material and wires glued to a slide. The invention was the first integrated circuit and provided the foundation for today's enormous computing and electronics industry.

CONSIDER THIS: Make the complex simple. Look around at the material you have to work with and determine how it can be used to its greatest benefit.

The Beginnings of EDS

"The mass of men lead lives of quiet desperation."
— Henry David Thoreau

H. Ross Perot was sitting in a barbershop reading *Reader's Digest* when he saw this quote from Thoreau at the bottom of a page: "The mass of men lead lives of quiet desperation." Perot thought, "That's me. There I am." He was a good salesman for IBM, but felt he was not meeting his potential. As a salesman, Perot noticed that people were buying computers but really didn't know what to do with them. He had the idea of selling companies not only the computers, but also the software and staff to run them—an entire data processing department. IBM listened to Perot's idea but said that 80 cents of the computer dollar (at the time) was spent on hardware and only 20 cents on software. The 20 cents looked good to Perot, but IBM turned down his idea.

After the episode at the barbershop, Perot made the decision of his life. He quit IBM and spent $1,000 to start Electronic Data Systems (EDS). He had no computer and no staff, "just" an idea. At first, Perot bought time on an IBM 7070 mainframe computer and traveled throughout the country trying to sell that computing time. He visited seventy-nine companies before making his first sale. Since he had no staff, Perot had to find IBM 7070 operators who would help him during their off-time. Those individuals have never worked another day for Perot, but they remain on the payroll and received EDS stock when it was issued. According to Perot, "If those guys hadn't done the job for me, there would be no EDS."

CONSIDER THIS: There is that one moment in our lives when we decide to break out of a rut and move on to something greater. Is that moment right now for you?

FlightSafety International

"When we cannot invent, we may at least improve." — Charles Caleb Colton

Al Ueltschi (yule-chee) was a military pilot trainer before World War II. Al particularly remembers the time he fell out of the plane as he was demonstrating a snap roll. He managed to struggle out of his seat and pull the ripcord just in the nick of time. Inspired by the likes of Charles Lindberg in the 1930s, Ueltschi began flying as a teenager. After World War II, as he piloted Pan American Airways Chairman Juan Trippe around the globe, he noticed a swell of interest in business travel. Ueltschi also noticed that, except for the military, there were few places where pilots could acquire training. With $10,000 he obtained by taking a second mortgage on his house, Ueltschi opened his first training facility in a leased space at New York's La Guardia Airport.

Ueltschi was also aware that small plane manufacturers wanted to get out of the pilot-training business, so he managed to contract with the manufacturers to provide that service. Several corporations that employed pilots became his first backers as Ueltschi sold them five years' worth of training to get the capital he needed to purchase his first flight simulator. Al Ueltschi continued to work as a pilot for Pan Am until 1968 when his FlightSafety International went public. Aircraft manufacturers increasingly became convinced that Ueltschi's company could provide better training, and as a result, FlightSafety has grown to include dozens of simulators. The company also has broadened its curriculum to include simulation training for employees of nautical shipping firms and power companies.

CONSIDER THIS: Can you offer a service for a company that is superior to its own in-house service?

Holiday Inns

"Learn the art of being aware; our success depends upon our power to perceive, to observe and know."
— Henry Miller

Before World War II, a large portion of the hotel-motel industry catered to the business traveler. After the war, families began to take to the road to discover America. The nation's new interstate highway system was expanding, automobile production had resumed, and postwar affluence put vacations within the reach of millions of American families. In 1952 Memphis businessman Kemmons Wilson took his family on a vacation. What he repeatedly found on that excursion were uncomfortable, inconsistent, and overpriced lodgings. As a result, Wilson came to believe that the hotel-motel market was "the greatest untouched industry in the country." Wilson constructed his first Holiday Inn on the outskirts of Memphis, Tennessee, his hometown. The facility had 120 rooms, each offering a private bath, air conditioning, and a telephone. Other features included a swimming pool, free ice, free parking, and a kennel. Children under the age of twelve stayed free.

This first Holiday Inn offered a wide range of amenities that were revolutionary for the hotel-motel industry of the mid-1950s. Kemmons Wilson's idea proved to be a major success, and his hotels began appearing across the country. The company went public in 1957, and its entire offering was sold on the first day. The first international Holiday Inn was built in Montreal in 1960, and in 1968 the company opened its 1,000th hotel.

CONSIDER THIS: If something bothers you, it probably bothers a lot of other people. Is this a business opportunity?

From Failure to Success

"Nothing is so contagious as enthusiasm; it moves stones, it charms brutes. Enthusiasm is the genius of sincerity and truth accomplishes no victories without it."

— Edward George Bulwer-Lytton

Success usually has less to do with one's innate talent than it does with one's attitude. Some people's lives are guided by negative attitudes, and as a result, they handicap themselves and never recognize their potential. Other people learn that by changing their attitude, they can improve their chance of realizing their dreams. The power that attitude can exert is illustrated by Frank Bettger in his autobiography, *How I Raised Myself from Failure to Success in Selling*. Frank started out as a baseball player in the minor leagues. He had ability but was traded from team to team, often at a lower salary. Then, someone told him that the reason he wasn't getting anywhere: He had no hustle, no enthusiasm for the game. Frank agreed and determined that he would improve his attitude. As a result, he turned his career around and was soon signed by the St. Louis Cardinals.

When Frank left baseball and embarked on a career selling insurance, he found himself in the same boring mold that had plagued him in the minors. Frank was getting nowhere fast. His sales were mediocre and he wasn't enjoying his what he was doing. The answer to his problem proved to be the same one that saved his baseball career. Frank began to deliberately cultivate enthusiasm for his work, and his improved attitude helped him move to the top of the sales force. Although Frank's solution may sound simplistic, it contains a key ingredient to the recipe for success.

CONSIDER THIS: Are you enthusiastic about your work? Are you deliberately cultivating enthusiasm?

Andy Griffith

"Act the part and you will become the part."
— Anonymous

Andy Griffith was born in Mt. Airy, North Carolina, and attended the University of North Carolina at Chapel Hill. At one time he considered becoming a minister but soon decided on an entertainment career. For seven years he appeared as Sir Walter Raleigh in the Carolina Playmakers production of *The Lost Colony*. He also taught music in Goldsboro and performed at various functions. Once, he was scheduled to appear before the same group a second time and was forced to come up with a different act. The result was a monologue based on a joke, called "What It Was Was Football." Orville Campbell, head of a small recording company, heard Andy's act and asked him to make the comedy routine into a record. A Capitol Records executive heard the recording on radio and signed Andy to a contract.

Griffith made his first nationwide appearance in January 1954 on *The Ed Sullivan Show*. "I was not an overwhelming success," he admits. Continuing to perform his act in the South, Griffith read the Mac Hayman novel *No Time for Sergeants* and believed he could play the part of Will Stockdale better than any one else. He was persuasive with the show's producer and got the part for the TV production, played 354 performances on Broadway, and starred in the movie version. In 1960, the William Morris Agency got Andy together with Sheldon Leonard, who created the pilot for *The Andy Griffith Show*, which was a spin-off from the popular Danny Thomas program. *The Andy Griffith Show* lasted eight years on television, often commanding the number-one position in the national Nielsen ratings.

CONSIDER THIS: Sometimes you just have to keep going and look for the breaks that will move you one step farther down the road toward success.

What the Customer Really Wants

"The customer is always right." — Anonymous

Some of the most successful American companies have a reputation for aggressively seeking to find out what it is their customers really want. Sam Walton visited each of his Wal-Mart stores every year and made a point to talk to the salespeople on the floor as well as to the customers. He worked only a half-day each week in the corporate office and spent the rest of the week "wandering around" his various stores. A former chief operating officer at PepsiCo spent as much as 40 percent of his time on the road in order to find out how business was faring on the front line. At Hewlett-Packard, computer engineers often leave their work on display so that co-workers passing by can play with it and offer their comments. At 3M, all of the corporation's research and development people are required to take part in sales calls.

A number of companies regularly send their accountants, assembly-line workers, and executives to local department stores to act as sales clerks for a day, selling the products their companies make and finding out what people actually think of those products. There is simply no substitute for direct human interaction. Statistics, reports, computer printouts, and seminars cannot accurately tell the story of what is actually taking place in the marketplace. To gain a real understanding of what people feel and what they want, you have to get out of your office and see it for yourself.

CONSIDER THIS: Are you sitting in a corporate ivory tower, believing that you really know what is going on in the real world? Wake up, and get out there and find out for yourself!

Pepperidge Farm

"An enterprise when fairly once begun, should not be left till all that ought is won."

— Shakespeare

How many people have become successful doing something other than what they set out to do? Margaret Rudkin had never baked a loaf of bread in her life. But her young son had asthma, and the doctor suggested that, as part of her son's treatment, she bake whole wheat bread from only natural ingredients. As her son remembers, the first loaf came out like a brick, but gradually, as Margaret experimented with the recipe, the bread became quite tasty. It was soon the only bread served at the Rudkin house, and visitors often would ask where they could purchase it. To see how marketable her bread really was, Margaret baked twelve loaves, took them to the local grocer, and had him taste it. The grocer immediately ordered more of the bread, and Margaret was in business.

The bread was first baked in the family kitchen, but as its popularity grew, the enterprise was moved to the family barns, which had been converted into kitchens. Margaret Rudkin was very particular about her product. If a loaf had not been wrapped neatly or if anything about the bread looked wrong, she would not let it be sold. Pepperidge Farm became well known for its tasty, high-quality products that consumers perceived to be a cut above other baked goods. Today, the company's products, including fresh baked products, biscuits, and frozen foods, are sold nationwide.

CONSIDER THIS: Even someone who has never tried his or her hand at a task can become a master, with patience and practice.

Michael Jordan

*"If you work hard, you will get the things
you want."* — James Jordan

As a youngster, Michael Jordan took sports seriously. He always wanted to win and he hated to lose. Standing only five feet ten inches tall, he made his high school's junior-varsity basketball team as a sophomore but was passed over in favor of another athlete when the coach needed a taller player for a state championship tournament. Michael never forgot that moment.

When he returned to school the next fall, Michael startled everyone, for over the course of the summer, he had grown five inches. "It was almost as if Michael willed himself taller," said his father. In order to gain more practice time, Michael began skipping classes. He eventually was suspended from school, and his father had to help the youngster strike a balance between academics and his commitment to sports. Michael took his father's advice but never lost any of his passion for winning. He continued to work harder than any of his teammates, and he also demanded more of himself. During his final season at the University of North Carolina, Michael was selected as college basketball's 1984 Player of the Year. Drafted that spring by the Chicago Bulls of the National Basketball Association, Michael Jordan became an instant sensation with his easygoing smile and slashing style of play. His formidable skills and dogged determination helped lift his new team from mediocrity to become one of the league's most successful franchises of all time.

CONSIDER THIS: If you know your talents and develop them passionately, you will earn success.

Alex and Richard Manoogian

"Nothing we develop is the stuff dreams are made of, they just make lots of money."
— Richard Manoogian

Alex Manoogian was born in Turkey and immigrated to America in 1920. He became a machinist and worked in a Detroit company until 1929, when he formed Masco Screw Products Company, a supplier of nuts and bolts to automobile makers. The company was successful, but Manoogian became concerned that his customer base was so small. In 1950 he decided to diversify and developed a single-handled faucet. Manoogian tried to market the device through major plumbing suppliers, but they were not interested, so he decided to market it himself. Known as the Delta faucet, it was advertised on NBC's *Tonight Show*, where it was the subject of several jokes by Johnny Carson and Ed McMahon. The attention only created more interest in the faucet.

Richard, Alex's son, joined the company in 1968 and began a further diversification into other non-glamorous businesses, such as auto parts and tools and oil equipment. The one venture that turned sour was the CB radio business. Masco had built up monthly CB sales of $10 million, but when the government raised the number of CB channels from 23 to 40, thousands of radios in its stock immediately became obsolete. Still, Masco's diversification has given it a solid foundation of mundane products that protects the company from volatile changes that can occur in other markets.

CONSIDER THIS: While others put up with feast or famine, there are solid markets that quietly and consistently make their owners rich.

Cracker Barrel

"There never was a day that couldn't be improved by some good country cookin'."

— Cracker Barrel menu

Dan Evins operated a small filling station business in Tennessee during the 1960s, about the time the interstate highway system was beginning to open up many rural areas. Wondering how he could take advantage of the traffic, Dan realized that travelers would be hungry as well as in need of gasoline, so he considered selling food at his stations. At first, he thought about adding fast food, which seemed to be the trend, but ultimately determined that many people would rather have "real food" instead.

Dan decided to create a highway restaurant that would buck the trend. He wanted his restaurant to be comfortable and reflect the nostalgia of rural America. It would be like a country store, with big jars of candies and homemade jellies, potbellied stoves, handmade quilts and other quality items. With the help of some investor friends, Dan opened the original Cracker Barrel Old Country Store in 1969 as a family restaurant, gift shop, and service station. Travelers liked the idea, and soon people were standing in line to eat his country cooking. Dan obtained more investors and built more stores, eventually omitting the service station. By the late 1990s, over 300 Cracker Barrels had been opened. Dan believes that authentic country cooking, American values, and an honest-to-goodness rural lifestyle can be preserved, and he intends to do his part in his stores.

CONSIDER THIS: When everyone is following one trend, perhaps there is another important part of the market that is being forgotten. Someone will find it and service it. Will it be you?

Daniel Boone

"Two men look out through the same bars: One sees the mud, the other the stars."
— Fredrick Langbridge

Our hopes and dreams today were fashioned by the people who first pioneered the American Dream. One of those people was Daniel Boone. At age thirty-five, living meagerly on a farm in North Carolina, Boone was disgusted by the taxes, lawyers, sheriffs, and the so-called "quit-rent" system that ensured people would never quit paying rent on land they had already purchased. To the north and west lay the Kentucky wilderness, which Boone saw as a hope for a better future. His first trip in 1769 yielded nothing but experience. Indians stole all of his pelts, and Boone was lucky to return home alive. In 1775 Boone tried again, this time after the land had been "purchased" from the Cherokees for $50,000. Boone and thirty men with pickaxes cut a passage across the Cumberland Gap through 100 miles of dense forest, establishing the settlement of Boonesborough in central Kentucky at the end of the trail, which became known as the Wilderness Road.

The settlement flourished but was attacked during the Revolutionary War by Indians who had been armed by the British. After the war, the Indians fought on and Boone lost a son. The Shawnees captured his sixteen-year-old daughter, but she left a trail of petticoat scraps that provided a trail for Boone's rescue party. When civilization finally came to the region, lawyers, speculators, sheriffs, and politicians came, too, and Boone lost all of his land and wealth. Daniel Boone and his reputation moved to St. Louis, where his extended family eventually numbered over 100 and where he spent the rest of a good life.

CONSIDER THIS: Our heroes have molded our thinking in ways we may not recognize. They taught us to despise injustice and to create a system of living that is fair and right for all.

Exampling

"Integrity is as integrity does."

— Phillip B. Crosby

In his book *Running Things*, author Phillip B. Crosby points out problems associated with decaying morality in business, and how company management is responsible for and can correct many of those problems. Crosby explains that most people have high integrity and do not usually do things they consider to be wrong. The problem lies in the fact that what is considered wrong often changes from time to time and from place to place. In many small towns, people do not worry about crime since they know everyone in the area and everyone generally lives up to the community's expectations. In a company, employees' perceptions of appropriate office behavior are shaped by managers and the examples they set.

Managers are sadly mistaken if they think "commandments" will convince people to behave in a professional manner in the workplace. Like children taking after their parents, employees will imitate the behavior of their employers. If supervisors come in late, take extra time for lunch, and run personal errands on company time, workers will feel justified in balancing their checkbook, making personal calls, and writing personal letters while on the job. In most companies, nearly everyone knows nearly everything that goes on. There are few secrets. The examples set by managers are seen by everyone, and they will affect the level of integrity of the company's work force.

CONSIDER THIS: If you are a manager, a supervisor, or an executive, workers will follow your example, whether it is good or bad. If you want your employees to meet certain standards of behavior and performance, you must meet those standards yourself.

Kleenex Tissues

"Don't put a cold in your pocket."
                                    — Kleenex advertisement

During World War I, the Kimberly-Clark company developed a super-absorbent material that could be used as a surgical dressing as well as a gas-mask filter. After the war, the same material was used in Kleenex brand tissues, which were originally intended to be used as a cold-cream remover. For years the product was promoted only for its ability to help remove cold cream. However, marketers kept receiving letters from customers that asked, "Why don't you say it's good for blowing your nose?" At first, no one paid much attention to the suggestion, but the letters came in so frequently that the marketing department decided the concept was worth some research.

To test the new idea, a novel advertising campaign was devised. Half of the newspapers in Peoria, Illinois, carried an ad urging people to use Kleenex for removing cold cream plus a coupon good for a free box of the tissues. Ads in the remaining newspapers also included a coupon but touted Kleenex as a handkerchief substitute. The handkerchief version drew the most response, accounting for 61 percent of the coupons redeemed. The experiment showed that Kleenex could be more popular if used as a disposable handkerchief rather than for the purpose it was originally intended. With that evidence, a new ad campaign was devised to promote both uses of Kleenex, with its role as a handkerchief getting most of the coverage. Eventually, Kimberly-Clark comprised a list of forty-eight "typical" uses for Kleenex.

CONSIDER THIS: Be alert for new or different uses of a product or service. This can be a natural avenue for expansion.

Malcom P. McLean's Shipping Containers

"Determine that the thing can and shall be done, and then we shall find the way." — Lincoln

There was a problem in the shipping industry. Goods were loaded onto ships in Europe in boxes or barrels, but when they reached the United States, some of the cargo would be gone. Such losses are called "shrinkage," and they cost American consumers millions of dollars. Malcom McLean recognized this problem and believed he had an answer. McLean had started a trucking company during the depression with a single used truck and had sold the company in 1955 for $6 million. He used the proceeds from that sale to purchase the Pan-Atlantic Steamship Corporation, which McLean renamed Sea-Land Services (SLS). Additional ships were purchased for SLS from the U.S. Navy by investors who then leased them to McLean. The investors were attracted by a highly favorable tax advantage. The navy vessels were fully depreciated, since they were over forty years old, but the reconstituted vessels were given a short seven-year depreciation life.

McLean's answer to the shrinkage problem came from his experience in the trucking industry. Instead of shipping goods in small containers, McLean utilized large sealed containers, the same type that fit onto the backs of trucks. With that system, the trucks pulled up to the dock, and the containers were hoisted aboard ship. At the end of the voyage, the procedure was reversed. In addition to reducing loading and unloading time, the sealed containers also made it difficult for thieves to get to the cargo. The idea has been adopted by other shippers and has saved untold millions of dollars in shipping costs.

CONSIDER THIS: A large deal takes more than a good idea. It also requires a smart financial plan.

KitchenAid

"If nobody else is going to invent a dishwasher, I'll do it myself." — Josephine Garis Cochraine

The automatic dishwasher took a long time to reach American homes after its invention in 1886. It all started when Josephine Garis Cochraine, the wife of an Illinois political leader, got mad at the servants who kept breaking her china. After one particularly bad evening, Josephine exploded at the kitchen staff and declared that she would invent a dishwasher, even though she had no mechanical experience and rarely washed dishes herself. Working in the woodshed, Josephine devised a contraption she dubbed the Garis-Cochraine, which proved to be such a good design that it was patented and won an award at the 1893 Columbian Exposition. Friends and business associates helped her establish a company, and the dishwashers it produced were sold to hotels and restaurants. Josephine directed the firm until her death in 1913.

In 1926 another company came into the picture. The Hobart company, founded in 1897, produced equipment for grocers and institutional kitchens. Hobart acquired the Garis-Cochraine but continued to concentrate on its heavy-duty dishwashers. It was not until 1949 that the company finally introduced a home model, called the KitchenAid. In its marketing research, Hobart found that many women of the period actually enjoyed washing dishes, so the company had to find a more compelling reason for women to buy the machine. Researchers also discovered that women felt guilty about leaving dirty dishes after late night snacks. That information, plus the added benefit of sterilization, led to dishwashers becoming a permanent fixture in many American homes.

CONSIDER THIS: A good idea may come before everyone is ready to use it. Timing must also be right.

Victor Kiam

"Entrepreneurs don't sit on their haunches,
waiting for something to happen. They make
things happen."   — Victor Kiam

In his autobiography *Going For It!* Victor Kiam is the first to admit that he is no entrepreneurial genius. He simply learned what it takes to operate and build a company by watching it happen. After graduating from Harvard Business School in 1951, Kiam spent the next few decades climbing the corporate ladder at Lever Brothers and Playtex. After a merger, Kiam became disenchanted with the direction the company was taking and left. As many executives do, he went to a corporate headhunter to begin the process of finding a new position. George Haley of Haley Associates had a different idea. "You should go out on your own," he told Kiam. "Find a company you are interested in, buy it, and run it yourself. Or start a new company."

Haley's advice took Kiam by surprise, but he let the idea settle and attended the worldwide seminar of the Young Presidents' Organization. After the conference, Kiam bought the Benrus company and in 1979 acquired Remington. Both companies were having problems, and Kiam was able to play a role in turning them around. He became a celebrity of sorts by appearing in television commercials and telling viewers about his purchase of Remington. Attired in a bathrobe, Kiam declared that he liked Remington's electric shaver so much, "I bought the company."

CONSIDER THIS: Never say never to an idea. What is it that you have been mulling over, thinking about doing, but have not had the courage to attempt?

The Wizard of Oz

"Toto, I don't think we're in Kansas anymore."
— Dorothy

Our own American Dreams are frequently fashioned by the ideas we hear about in stories, particularly those stories we encounter in our youth. *The Wonderful Wizard of Oz* is one of those stories. Its author, Lyman Frank Baum, began his career as journalist. He frequently entertained neighborhood children by telling stories, often making up the tales on the spot. In 1899 Baum penned his first children's book, *Father Goose*, which was commercially successful and encouraged him to write more.

One story he told that the neighborhood children seemed to enjoy was about a girl named Dorothy who was swept from her Kansas home by a twister and stranded in a magical land. When one of the neighborhood youngsters asked Baum the name of the land, he was stumped at first. Then, so legend has it, he looked over to his file cabinets and the drawers labeled A-G, H-N, and O-Z. Baum quickly dubbed the magical land "Oz" and the children seemed to like the name. When he originally titled this story, he called it *The Emerald City*, a title over which he and his publisher disagreed. They considered *From Kansas to Fairyland* and *The City of the Great Oz* before finally deciding on *The Wonderful Wizard of Oz*. Baum went on to write more than sixty children's books, many about the wonderful land of Oz.

CONSIDER THIS: Try out your "product" on potential consumers until you get it just right. Listen to their ideas and concerns, and incorporate them into the name and marketing of your goods.

Persistence Pays Off

"In the long run a man becomes what he purposes,
and gains for himself what he really desires."
— H. Mabie

Time after time, biographies tell the story of a person who had a great idea that was rejected or who was turned down for a job. But that person was incredibly persistent and eventually became a success. Such was the case of Becky Heflin. After applying for a job that she really wanted in state government, Becky virtually camped out on the doorsteps of the governor's office until she was hired. Over the next several years, she was named to a number of high-level positions. When Carol Channing went looking for a job, she continually hung around a talent agent's office until she was accidentally invited to audition for a part.

Steven Spielberg went to the film studio where he wanted to work, found an empty office, put his name on the door, and began to create. Almost no one at 3-M believed that Post-It notes had a future, but Art Fry kept handing them out to people until the company gave the product a chance. Even after the first marketing attempt failed, Art refused to give up on the idea and kept plugging away. A new idea can go nowhere unless someone has the faith to believe in it after others have stopped doing so and possesses the persistence to keep trying after most reasonable people would quit. Who knows what inventions or ideas have been overlooked because they weren't pushed hard enough?

CONSIDER THIS: What ideas have you given up on too soon? What opportunities have you left because the "door closed?" Why aren't you outside that door trying to pry it open again?

Cracker Jack

"It is a difficult matter to argue with the belly,
since it has no ears." — Marcus Porcius Cato

In 1871 F. W. Rueckheim came to Chicago to help with the clean-up after the great fire had destroyed much of the city. Rueckheim was a German immigrant who had saved $200 working as a farmhand and wanted to carve out his own piece of the American Dream. Once in Chicago, he decided to use his money to go into the popcorn business, and he and a partner set up a small stand at 113 Federal Street. Rueckheim eventually bought out his partner, and his brother Louis joined him in 1873. Together the brothers purchased some candy-making equipment to expand their product line. They added marshmallows and other confections to their growing business and in 1893 began selling their wares at the Chicago World's Fair. One of the Rueckheims' products was a tasty blend of popcorn, peanuts, and molasses.

Demand for the new treat continued to increase, and the brothers outgrew their production capacity more than once. When Louis gave a sample of the product to a salesman, the man exclaimed, "That's a Cracker Jack!" "So it is," replied Rueckheim, who the proceeded to trademark the name. Another customer provided the slogan "The more you eat, the more you want." In 1910 the Cracker Jack box began carrying coupons that were redeemable for prizes, and the company's hallmark "prize in every package" made its first appearance in 1912.

CONSIDER THIS: Give the customers what they want, then give them a little extra. Without satisfied customers, there is no business.

Telly Savalas

"There is an hour appointed in each man's life to make his happiness, if he then seizes it."
— Beaumont and Fletcher

You never know where life will take you. Aristotle (Telly) Savalas graduated from Columbia University with the intention of pursuing a career in diplomatic service. He began working at the State Department and expected to remain there until retirement. After a few years, however, he accepted an executive position with ABC's television news division. While there, he won several major awards. As a favor to a talent-agent friend who was having trouble finding an actor with a certain accent, Telly took a small role in a motion picture. Burt Lancaster saw the film and recruited Savalas to appear in *Birdman of Alcatraz*. In this first major role, Telly was nominated for an Oscar.

After his triumph in *Birdman*, Telly next played Pontius Pilate in *The Greatest Story Ever Told* (in which he first shaved his head) and landed starring roles in *The Dirty Dozen* with Lee Marvin, *Kiss of Death* with Richard Widmark, and many other movies. But even though he had appeared in sixty films, Telly admits that people still called him "what's-his-name." Finally, in 1973, the television series *Kojak* elevated Savalas to superstar status. Even though *Kojak* has been out of production since 1978, it is still seen throughout the world in reruns. Telly Savalas never planned to become an actor, but he took a chance to do something different with his life and made the most of the opportunity when it came.

CONSIDER THIS: Keep your mind open for opportunities that may provide you with new adventures you never expected could happen.

Selling Yourself

"A man's success in handling people is the very yardstick by which the outcome of his whole life's work is measured." — Dr. Paul Parker

There is a difference in being an "order taker" and being a salesperson. High school students can be hired to "take orders" at McDonald's or at the local department store. In sales, there is an important step to becoming a professional. Most professional sales relationships are more than just a single chance encounter, such as would occur at a grocery store or a fast-food restaurant. In fact, the relationship is much like a marriage. There is a courtship, a consummation of the deal, and involvement that continues after the sale is made. The quality of the "marriage" depends on how well the seller manages the relationship. If the marriage is good, the seller's reputation is enhanced and there will be opportunities for more sales. If it is bad, the seller's reputation is tarnished and sales will dry up.

This sales relationship occurs even if we are not pursuing sales as a career. We sell ourselves to our employer, to other business associates, and to our friends. In every case, we must follow through after the sale. We must recognize that there are competitors lurking around every corner. Service after the sale builds the relationship generates repeat business. Honesty in the relationship builds trust. Being there when troubles surface builds loyalty. Good sales relationships build referrals, recommendations, and more opportunities to make another sale.

CONSIDER THIS: Relationships do not just happen. Like a marriage, they require time, commitment, and energy. Give of yourself to others, and you will see friendships develop.

Amelia Earhart

"As soon as we left ground, I knew I myself had to fly." — Amelia Earhart on her first flight

Amelia Earhart was barely five years old when Orville and Wilbur Wright made their famous first flight at Kitty Hawk, North Carolina. She may not have known it at the time, but it was a turning point in her life. As a bright student, Amelia dreamed big dreams. She read the newspaper and cut out clippings of famous first events. She was particularly impressed when a woman achieved a great feat or landed a notable job. However, Amelia had trouble finding a field in which she could make her own mark on history. Then, one day in 1920, her father took her to an air show.

Inspired by what she had seen, Amelia took her first plane ride a few days after the show. She was exhilarated! She found a woman pilot and began taking lessons—which cost $1 a minute—and in time became an accomplished pilot herself. Amelia set a women's altitude record while still a student pilot, climbing to 14,000 feet above sea level without bottled oxygen. In 1928, accompanied by two male aviators, she became the first woman to cross the Atlantic by plane, and in 1932, Amelia became the first woman to fly solo across the Atlantic. Taking off from Canada, Amelia began experiencing trouble just four hours into that journey. She encountered a severe storm and lost her fuel gauge and two navigational instruments, but doggedly continued flying east until she spotted Ireland. Amelia Earhart continued to set aviation records, but she was lost over the Pacific in 1937 while on her greatest adventure, an attempt to circumnavigate the globe.

CONSIDER THIS: If you dare to be great, set high goals for yourself. Go where no one has dared go before, and enjoy the ride while it lasts.

The Pet Rock

*"Some Pet Rock owners have found that the
ticking of an alarm clock placed near the box has
a soothing effect, especially at night."*
— From the Pet Rock manual

In 1975 Gary Dahl introduced what is perhaps the most un-usual fad of all time, the Pet Rock. The craze lasted only one Christmas season, then it was gone. Some called the pet rock stupid, but the concept made Gary a millionaire. The idea came to Gary while he and some friends were relaxing at a local pub. After listening to everyone else talk about the woes of owning a pet, Gary said, "My pet is no trouble at all. . . . I have a pet rock." Making up the tale as he went, he told his friends about the care and feeding of his imaginary companion. Everyone had a good laugh and then swapped jokes for another hour. Gary left the pub feeling that the pet rock was an idea worth thinking about.

A former copywriter, Gary at first wrote a book about own-ing a pet rock, following the format of a popular dog owners' manual. He soon revised his idea and decided to market an ac-tual rock with a small instruction manual attached. Luck, cou-pled with persistence, resulted in publicity about Gary's novel idea in major newspapers and magazines. As word of the nov-elty spread, the Pet Rock began to sell like gangbusters, and Gary had to work virtually twenty-four hours a day to keep up with the orders. But he sensed that the craze would remain popular for only one Christmas season. Gary was correct, and sales fell off as quickly as they had soared. Although its popu-larity was short-lived, very few things have ever approached the success of the Pet Rock.

CONSIDER THIS: Fads have short life spans. If you can't get in and make a profit quickly, you may lose your shirt.

Maytag

"All will come out in the washing."

— Cervantes

At the turn of the century Fred Maytag and several of his friends were busy running a small business in Newton, Iowa, that made farm machinery. They were fairly successful, but sales were very seasonal. In an attempt to stabilize sales, the partners decided to diversify and began to make other products. One of their ideas was the Pastime Washer, which they introduced in 1907. The device consisted of a cypress-wood tub that was fitted with hand-operated washing blades and had grooves in the interior that imitated the function of a conventional washboard. Fred's company tried other products as well and, like almost every other manufacturer in America at the time, attempted to crack the burgeoning automobile market. The Maytag automobile was introduced in 1909, but it was not successful.

By 1920, when Fred resigned from the company, Maytag washers were its dominant product. The company continued to concentrate on making its washers more innovative and introduced such features as an all-aluminum tub and gentle blades that worked better than those of competing brands. In 1923 Maytag dropped its other product lines, and as a result, its sales rose from the 1921 level of $1.25 million to $28.7 million in 1925. The company continued to hold a leadership position in the washer industry until it was overtaken by Whirlpool in 1950.

CONSIDER THIS: Once you know what you do best, focus your attention on that one occupation and eliminate those tasks that distract you from your main business.

The Backward Broad Jump

*"Every problem contains within itself the seeds of
its own solution."* — Stanley Arnold

When something has been done a certain way for a long period of time, we often lose the ability to consider other techniques that might work better. This is much like not being able to see the forest for the trees. If we lack the ability to duplicate a feat that someone else has accomplished, maybe we should look at the problem from another perspective or try to overcome it in a different way. In *The Executive Breakthrough*, author Auren Uris relates the story of a young teenager named Stanley Arnold. Stanley was not athletic; he did poorly in most sports and was no match for the rest of his class in the broad jump. As Stanley tried to practice, without success, an idea occurred to him: Maybe he could jump backward! It was at least worth trying, and as it turned out, the idea worked and Stanley was soon beating his classmates. After perfecting the technique, Stanley eventually became the world's first backward broad jumper.

As an adult, Stanley formed his own company, Stanley Arnold & Associates. Employing the same concept of creative thinking that changed his athletic life, Stanley now specializes in finding unique ways for companies to solve business problems. His novel approach to broad jumping taught Stanley an important lesson: Look at problems from all angles and without prejudice for how others have approached the problem in the past. The solution may be simple if we can set aside our preconceived notions about how things *ought* to work.

CONSIDER THIS: Do you have some problems that deserve a fresh and unique look?

Post-It Notes

Self-trust is the essence of heroism." — Emerson

Art Fry, a scientist at 3M, was singing in the choir of North Presbyterian Church in St. Paul, Minnesota, and trying to mark his place in the hymnal with small pieces of paper. However, when he opened the book, the slips would invariably fall out. "What if there where a little adhesive on the paper to keep it in place?" Art thought to himself. He remembered a novel adhesive that had been invented some years earlier by another 3M scientist, Dr. Spencer Silver, and for over a year, Art conducted experiments to bring his adhesive bookmark to fruition. The work was not officially sanctioned, but 3M's corporate culture allows people to spend some of their time developing new ideas.

The right formula for the adhesive was difficult to determine. It had to be strong enough to hold the paper in place, but not so strong that it damaged the surface to which it adhered. Instead of using the pieces of paper as bookmarks, Art began to write notes on them and then stick them on things. He called the invention Post-It Notes. Sensing success, Art began to pass the notes out at meetings and finally got people at 3M to take notice, although there were still those who failed to see the value of the product. The company's first attempt at selling Post-It Notes was a disaster, but when the marketing department finally began passing out samples, the product took off like wildfire. Today, Post-It Notes are considered to be possibly the most important invention at 3M since Scotch brand transparent tape.

CONSIDER THIS: It often takes a champion, someone who really believes in a product, to push it past the corporate doubters to success in the marketplace. Does your organization encourage such champions?

The Levi's Mystique

"Chance favors the prepared mind."
— Louis Pasteur

Since their introduction during the California gold rush of the mid-1800s, Levi's jeans have been known for their durability and comfort. Yet, there are probably other brands of pants that are just as comfortable and durable. What has made Levi's jeans stand out among the literally hundreds of brands of slacks that can be found on clothing racks throughout the country? Part of the success of Levi's jeans can be traced to their association with the culture of the West. Until the 1930s, when Easterners discovered Levi's at popular dude ranches, the jeans were mostly sold to Westerners and real cowboys. Their popularity was on the rise when World War II began. When the government declared the jeans to be an essential commodity, available only to defense workers, Levi's became even more scarce and valuable.

In the westerns of the thirties and forties, heroes like Gary Cooper and Roy Rogers wore jeans. Then, in the fifties, a new crop of screen idols, among them James Dean and Marlon Brando, further popularized jeans by wearing them in such generational classics as *Rebel Without a Cause* and *The Wild Ones*. Levi Strauss & Company has continually capitalized on the mystique of its jeans through heavy advertising in virtually all media. However, the most important advertising is the kind that cannot be bought. The association of the product with heroes and matinee idols has made Levi's jeans a staple of almost every American family.

CONSIDER THIS: It is often those chance (or planned) exposures of a product through popular media that are more valuable than any paid advertising.

Grace Hopper on Leadership

"If everyone is thinking alike, then no one is thinking." — Gen. George S. Patton

To many people in the computer industry, Grace Hopper is known as the "mother of computer programming." In an industry usually dominated by men, she stands as a pioneer. When Hopper worked on IBM's first computer, the Mark I, during World War II, computers consisted of a series of delicate electro-mechanical switches. Hopper recalls that the computer wouldn't work one day and that a painstaking search of the equipment revealed a dead moth in one of the switches. The moth was removed and taped in the day's journal. Hopper, who was an ensign in the navy, noted that she had "debugged" the computer—thus becoming the first person ever to use that phrase. Hopper played a major role in developing programming languages for computers. She remained in the navy until 1986, when she retired as a rear admiral.

In a CBS interview, Hopper related her thoughts on leadership: "Somewhere along the line we lost our leadership. Quality of leadership is a two-way street. It is loyalty up and loyalty down. Respect your superior; keep him informed what you're up to, and take care of your crew. When the going gets rough, you cannot manage a man into battle, you must lead him. You manage things, you lead people." Then she revealed a secret: "[Leaders], when in doubt, don't ask, just do; many times it is easier to apologize than to get permission. The big rewards go to the people who take the big risks. A ship in port is safe, but that's not what a ship is built for."

CONSIDER THIS: Do you believe in something enough to be a leader? Will you take the risk involved? Are you prepared to take the responsibility for failure as well as for success?

Buster Brown

*"Never forget a customer, never let a customer
forget you."* — Unknown

I f you don't know the Buster Brown Shoes character, you must have been living somewhere other than the United States. It is one of the most widely known symbols in American marketing. Buster Brown is also one of the first characters ever used to promote a product. The Brown Shoe Company was founded in 1878 and produced a line of shoes for boys and girls. In 1902 cartoonist Richard Outcault introduced a comic strip based on Buster Brown, his sister Mary Jane, and their dog Tige. John Bush, a sales executive for the Brown Shoe Company, recognized the sales potential that a tie-in with the cartoon character would create, and he soon purchased the rights to use Buster Brown to promote Brown Shoes. The problem was that the Brown Shoe Company did not buy exclusive rights to the character, and the firm's owners were taken aback when the Buster Brown character was also used to promote whiskey and tobacco.

Bush was determined to make Brown Shoes' image of Buster Brown stick and hired a series of midgets to tour the country in costume. Ed Ansley devoted twenty-eight years to performing in a Buster Brown outfit and wore out five dogs in the process. With the advent of radio and television, Ed McConnell became Buster Brown. Today, surveys show that the Buster Brown logo is still widely recognized. In fact, many of the customers who bought their own pair of Buster Brown Shoes in the forties and fifties are now buying the same brand of footwear for their children.

CONSIDER THIS: The recognition of a logo can have long-term benefits and can even last from generation to generation.

W. Edward Demming

"I told them Japanese quality could be the best in the world instead of the worst."

— W. Edward Demming

American industry wasn't interested in his message, so W. Edward Demming took his quality gospel to Japan. In the years following World War II, everyone knew that the label "Made in Japan" was synonymous with cheap and poorly constructed products. In 1949, to help get Japanese industry back on its feet, Demming presented an eight-day lecture series. He described to Japanese business leaders how they could stop making the worst products in the world by adopting the management principles of statistical quality control. Some of the industrialists adopted Demming's advice, implemented his techniques, and launched what many contend is the world's most influential quality revolution.

After World War II, U.S. companies didn't have to worry much about quality. They could sell virtually everything they made. It was not until Japanese cars and electronics surpassed American products in reliability and sales that American industry began to consider Demming's quality message. It was Demming's belief that, rather than placing responsibility for product quality on inspectors at the end of the manufacturing process, quality should begin at the design stage and continue throughout production to give workers at every level the power to make improvements. Today, companies that have adopted Demming's quality message have seen vast improvements in product quality and in their ability to compete globally.

CONSIDER THIS: A memo does not implement quality. Quality comes from a passionate commitment to be the best.

Charles Spahr

*"A business may prosper temporarily because of
fortuitous circumstances, but in the long run an
enterprise needs a management team that can
effectively respond to change in the environment in
which it operates."* — Charles Spahr

Until the 1950s, Sohio, a part of the original Standard Oil
empire, was content to operate within the borders of Ohio and
to stay only in the oil business. When Charles Spahr, a longtime Sohio veteran, became president in 1959, he began looking at ways to move the company into a new era of growth and
prosperity. "He shook the company like a terrier grabbing a
mouse," as one executive put it. Sohio expanded its gasoline operations outside Ohio in 1962. It also diversified into such related fields as plastics and oil-shale mining, and intensified its
research on synthetic fibers and other oil-related products.

To make those changes work, Spahr had to transform company management and employee thinking. Placing a high priority on productivity, Spahr put people in responsible positions
because of their ability and not because of seniority. He developed systems for inspiring and rewarding all employees for superior achievement. An innovative compensation program
helped both managers and employees develop an "ownership
attitude" and unity of purpose. Sohio's streamlining and positive
motivation worked because of Spahr's ability to sell his ideas.
The result was a memorable turnaround for Sohio from a stale
company to a growing concern.

CONSIDER THIS: When an organization becomes stale, it is
time for a new look at how things are done. Perhaps it is time
to shake up the *status quo* like "a terrier grabbing a mouse."

Booker T. Washington

"You must understand the troubles of that man farthest down before you can help him."

— Booker T. Washington

America has long been a country of opportunity, but for African Americans in the South, there have been special problems to overcome. One person who provided a model for education and advancement of his people was Booker T. Washington. Born a slave in 1856, his family walked to West Virginia when he was nine, and he began attending school at night after working in a mine during the day. Adopting the name Washington, he left home at age sixteen to attend school in Hampton, Virginia. When he graduated, he was given a place on the faculty.

Sometime later, in Tuskegee, Alabama, a white merchant and a black workman joined together to establish a school for African Americans. After securing $2,000 in funding from the state legislature, they invited Washington to become the school's principal. When he arrived, Washington asked to be shown the school. "There isn't any—yet," he was told. The school opened in a borrowed church, and Washington began searching for money. People from both races contributed to the school, and many white Southerners were greatly impressed by Washington's sincerity, intelligence, and commitment. He called on people to "invest in the Negro race" and was an able spokesman for the cause. When he approached railway magnate Collis Huntington for a donation and he was offered just $2, Washington persisted. As a result, Huntington gave $50,000 to the school and later donated the money for a new building, which was named Huntington Hall.

CONSIDER THIS: Gentle and persistent persuasion is often the best method for bringing a person to your way of thinking.

Sheldon Adelson and COMDEX

"If at first your don't succeed, try, try again."
— Anonymous

Sheldon Adelson first became an entrepreneur at the age of sixteen when he used his paper-route savings, a $3,000 loan, and a note from the seller to buy a small vending machine company. He placed the machines in nearby factories and collected the nickels to pay back the loan. Later, he bought a truck and began selling ice cream. Adelson went into the service during the Korean War and afterward took a job as a secretary to the owner of a financial magazine in New York City. In 1962 he co-founded a firm that acted as a finder for companies trying to locate capital, but the stock market reversal of 1970 left Adelson over a million dollars in debt.

Leaving Wall Street, Adelson went into condominium conversions, but he soon returned to publishing with his purchase of *Communications User* magazine in 1972. While attending a condominium-conversion trade show, he recognized the need for a similar show in the communications industry. Adelson staged his first trade show in 1973, when the microcomputer began making its way to the marketplace. Called COMDEX, his trade show for microcomputer dealers quickly became one of the world's most respected computer trade shows. While others have failed, COMDEX continues to be one of the best. As a "side show," Adelson's company, The Interface Group, began providing attendees with travel packages and became one of the top ten tour businesses in the United States.

CONSIDER THIS: A successful device used in one industry, such as the trade show, can often be tailored to meet the needs of an emerging industry. However, it is often those who get there first who establish themselves as the front-runner.

IBM's Secret of Success

"It's a funny thing about life, if you refuse to accept anything but the best, you very often get it." — W. Somerset Maugham

Throughout the much of the twentieth century, IBM has been one of the most respected corporations in America. Among the reasons for its success are the corporate beliefs that have been a part of the company from its beginning. The father-son team of Tom Watson and Tom Watson Jr. doggedly promoted a three-part mission for the corporation that became ingrained in every aspect of IBM's operation. The principles are:

1. Respect for the individual.
2. Unparalleled customer service.
3. Excellence and superior performance.

What's the big deal? Nearly every company espouses similar principles. The difference is the importance placed on the principles by IBM's upper management. Tom Watson drilled the importance of the principles into the very fabric of his company. Rewards were given to those employees who exhibited outstanding support of the corporation's values. One story tells about an IBM representative who needed to deliver a part for a broken computer across town. Bad weather had closed most of the bridges in the city, and traffic on those that remained open was backed up for miles. Not to be deterred, the quick-thinking IBMer put on a pair of skates, wove his way through the gridlock, and got the part to the customer in time.

CONSIDER THIS: We all pay lip service to our principles. Do you believe in yours enough to make them an everyday part of your life? Expect the best of yourself and very often you will get it.

The Law of Venture Capital

> *"Great moments start in obscurity with obscure people and sweep on to success if those obscure people are servants of great ideas."*
> — Nashua Cavalier

In his book *Entrepreneurial Megabucks*, A. David Silver invents "Silver's First Law of Venture Capital:" $V = P \times S \times E$. In the equation, P, S, and E represent qualities of a new venture. P is the size of the problem to be solved, S is the elegance of the proposed solution, and E represents the quality of the entrepreneurial team. By assigning numbers to each attribute, they can be multiplied together to calculate the worth of the enterprise (V). Using this technique, you can compare several potential investments and determine which has the highest chance of success (the highest value of V). Silver claims that many venture capitalists use the formula to determine where they will invest.

To be worthwhile, the size of a problem and the resulting solution must be large. In other words, there must be a market that is sufficiently large to pay for the venture. The elegance of the solution is also important. If the solution is elegant and difficult to reproduce, then it is reasonable to expect that it probably will not soon be copied by competitors. Perhaps the solution might be patentable. Finally, the quality of the entrepreneurial team is important. Many people have good ideas, but it takes a team with good ideas as well as the management ability to make things happen for a venture to be successful. All components are necessary for the final outcome (V) to make the value of the enterprise sufficiently high to warrant consideration by investors.

CONSIDER THIS: What large problem is out there now waiting to be solved? What special interests or skills do you have to begin to solve such a problem?

Gerber

"The advertising man is a liaison between the products of business and the mind of the nation."
— Glenn Frank

Dan Gerber had to take his turn feeding his six-month-old baby hand-strained foods. Since his family business, the Freemont Canning Company, was involved in food processing, Dan naturally wondered if there might be a market for canned baby foods. However, there were some problems. The baby-food business was viewed as very risky. If a mistake were made, it could destroy the reputation of the entire company. Also, baby food would be more expensive to produce than conventional canned goods. A 4.5-ounce can of baby food would sell for 15 cents while a 10.5-ounce can of regular vegetables would sell for just a dime. The company was aware of the potential problems, but a survey of mothers and pediatricians yielded encouraging results.

In 1928 Fremont came out with a line of five canned baby foods, which was initially promoted with a coupon campaign. When the country began to slide into the Great Depression, the company decided to continue promotion of its baby food, and sales continued to rise. Competitors soon began to enter the market, and to garner a competitive edge, the firm sought to gain the trust of mothers by becoming experts in baby care. Part of the approach included providing informational pamphlets to pediatrician's offices. Dorothy Gerber, Dan's wife, helped to answer the more than 20,000 letters sent to the company by mothers seeking help with problems ranging from how to get babies to sleep to the best way to remove stains from bibs. In 1941 the enterprise changed its name to Gerber Products Company.

CONSIDER THIS: A good idea must still be followed up by smart marketing and continued awareness of those who use the product.

The Magna Carta

*"Look back often and see what made our country
the great nation it is today."* — E. S. March

The American Dream has been shaped by a few significant documents that have defined the methods by which people could seek freedom and happiness. Among those usually mentioned are the Mayflower Compact, the Declaration of Independence, and the Constitution. However, on June 19, 1215, nearly three centuries before Columbus arrived in the New World, King John of England signed the Magna Carta. That parchment was to become the first stepping-stone to the great documents of freedom written in early America. The Magna Carta guaranteed for the first time that a king must rule by law and that the king himself is subject to the law.

The Magna Carta was instrumental in shaping the foundation of America and in many ways influences how we run our households, our clubs, and our businesses today. The U.S. Constitution provides a framework under which our country is governed, defines the powers and limits of law, and seeks to ensure that the law applies equally to all people. In our homes, even when one parent has "power", he or she is subject to societal constraints. In business, workers may put up with a little tyranny if they think it is for their own good, but Americans have a long tradition of rebelling against ill-used power. Americans tend to work well together in a society that strives to treat all people fairly and works toward the common good. History has shown that the American system of government has provided society with the greatest opportunities for all its people.

CONSIDER THIS: Never forget or underestimate the heritage of the American Dream. Remember how the struggles of others won the freedom we enjoy today.

Inventors vs. Entrepreneurs

*"The conditions of success in life are the possession
of judgment, experience, initiative and character."*
— Gustave Le Bon

Many people tend to lump inventors and entrepreneurs together. While this may be correct in some instances, the process of inventing is much different from that of creating a company to bring the resulting product to the market. An inventor creates a solution to a particular problem; the entrepreneur organizes, manages, and assumes the risks of making the solution commercially viable. When Rudolph Diesel invented the diesel engine, it was probably the worst thing that could have happened to him. His poor business acumen led him on a roller-coaster ride of riches and poverty that ended in his suicide. Ole Evinrude invented the outboard motor, but without the business sense of his wife, Bess, his engine may have faded into obscurity. James Murray Spangler invented the vacuum cleaner, but it was William Hoover who made the invention a household word.

Many times an inventor may have enough business sense to start a small company and carve out a niche for the product. But if the enterprise becomes large, it often becomes unmanageable, and the inventor will have to find the proper management to help, sell the company to others, or watch it fail. Entrepreneurs may not actually invent anything. They may find an inventor and develop a team that can bring the idea to fruition, as in the case of Hoover. A good invention does not in itself make a viable business. The formula must include not only a good idea, but the entrepreneurial passion to take risks and the management skill to make it all work together.

CONSIDER THIS: Ideas don't mean a thing unless there are the other parts of the formula to make the idea successful in the marketplace.

Winton Blount

> *"This is the age of the specialist. Charm and good manners are worth up to $30 a week. After that the pay-off is in direct ratio to the amount of specialized know-how in a fellow's head."*
>
> — Billy Rose

After World War II, Winton Blount and his brother Houston decided to try to revive their family sand and gravel business, which had almost gone under during the war. When Winton went to Atlanta to purchase some surplus army equipment, he couldn't resist some attractively priced tractors and scrapers. He figured the company could also go into the contracting business. The Blounts took small jobs and gained experience that allowed them to bid on and complete a wind tunnel for the air force in 1952. The experience they gained enabled them to successfully bid on other technical buildings for the air force and NASA. As America's space program moved into high gear, those building projects were the first of many that required the kinds of specialized experience the Blounts had obtained on previous projects. Projects included an indoor ocean for the navy, nuclear reactors, a cyclotron, and an airline terminal at the Atlanta airport.

Construction is always cyclical, and to smooth out the business cycles, the Blounts diversified into manufacturing machinery and equipment. As a result of specializing in the construction of technically complex buildings, the Blounts were able to secure contracts that offered higher profit margins. By 1985, Blount, Inc. employed over 8,000 workers. Winton Blount used much of his fortune to benefit numerous charities. He also took leave from his business in 1968 to serve as America's postmaster general.

CONSIDER THIS: Specialization and expertise in doing the hard jobs often provide you with less competition and more chance for profit.

Alex Haley's Roots

*"Our belief at the beginning of a doubtful
undertaking is the one thing that assures the
successful outcome of any venture."*

— William James

Alex Haley, in his book *Roots*, contributed a new chapter to
the American Dream. Haley showed millions of Americans the
value of knowing who you are, where you came from, and the
value of your heritage. The pinnacle event of the *Roots* miniseries
was a long time coming for Haley. After retiring from the Coast
Guard, he was determined to become a writer. During his first
year, he eked out a measly $2,000 working sixteen-hour days. At
one point, Haley took stock of his situation. He had two cans of
sardines and eighteen cents to his name. Sensing that he had hit
his lowest point, Haley put the items in a sack as a reminder. The
next day, he received a check for an article he had written. For
years, Haley kept that sack hanging like a trophy in his library.

Haley had made some progress as a writer when he began to
write *Roots*. He remembers going deeply into debt as he spent
much of his time sifting through old records in courthouses. "I
owed everybody I had been able to borrow from." Haley
missed five deadlines and was bogged down trying to describe
Kunta Kinte's journey from Africa to America aboard a slave
ship. Somehow, he found someone who would loan him more
money and booked passage on a freighter. Haley spent ten days
in the vessel's cargo hold, stripped to his underwear and trying
to imagine what it had been like for Kunta. The experience
helped him gain an understanding of his forebears' feelings, and
he finally was able to complete the story.

CONSIDER THIS: If you believe in what you want to become,
you will gain the strength to overcome the valleys of depression
and humiliation, and rise up to accomplish the task at hand.

Business Passion

"A certain excessiveness seems a necessary element in all greatness." — Dr. Harvey Cushing

Many Americans are content with not stepping out of bounds. Peer pressure and cultural mores tend to keep people in check and often prevent them from doing something fantastic. When Tom Peters and Nancy Austin were writing a book about American businesspeople who made things work when others merely limped along, they could find no better word to describe the phenomenon than *passion*. Passion is that quality that moves a person beyond the ordinary execution of a task. With passion, the objective becomes a personal quest. Extra hours do not mean anything. Skipping meals is a natural occurrence. The objective has given a certain meaning to existence, and the fulfillment of the goal is a journey of excitement and often joy.

People who have broken out of the ordinary learn to love their participation in life. They often go against the grain. When others shy away from a task, they seek it. They may be the first to volunteer. Then they tackle the task with excitement. That kind of attitude spreads to others, and the person who exhibits that attitude may become what Tom Peters calls a "champion." Champions are the building blocks of many businesses. They may be the owners of a small enterprise or up-and-coming employees in a corporation. It is inevitable that champions will make mistakes, fail, and have successes. They will seek to make a difference in whatever they do. If they are allowed to make progress, they will attract people to their goals. If they are discouraged from making progress, they will go elsewhere.

CONSIDER THIS: The organization that can tap into the energy of a champion can perform tasks that are impossible to accomplish by ordinary means.

Rose Blumkin's Superstore

*"Probably the world's greatest humorist was the
man who named them easy payments."*

— Stanislas

Even at age ninety, Rose Blumkin could "run rings around"
the top graduates of America's business schools and the Fortune
500 CEOs, stated a 1984 article in the *Wall Street Journal*. Rose
emigrated from Russia to the United States in 1917, bribing her
way past a border guard and traveling through China and
Japan. The daughter of a poor rabbi, her success was due to a
combination of brains, wit, and the determination to make
something of herself. She told *Journal* reporter Frank James in
1984, "I'm born, thank God, with brains. In Russia you don't
have no adding machine or nothing, so you have to use your
head. So I always used it."

Rose Blumkin began her business career in a pawnshop at
the age of forty-three. She ran the shop with her husband until
his death 1950, and at that point she took off on her own. She
established the Nebraska Furniture Mart, which became one of
the largest furniture retailers in the U.S. However, things did
not always go smoothly. During the Korean War, Blumkin had
to borrow $50,000 on a short-term note to pay suppliers. Hold-
ing a special sale, she quickly made $250,000 in cash and paid
off the loan. Once out of debt, Blumkin operated on a cash-
only basis and provided her customers with a wide range of
quality products selling for 20 percent to 30 percent below normal retail. One of the first to use the "superstore" concept successfully, Rose Blumkin sold Nebraska Furniture Mart in 1983
for $60 million in a "handshake deal."

CONSIDER THIS: When times are good, getting into debt is
easy, but when times are bad, debt can be fatal.

J. B. Fuqua

"The strength of an organization is not I. It is we."
— A. B. Zu Tavern

John Brooks (J. B.) Fuqua was raised on a Virginia tobacco farm, but his sights were not set on farming. As a young schoolboy, a schoolteacher told Brooks that he could borrow books from Duke University by mail. That, he believes, was a turning point in his life. He ordered books on business and finance and read them from cover to cover, even though he understood only part of what he was reading. By the time he got out of high school, J. B. knew plenty about the business world. At age fourteen he became a ham-radio operator and by age nineteen was the chief engineer at a radio station. At age twenty-one he went to Augusta, Georgia, with a plan to start a new radio station. J. B. knew no one in the city, but within a few days, he had found people who would back his venture with their money, give him a share of the ownership, and let him manage the operation.

There are two important elements in Fuqua's strategy: using other people's money and using other people's brains. Since he began with little money, Fuqua had to learn how to find people with money who would back him. Since there were many things about business he did not know, he hired people smarter than he to perform those tasks. Fuqua has become an expert on financial reports. Calling the footnotes the most important part of any report, Fuqua has bought and sold scores of businesses on his way to taking Fuqua Industries, Inc. into the Fortune 500.

CONSIDER THIS: One person cannot have all the money and brains to build an empire. It takes resources and knowledge beyond what one person can muster—and it takes someone with the ability to bring those resources together.

Roger Horchow

"Satisfied customers almost invariably become active agents for the advancement of the company's business." — Unknown

Since the first Montgomery Ward and Sears catalogues appeared in the late 1800s, everyone had known that mail order was a viable business, but most thought that the customers were rural households. Then came Roger Horchow, who discovered that the rich like to do their shopping from home as well—if the products are right. Using his savvy for picking good products, Horchow put together a company that defined the luxury mail-order business. A Yale graduate, Horchow chose to enter the retail field after working a summer job at the Lazarus store (the forerunner of Federated Department Stores) in Columbus, Ohio. After serving in the army during the Korean War, he accepted a job at Foley's in Houston, where he eventually worked his way up to buyer.

Later, Horchow received direct-marketing experience at Neiman-Marcus as its vice president of mail order. In 1971 he became president of Kenton Corporation, a new mail-order business selling upscale merchandise. The business sustained losses of over a million dollars in its first two years. But despite such a poor beginning, Horchow saw great possibilities, and when Kenton was ready to sell, he scraped together $1 million to buy the company. With its name changed to The Horchow Collection, the business began showing a profit in 1973 and over the next several years carved out a substantial niche in the luxury mail-order business. One of the primary factors in Horchow's success is his ability to select items that will appeal to his clientele. If he can't think of someone for whom a particular item would make an appropriate gift, that item will never appear in his catalog.

CONSIDER THIS: What kinds of clientele is your business leaving out?

Curt Carlson and Gold Bond

"Success is sweat plus effort." — A. A. Milne

The son of Swedish immigrants, Curt Carlson was born into a family that stressed hard work, religious training, and the importance of family. By the time he had reached the age of eleven, Curt had his first paper route. While he was in college, he operated a corner newsstand and sold advertising. After Curt graduated with a degree in economics, he went to work as a soap salesman for Procter & Gamble. When he noticed a department store giving away redeemable coupons for each dollar's worth of merchandise purchased, Curt thought the trading stamps also could build business for grocery stores. In 1938 he started the Gold Bond Stamp Company, and spent his evenings and weekends selling the idea to mom-and-pop groceries in Minneapolis, Minnesota. The concept caught on slowly at first, but soon Curt quit his full-time job to devote time to his new venture.

Just as the business was starting to take off, World War II paralyzed the market. The company managed to survive, and by the 1950s Gold Bond stamps were being offered by national chain stores. In the 1960s the trading stamp business peaked, and Curt Carlson began to diversify. He purchased the prestigious Radisson Hotel in Minneapolis and began to build a large chain of hotels throughout the United States and Canada. Other Carlson holdings include restaurants, marketing companies, travel agencies, and investment firms. Carlson has also taken a leadership role in supporting non-profit organizations. His company is a charter member of the Minnesota Keystone Club, which consists of businesses that donate 5 percent of their earnings to selected local organizations.

CONSIDER THIS: Working hard and smart can still get you to the top. But don't leave it at that, add persistence and patience.

Boys Town

"He ain't heavy, Father . . . he's m'brother."
— Boys Town slogan

While operating a haven for homeless men in Omaha, Nebraska, Father Edward J. Flanagan began to understand that such men had often begun life as neglected or abused children. That realization made him want to address the problem at its source—to work with neglected young boys and provide them with a way to escape from certain poverty. With support from his archbishop, Father Flanagan decided to change the direction of his ministry and open a home for such youthful castoffs.

On December 12, 1917, with a $90 donation, Father Flanagan began his ministry by taking in five troubled youngsters at a modest home in Omaha. News spread quickly, and by Christmas he was caring for twenty-five boys. Judges soon heard about the effectiveness of this ministry and sent so many boys that only those whose conditions were most desperate could be accepted. At first, local residents were generous with donations, but some complained about the growing number of delinquent boys in the neighborhood. Therefore, with support from friends and business owners, a farm was purchased ten miles outside Omaha where a "Boy's Town" was erected. On October 22, 1921, Father Flanagan and the boys moved into their new home. The hastily constructed temporary buildings soon housed a growing "family" of more than 200 boys. Omaha citizens conducted several campaigns to raise support for the town, and in March 1922 ground was broken for a permanent five-story main building. Thousands of boys (and later girls) have experienced the benefits and responsibilities of a loving family though the ongoing ministry of Father Flanagan's Boys Town.

CONSIDER THIS: The best way to create a safe and free society is to give everyone an opportunity to succeed.

The Company Hero

"Lives of great men all remind us we can make our lives sublime, and departing, leave behind us footprints on the sands of time." — Longfellow

In business, as in all organizations, it is helpful to have a role model to follow. Heroes are not easy to come by, and when one appears, the most should be made of the moment. In many businesses the founder is the hero, the one who took the business from nothing to something with hard work, sweat, and commitment. The hero may have fallen at one point, only to rise above the situation and pursue the goal again. Tom Watson's piano-selling days are well known to every IBM employee. His simple directives to "Think" and "Aim High" are repeated again and again, years after his death. Other heroes at IBM are treated royally with recognition, promotions, and monetary rewards.

What would Mary Kay Cosmetics be without the dynamic story of how its founder rose from nothing to become a giant in the industry? The story of Charles Steinmetz, the Austrian immigrant who worked for Thomas Edison, is a well-known part of the corporate lore at General Electric. And you can bet that the employees of Hewlett-Packard know the history of their founders. Even in smaller companies, heroes can be honored. The top salesperson or the employee who discovers how to save thousands of dollars should be recognized. This recognition not only inspires others, it also heightens their awareness of possible opportunities for them to excel. The result is a more motivated and usually happier employee and a more productive organization.

CONSIDER THIS: Being shy about recognition is not a desired character trait. Your accomplishments can inspire others. If you keep your achievements to yourself, you are preventing others from recognizing their own potential.

Warren Buffet's Good Investments

> *"Behold the turtle. He makes progress only when he sticks his neck out."* — James Conant

There is no training you can receive in school that will thoroughly substitute for the lessons gained from hands-on experience. Warren Buffett started learning about business at age fifteen by buying some coin-operated pinball machines and putting them in local barbershops. Warren became interested in the stock market and studied it with a vengeance. He searched for the brightest investment firm and then applied for a job. Although he made good money, Warren felt the business was too mechanical and moved home to Omaha, where he eventually acquired control of Berkshire Hathaway, a textile manufacturer. Once he had control, the company's earnings grew by more than 20 percent per annum for over fifteen years. Part of the growth was the result of Warren Buffet's knack for picking sound investments.

A company that is a good investment, according to Buffett, exhibits the following traits: It offers a high return on investment capital. Its business is easy to understand, and most profits are generated in cash. It has a strong franchise and can raise prices. Its earnings are predictable, and it is not in an industry that is a natural target of regulation. Inventories are low, but there is a high asset-turnover ratio. The business is easily run and management is owner-oriented. Finally, the best business is one that receives royalties on the growth of others, requiring little capital itself.

CONSIDER THIS: If you find an excellent business, invest! If you don't know of such a business, study the market to find one or decide to start one on your own.

Ford's V-8

"Few things are impossible to diligence and skill."
— Samuel Johnson Rasselas

People with vision often butt heads with the more practical world. One person often sees in his or her mind's eye how something could be accomplished, but convincing others is no easy matter. A select few can ignore the nay-saying of others and push to make their vision become a reality. Henry Ford wanted to build a V-8 motor with all cylinders cast in a single block. Engineers could design it on paper, but they all agreed that it simply could not be built. "Produce it anyway," was Ford's reply. Reluctantly, the engineers tried. For months and months they tried, and came to Ford saying, "It can't be done!" But Ford continued to insist, and the engineers tried more ideas.

After more than a year of experimentation, there seemed to be no reasonable solution to the problems. The engineers reiterated their first assessment: "Impossible." Ford again said, "Keep trying." Although the engineers remained convinced that the task could not be accomplished, a solution was eventually found and Ford had his V-8 motor. Some called Ford hardheaded, and they were right! However, had it not been for his stubborn determination, Ford would not have pioneered many of the advancements that revolutionized the fledgling automobile industry. A visionary may see capabilities far beyond what is currently possible. If there were no visions of the future, we would not strive to reach them.

CONSIDER THIS: The solution to a problem may not be readily available. It may be thousands of man-hours away. But if you can conceive that there is an answer, you can eventually find a way to make it happen.

The Slinky

*"The man with a new idea is a crank until his
idea succeeds."*   — Mark Twain

Opportunity often knocks at odd times and in odd ways.
When the knock occurs, some people answer the door, say
"What a great idea!" and then proceed to do little or nothing
about it. A few people will grab the opportunity and make
something happen. The Slinky, the spring-like toy that walks
down stairs, essentially invented itself. One day in 1943,
Richard James, a marine engineer, was startled by a zero-com-
pression spring that fell off a shelf, proceeded to "walk" across
a row of books, and then bounced to the floor. James took the
spring home, and his toddler played with it for hours. The
spring represented an opportunity. What could be done with it?
Along with his wife, Betty, James decided to test the potential
of marketing the spring as a toy. They made 100 of the springs
and arranged to show them at Gimbel's department store in
New York City. Customers loved the Slinky's "personality" and
bought the entire stock.

Manufacture, promotion, and distribution of the Slinky was
haphazard at first, but sales soon flourished. Unfortunately,
Richard had a difficult time coping with success. By the mid-
1950s, he had drained the company of most of its assets. After
Richard left his wife and the Slinky organization, Betty continued on her own and returned the business to prosperity. After
more than forty years, and with only small modifications, the
Slinky still has the appeal to become a favorite toy of each
new generation.

CONSIDER THIS: Look at simple things. Get good ideas.
Get feedback. If the idea is good, then add very hard work. The
formula spells success.

Moving Up the Ladder

"The life that is unexamined is not worth living."
— Plato

Everyone has heard the phrase, "It's not what you know but who you know that counts." This bit of folk wisdom has found some verification in studies about how people move up the corporate ladder. Relationships with the people higher up can be very helpful or dangerous to your career path. Most managers tend to promote people they can work with, whom they can trust, and who will be team players. The employee who ignores the role of business relationships is probably the same one who will stay in the mailroom the rest of his career. In a corporate study, Robert Jackall researched the factors that help to move people up the managerial ladder. It was his understanding that, once a person reached a certain level, managerial ability was taken for granted. After that, there were five other key factors.

The top factor Jackall discovered was Patron Power. A manager must have a mentor, sponsor, or champion who can pull him or her up the ladder. Often, when the mentor moves up, his or her favorite workers move up as well. Style is an important component for a potential upward move. The manager must be well organized and be able to give slick presentations and think fast. Also, the manager must be perceived as a team player. He must have self-control, manage his stress, and always exhibit a smiling and agreeable demeanor in public. Finally, the manager must look and dress the part. Shakespeare said we are all actors. It is only those actors who can play the part well that wind up in the starring role.

CONSIDER THIS: Which of these factors do you need to work on? Are any of them holding you back?

The Risk of Freedom

*"Gentlemen, I make the motion that the United
Colonies are, and of right ought to be free
and independent."*
— Richard Henry Lee, June 7, 1776

What does Independence Day have to do with your personal success? A unique government was formed as the United States created opportunities like the world had never seen. Americans have the freedom to succeed, to fail, to choose their lot in life. It all started when a few entrepreneurial patriots risked their lives to make it happen. In the summer of 1776, a group of fifty-six men met and fashioned the greatest nation in the world. They knew they were at risk. Patrick Henry boldly declared, "If this is treason, make the most of it." Thomas Jefferson was called upon to form a committee and draw up a Declaration of Independence. Every man knew that a signature on such a document could be a warrant for his death.

War was inevitable. People would die, and the outcome of the revolution could not be predicted. Yet, those patriots held fast to their strong belief in freedom and the rights of individuals. They were willing to take the risk—and willing to hope, work, and fight for victory. On July 4, 1776, after extensive debate, arguments, and modifications, each man signed the Declaration, which provides each of us the freedom to choose how we want to live our lives, what occupation we wish to pursue, and what beliefs we want to hold. But without those who risked their lives to secure those freedoms, America's Declaration of Independence may have been relegated to footnote status in history books.

CONSIDER THIS: The United States is based on the belief that each person can and should be able to exercise the freedom of choice. What have you done with your freedom?

Discovering Problems

"Leadership is like the Abominable Snowman, whose footprints are everywhere, but who is nowhere to be seen." — Warren Bennis

In their book *Leaders*, authors Warren Bennis and Burt Nanus describe some of the characteristics that make managers different from leaders. Managers deal with problem solving. Their focus usually is reactionary, that is, they deal with problems as they arise. Leaders, on the other hand, discover problems. Problem finding in an organization is the identification of a new direction or a new vision. Problem finding looks beyond the current daily crises to the discovery of something beyond the everyday order of things. It brings to light undercurrents and perceives situations that have not yet risen to the surface. Leaders look for trouble well before it has a chance to happen.

Leaders challenge the old conventions. They care about the "know-why" rather than the "know-how." Like a scientist doing research, leaders often believe that knowing the right questions is often more important than knowing the answers. Why does the organization do this or that? Why must the solution to the problem be such-and-such? If an organization can look forward to what questions will be important in the future, its managers will be more able to make decisions today that will lead them toward the solutions to future problems. Let the managers keep the ship on a safe course; let leaders steer the ship into the future.

CONSIDER THIS: Forget about the daily problems for a moment. What are the important questions you need to be asking? Are you on the leading edge of your organization's growth, anticipating what comes next?

Änsa Bottles

*"An idea, to be suggestive, must come to the
individual with the force of a revelation."*
— William James

Bill and Nickie Campbell were like most new parents, doting
over their new daughter, Mary Kathryn. One day grandfather
Rex Gore made a simple observation: The baby was having a
hard time holding onto her baby bottle. "Someday someone
will put handles on these bottles so they'll be easier to hold,"
Rex predicted. Bill and Nickie jumped at the idea. Why not us?
Using some modeling clay, Nickie began to fashion bottles of
various shapes. The couple tested the clay bottles on Mary. The
three-sided one didn't work, nor did several other designs. Finally, Nickie created a bottle shaped like an elongated dough-
nut. The shape had promise. It had two handles, and each could
hold formula.

The Campbells used their own money to have a plastic mold
made by a company in Arkansas. They then had to find a company to manufacture their novel bottle and finally located one
in Florida. The name *Ansa* was chosen for the bottle because it
is Latin for *handle*. An umlaut was added to the first A to give the
name a European flavor, even though the company is based in
Muskogee, Oklahoma. The Campbells received bad news at
their first trade show. They had made opaque bottles in bright
colors, but parents wanted to be able to see the formula inside.
The couple quickly changed to a see-through design and in the
first sixty days of production sold 50,000 Änsa bottles. Within
months, they had moved to a larger warehouse, and their first
year's sales were $1.5 million.

CONSIDER THIS: You may not be the first to think of an
idea, but you can still be the one who does something about it.

Lemons to Lemonade

"When life gives you lemons, make lemonade."
— Unknown

The person with an easy life is the exception rather than the rule. At some point in life, most people find themselves in a state of depression or on the edge of ruin. This may be the very time when something wonderful can happen. It is often when we hit our lowest point, when we have nothing else to lose, that we are willing to take those risks that we would otherwise deem to be too foolish or too dangerous. Adversity may bring out the best in us. John Bunyan wrote the classic *Pilgrim's Progress* after being imprisoned for his religious beliefs. O. Henry (William Sydney Porter), the great short story writer, discovered his writing talent while in prison. Charles Dickens had a tragic first romance and, drawing on his personal life experience, produced the story of David Copperfield.

Beethoven was deaf, Milton was blind, and Helen Keller was deaf, mute, and blind. Yet, their contributions to the world live on. These people with severe handicaps became overcomers. Life had given them little, but they made the most of what they had. Perhaps you will not face these particular handicaps. However, what if you were fired or laid off? What if you were to lose a loved one or all of your wealth? What if you were physically or emotionally handicapped? Consider how much you could contribute to the world if you pushed aside those things that are holding you back. Can you, like those individuals mentioned above, overcome your shortcomings and release the power of your talents?

CONSIDER THIS: Unleash the talents within you. Overcome those areas in your life that you feel are "handicaps." Succeed despite those things that would hold you back.

An Wang

"Whoever wants to reach a distant goal must take many small steps." — Helmut Schmidt

In 1988 Dr. An Wang was elected to the National Inventors Hall of Fame in Arlington, Virginia, joining a prestigious group that includes Thomas Edison, Henry Ford, Louis Pasteur, and the Wright Brothers. An was the son of a Shanghai English teacher. After studying in his native China, he came to the United States and entered Harvard. He emerged with a Ph.D. in physics and an idea for a revolutionary way to store information in a computer's memory. An's invention, a doughnut-shaped device called a magnetic memory core, increased the response speed of a computer's memory. The device was sold to IBM and remained the standard computer core memory for two decades.

Dr. Wang founded his own computing company with $600 in capital in a walk-up loft in Boston's South End. In 1951, his first year, Wang's sales were a meager $15,000. To make his company grow, Wang had to inspire himself and his employees to come up with more innovation and more invention. Over the next several decades, with the help of a continuous stream of new computing products, the company grew steadily. Instead of competing with such computer giants as IBM, Wang found a niche in the small-business computer industry and later became a leader in the development of word processing and office automation. Wang grew his operation, Wang Laboratories, into a Fortune 500 company with annual revenue in excess of $3 billion.

CONSIDER THIS: One invention does not make a company. Particularly in the high-tech industry, success results from a long series of good ideas.

Arthur Fiedler

*"A spoonful of sugar makes the medicine
go down."*   — Mary Poppins

When the history of the twentieth century is written, it will likely be said that the person who sold classical music to the American public was Arthur Fiedler. Born in 1894 into a musical family, young Arthur took violin lessons but found them to be a chore. He attempted an apprenticeship in publishing but became disenchanted. At his father's urging, Arthur decided to become a professional musician and by 1915 was with the Boston Symphony Orchestra, where he ended up playing, at one time or another, almost every instrument. He began making a mark as a conductor as early as 1924 and by 1930 was named the director of the Boston Pops.

Fiedler had the desire to take music to the public. He reasoned that since people freely enjoyed fine books and paintings at libraries and art centers, they should be able to enjoy fine music as well. Therefore, he instituted a series of free open-air concerts that soon became the model for other orchestras and bands around the country. Fiedler offered the public a variety of music, from current popular music to unknown classical pieces. In addition to Chopin and Wagner, he conducted a piece based on radio commercial jingles. His version of "Jalousie," a hitherto unknown tango by a Danish composer, was the first symphonic recording to sell a million copies. Like a spoonful of sugar to make the medicine go down, Fiedler's skillful blending of popular and classical styles soon had Americans enjoying music they otherwise would never have heard.

CONSIDER THIS: Bring something to the market that people enjoy, package it with excitement, and you will always have an audience.

William McGowan of MCI

"Experience is the best teacher, only the school fees are heavy." — Anonymous

As a teenager, Bill McGowan earned his money working night jobs with the railroad while making his way through high school and college. He became qualified in as many jobs as he could and was often making more money than his teachers, thanks to union wages. After a year in a pre-med curriculum, Bill served a stint in the army and then returned to college, majoring in chemical engineering. Seeing that chemists rarely reached the top of a company, he switched to a business major and eventually received an M.B.A. from Harvard. Because he preferred small businesses to major corporations, Bill worked with Mike Todd on a new wide-screen cinematography process, then did management consulting for failing businesses.

In 1959 McGowan started his own business, Powertron, specializing in ultrasonic equipment, which was relatively successful. In 1962 he formed U.S. Servicator, manufacturing diagnostic devices for machinery. In 1968 McGowan was looking for a new venture when he was introduced to a group of men who were trying to take on AT&T's long-distance telephone monopoly with a microwave system. Microwave Communications Inc. (MCI) needed help working with the FCC and raising capital. McGowan joined the group and provided much of the expertise that put MCI on line in 1972 and revolutionized long-distance calling.

CONSIDER THIS: Experience with many enterprises can prepare you for that one venture where all your previous work will come together to create a gigantic success.

Harriet Tubman

*"That this nation, under God, shall have a new
birth of freedom."* — Lincoln

Without freedom, there would be no American Dream. The freedom that allows us to have such a dream has been secured by many great Americans who risked their own lives for the benefit of others. Harriet Tubman, a slave born in Maryland in 1820, became one of America's fighters for freedom. She had heard stories about a land in the north where black people could be free. At night, she dreamed of that land and looked into the deep night sky to find the North Star. That was the star that would lead to "the promised land." Other slaves talked about an Underground Railroad, a network of people who would help slaves find freedom. Harriet knew she had to find that railroad before it was too late. One day she learned that she was to be sold away from her husband and sent farther south where it was much more difficult for slaves to escape. That night, Harriet made her move.

She escaped first to the house of a woman she knew was a member of the Underground Railroad. From that point, Harriet was led farther and farther north, from station to station, until she walked into Pennsylvania and freedom. Former slaves worked as conductors on the railroad and would return to the South to lead slaves out. Harriet joined the railroad and risked her life to lead over 300 slaves to freedom. She became known as Moses, after the biblical figure who cried "let my people go." After the Civil War, Harriet tended to the poor in her house in Albany, New York, until her death in 1913.

CONSIDER THIS: Freedom is a first and necessary step in realizing our dreams.

General Motors

"Give a man a clear-cut job and let him do it."
— Alfred P. Sloan

More than 1,000 companies attempted to enter the automobile business at the turn of the century. Only about 200 ever made commercial products, and only a handful went on to success. As in all new areas of technology, the "shakeout" left only the smart and able companies. One such manufacturer was the General Motors Company, formed in 1908 by W. C. Durant. Durant brought together several of the new auto companies, including Buick, Oldsmobile, Cadillac, and Oakland (Pontiac). The Chevrolet Motor Company, formed in 1911 by racing car driver Louis Chevrolet and Durant, became a part of General Motors in 1918. But, as so often happens in business, the genius who brought the idea to fruition found the company too big to manage, and in 1923 Alfred P. Sloan took the helm.

During the thirty-three years of Sloan's leadership, GM progressed from producing only 10 percent of the world's cars to making over half the world supply in the mid-1950s. Perhaps Sloan's greatest gift to GM was a superior management style, which has been studied and replicated in countless businesses since. Sloan described his style as "decentralized operations and responsibilities with coordinated control." His goal was to maintain a balance between individual and group management, giving each worker a clear task and the responsibility to carry it out.

CONSIDER THIS: In every new industry, there will be a shakeout. Those companies that survive will do so because of better ideas and superior management.

Aluminum Foil

"When you're curious, you find lots of interesting things." — Walt Disney

A number of products that we consider to be indispensable today were developed or discovered by accident. That invariably happens when some keen-minded individual suddenly realizes a use for an item that was originally developed for another purpose. The microwave oven, facial tissues (Kleenex), Silly Putty, the Slinky, the Frisbee, and even the Band-Aid were all derived from some other product. Another item that was discovered "by accident" was aluminum foil.

The Reynolds Metals Company had developed a foil in the 1920s for use as a candy and cigarette wrap. Other aluminum products they produced included house siding, pots and pans, and windows. One Thanksgiving in the 1930s, the wife of a Reynolds executive was looking for a pan in which to roast a turkey. When she couldn't locate one, her husband came up with the idea of wrapping the bird in some of the company's foil. The result was promising, but nothing came of the experiment until after World War II. After further development of the foil for consumer use, Reynolds introduced its aluminum foil to the world in 1947. Sales grew quickly until the Korean War, when Reynolds voluntarily limited its production of foil to support the war effort. At the end of the conflict, sales of the company's hallmark product again soared, and aluminum foil has since become a staple of virtually every American kitchen.

CONSIDER THIS: Look for new uses for the products you sell or use today. Listen to how customers use your products. You might discover a whole new industry.

Proverbs in Business

"Wisdom . . . is more precious than jewels; and nothing you desire compares with her."

— Proverbs 8:11

Mary Crowley never went to business school, but when she needed help training the sales force for her home decorating company, she turned to Proverbs, a book of wisdom in the Bible. For Mary, the graduate education of life was the realization that truth, including business truth, can be found in the wisdom of the Bible. She based her successful company, Home Interiors, on the many common-sense principles that are found in the Bible's book of Proverbs. On laziness: "The soul of the sluggard craves and gets nothing, but the soul of the diligent is made fat." On seeking help: "The way of the fool is right in his own eyes, but a wise man is he who listens to counsel." The work ethic: "In all labor there is profit, but mere talk leads only to poverty." The reality that business is messy: "Where no oxen are, the manger is clean, but much increase comes by the strength of the ox."

Along with business principles, Proverbs also gives personal advice. Dealing with anger: "A gentle answer turns away wrath, but a harsh word stirs up anger," and "He who restrains his words has knowledge, and he who has a cool spirit is a man of understanding." Dealing with pride: "Pride goes before destruction, and a haughty spirit before stumbling." Avoiding confrontation: "Keeping away from strife is an honor for a man, but any fool will quarrel." Priorities: "He who loves pleasure will become a poor man; he who loves wine and oil will not become rich."

CONSIDER THIS: The reason that the Bible is the world's all-time best-selling book is because its wisdom is as fresh today as it was thousands of years ago.

Patrick McGovern

"What we try to do is build a total common family." — Patrick McGovern

In the tenth grade, Patrick McGovern read a book about computers, entitled *Giant Brains, or Machines That Think*. It was then and there that he caught the computer bug. Soon, Patrick built a small computer that played tic-tac-toe and won a scholarship to MIT. While there, he helped edit a Boston-based computer magazine. After graduation, in 1964, Patrick decided that there was a need for gathering statistics on the emerging computer industry. He presold his service to Xerox, Burroughs, and Univac, and hired high school students to count computers throughout the country. Patrick's company, International Data Group, was successful, and in 1967 he ventured into publishing with the periodical *ComputerWorld*.

McGovern felt that his leadership style was closely akin to cheerleading. He sent reporters congratulatory notes and regularly visited employees at their desks. He personally visited each of his employees at least once every year and handed out millions of dollars in cash bonuses on the spot. McGovern was known to work on the beginning of an idea and then leave the rest of the concept to be developed by others. His successful publications include *PC World*, *Mac World*, and a host of other American and international computer-related magazines. From its infancy at the birth of the personal computer era, McGovern's International Data Group (IDG) grew to become the world's leading computer publishing, research, and exposition-management company.

CONSIDER THIS: In a growing business, someone has to have the vision to lead and to cheer on others. Hire competent managers to keep things in order.

Celestial Seasonings

"Good taste is the flower of good sense."
— A. Poincelot

Just for his own pleasure, Mo Siegel picked herbs in the mountains of Colorado and blended them to make an herbal tea. His friends loved the tea and encouraged him to sell the blend. Mo experimented with selling small amounts of his concoction at some local health food stores, and customers seemed to like it very much. Although his small experiment was successful, Mo found that creating a company to produce and sell large amounts of tea was not easy. However, the dream of success was fixed in his mind, and it urged him on. Mo and his wife, Peggy, crisscrossed the country, introducing their tea to skeptical store owners. Back home, there was no money to hire herb pickers, make the teabags, print the boxes, or pay the helpers. Times were very lean.

Mo believed that his company would make it. A college drop-out, Mo's business acumen and success-oriented attitude came from reading the writings and biographies of his American heroes, among them Abe Lincoln, Walt Disney, Tom Watson, and others. He also had a deep belief in God and had studied carefully the teachings of Jesus. Work, work, and more work slowly moved the business into prosperity. Mo Siegel was smart enough to realize that he could not know everything, and as his Celestial Seasonings company grew, he hired key people from Coca-Cola, Pepsi, Pepperidge Farms, General Foods, and other successful corporations. Workers were given ownership in the company, and their commitment to excellence in quality and production made Celestial Seasonings a classic success story.

CONSIDER THIS: Work, work, work. Think, think, think. Working hard and thinking smart are still two main keys to success.

Norm Brinker

"Norman epitomizes the spirit of American entrepreneurship." — Dave Thomas

While only a first grader, Norm Brinker dreamed of owning a horse. His family couldn't afford one, so Norm earned the money himself by picking cotton, delivering newspapers, raising rabbits, and kenneling dogs. Those early businesses taught him both success and failure. Norm's skill and love of riding earned him a spot on the 1952 Olympic equestrian team. Two years later, at the Modern Pentathlon in Hungary, Norm's horse stumbled during a jumping competition, catapulting him out of the saddle. Even though he sustained a broken collarbone, Norm got back on his mount and finished eighth in a field of sixty.

To pay his way through college, Norm sold cutlery door to door. Upon graduation, he received a number of job offers and chose the one that promised to be the most "fun." With an energetic and honest approach to business, Norm played an important role in the expansion of Jack-in-the-Box restaurants during the 1960s. However, his own first restaurant, Brink's Coffee Shop, was a failure. After rethinking and studying the market, he conceived and opened a restaurant based on an Old English theme. Steak & Ale was an instant success and became the model for an entire "casual dining" industry. Norm Brinker's zest for life was put to the test in 1993 when he was almost killed in a polo accident. Doctor's gave up on him, but family and friends prayed and pulled for his recovery. After weeks in a coma, he woke up, responded to therapy, and eventually returned to work.

CONSIDER THIS: Persistence, fortitude, and hard work are the foundations of success. When you are knocked down, get back up and keep fighting.

The Typewriter

"Events are never absolute, their outcome depends entirely upon the individual."

— Honoré de Balzac

Christopher Sholes was not the first person to invent the typewriter—in fact, he was the fifty-second. As early as 1843, patents had been sought and awarded for writing machines. It was in 1866 that Sholes, a printer and newspaperman, was tinkering with a machine to number book pages when a friend remarked that a similar machine could be built to type letters. For seven years, Sholes worked on versions of the machine, but money was running out. Writing letters on the new device, Sholes contacted a Pennsylvania businessman and promoter, James Desmore. Desmore agreed to pay Sholes's bills of $600 and provide future financing in exchange for a 25 percent stake in the invention. Sholes agreed, not knowing that the $600 represented all of Desmore's liquid assets.

Desmore embraced the new venture with enthusiasm. Realizing that they needed more mechanical expertise and financing, the pair sold rights to the machine to Remington. Sholes took a $12,000 payment for his share, and Desmore negotiated a royalty that would eventually pay him $1.5 million. Remington promoted the machine but was a little off in its initial marketing of the typewriter: "Persons traveling by sea can write with it when pen writing is impossible." Finally, the business advantages of typewriting were recognized, and with the help of the YWCA, many thousands of women were trained as typists and gained their first entry into the business world.

CONSIDER THIS: You may not be the first to think of a new idea, but if you keep at it when others quit, you may well be the one who gets the prize.

Amway

> *"Go into business for yourself. Don't be afraid to take risks. It's the only way to succeed."*
> — Richard DeVos's father

Richard DeVos and Jan Van Andel met in high school and became close friends. Both were from a Dutch background that instilled the ethics of hard work and self-esteem. After high school, DeVos and Van Andel fought in World War II, after which they started a flying school and operated a hamburger stand. After selling their first business, they attempted to travel to South America in an old sailboat, but it sank by the time they reached Cuba. After returning to their home in Grand Rapids, Michigan, they were introduced to the direct selling of food supplements through a friend. They were good at it and soon built a distribution network of 5,000 people that they named the American Way Association (Amway).

Amway began when DeVos and Van Andel introduced their own product, an all-purpose cleaner derived from coconut oil. Amway provided a way for people to make money on a part-time basis, but it also provided the full-time worker the opportunity to become a distributor with an unlimited income. DeVos was the team's cheerleader and encouraged more than a million salespeople with positive thinking and risk-taking dares. Van Andel kept the team's head out of the clouds by telling the distributors that "Amway isn't a fast-buck, easy-money scheme. It requires all the attention you would expect to put into a business of your own." Like any business, growth cannot be based on hype. Superior products, research and development, factories, and distribution centers are all crucial to a business's expansion.

CONSIDER THIS: Hype must be backed up by excellent products or the business will eventually fail.

The Potato Chip

"Common sense in an uncommon degree is what the world calls wisdom.
— Samuel Taylor Coleridge

In 1853 George Crum was chef at a resort in Saratoga Springs, New York, when he came up with a new way to fry potatoes. Everyone liked the idea, but people constantly told George to cut the potatoes thinner and thinner. Finally, he began slicing the potatoes so thinly that they were transparent, then fried them in deep oil and salted them. The potatoes were a big hit at the resort and became known as Saratoga Chips along the East Coast. Once a good idea materializes, it takes no time for enterprising imitators to try their hand at the task.

In the 1890s George Sleeper also made a contribution to the potato chip. He was a caterer in Massachusetts when he began placing potato chips in box lunches. They proved so popular that he built a business around the chips and popularized their use in packaged lunches. In 1921 Earl Wise used the potato chip to get him out of a bind. As a grocer with far too many potatoes, he decided to slice them on his cabbage cutter and make them into chips, which he sold in bags for a nickel each. His idea soon grew into a business, and Wise Potato Chips became one of the first producers of processed foods sold in grocery stores. Literally hundreds of independent chip makers sprang up throughout the United States in the twenties and thirties and after World War II. Many of those enterprises eventually were assimilated into larger food companies.

CONSIDER THIS: Good ideas do not have to be original. It may be less risky to duplicate someone else's success from another part of the country.

Edwin Hewitt

"An institution is the lengthened shadow of one man." — Emerson

Like many young men in their early thirties, Edwin (Ted) Hewitt had a dream about his career. He enjoyed being an insurance salesman and was making a good living, but the lure of owning his own business tugged at him. In 1940 Ted made the decision to start his own company. He planned for a year, working out the details of the structure and philosophy his organization would have, the kinds of people to hire, and the business principles the company would follow. Ted's intention was to develop a business specializing in financial planning, and he soon began recruiting his team. With his small company situated in the Chicago's financial district, Ted and his associates began approaching local corporations.

Parker Pens was an early client, and Hewitt helped that company set up a formal retirement plan. That project caused Hewitt to re-examine his business plan. There was a conflict. Although he felt that insurance was not always the best answer to retirement plans, he had made most of his money selling insurance for retirement. World War II interrupted his company's growth, but after the war, Hewitt made the decision to concentrate on providing consulting services for benefit planning on a fee basis. Although his business was headed in a new direction, Hewitt's work in planning the company's philosophy before it hired a single person made it one of the most desirable places to work in America.

CONSIDER THIS: The tools of the trade may change, but the importance of human values and relationships to success remains constant.

Martha Berry

"Not to be ministered unto, but to minister."
— Berry College motto

One Sunday Martha Berry, the young daughter of a well-to-do family in northern Georgia, went out to an old log cabin to read and write. She noticed that mountain children were peeking in to watch her. Inviting them in, she told them Bible stories. Week after week, more children and even adults came to listen. Martha was taken with the bright youngsters, who had virtually no chance of obtaining an education, and started a small school in an old church near Lavender Mountain. The church was named Possum Trot, and it became the cradle of one of the most fantastic educational institutions in America.

Students worked at the school to pay their tuition, and Martha never turned away anyone for lack of funds. She named the gate leading to the campus The Gate of Opportunity and believed that every building on the site should have a spire, "to keep people looking up." As needs grew, Martha searched for outside funding. Martha Berry and her school inspired the world and attracted such benefactors as Andrew Carnegie, Henry Ford, presidents from Theodore Roosevelt to Franklin Roosevelt, the king and queen of England, and many more. Each time a new project was needed, Martha announced, "We are stepping out on a plank of faith." Even today, according to Martha Berry's wishes, Berry College continues to be a different kind of institution, with a strong commitment to "educational quality, Christian values, insistence on the work ethic, and adherence to the principles of American private enterprise: personal responsibility, individual initiative, service to others, courage to take risks, belief in self and in our nation."

CONSIDER THIS: One person *can* change the world. Could you be that one person?

Irving Berlin

"Simplicity is the badge of genius. Simplicity is the badge of distinction." — Milne

As one of the most published songwriters in America, Irving Berlin surely must have studied with the great composers, learned music theory from European masters, or received training at a great conservatory. In reality, Berlin had none of those advantages. After only two years of formal education, he took to the streets as an entertainer. He sang in saloons and learned to pick out tunes with one finger on the keyboard. He never learned harmony and could only play in the key of F sharp. Yet, in 1907 Berlin began to compose. It was not until 1911 that he had his first big hit, "Alexander's Ragtime Band," which sold over a million copies in the first few months. Drafted in 1917 for service in World War I, Berlin wrote a soldier's show that included the popular "Oh, How I Hate to Get Up in the Morning."

Berlin's songs seem to be spontaneous inspirations. Yet, his process of writing was long and painful. He often struggled with lyrics, going through many revisions to get them right. Then, with his limited mastery of the piano, he would bang out a tune. Somehow, after all the agonizing, the song would begin to flow naturally. Unlike a Gershwin song that can be identified after hearing its first measure, Berlin's songs have never had a distinctive style. Berlin never initiated a new musical trend; he just took an existing trend and adapted his music to it. He wrote for the Ziegfeld Follies, Marx Brothers movies, and Broadway shows. His best-known hits have included "White Christmas" and "God Bless America." In his own simplicity Irving Berlin has managed to tell the ever-changing story of America in song.

CONSIDER THIS: You don't have to be complex to be good. Simplicity goes a long way and has staying power that no fad will ever match.

Shareware

*"True creativeness is finding new possibilities in
old situations."*   — Unknown

There may be nothing new under the sun, but there are plenty of people who are still discovering interesting marketing ideas—or developing new twists on old ones. Chrysler made the rebate a part of Americana. Horchow brought a new concept to mail order. Television shopping channels are hot. But one of the most radical concepts in marketing in recent years is Shareware, also known as Freeware or User-supported Software. Originally, the Shareware concept allowed people to freely copy evaluation versions of computer software and pass them along to friends. Clubs soon popped up all over the world offering vast libraries of the "free" software. The question is, how can such software be written, supported, or improved?

People who use Shareware programs are asked to send a registration fee to the author if they like and use the software. Such payment usually entitles users to receive a printed manual, phone support, and additional goodies. You might be tempted to think that the programmers who make the software are hobbyists. Some are; however, some of the programs bring in over a million dollars in fees each year. Many Shareware programs are as good as or better than their retail equivalents. Many well-known current or former Shareware programs, among them DOOM, Procomm, WINKS, and Automenu, are a testament to this creative marketing concept.

CONSIDER THIS: There are new ways to market your product or idea. Look around and learn from other industries. What is working there? Can a similar concept be used by your organization?

A New Disney

"As long as you act as if you're coming from behind, you have a shot at staying ahead."
— Michael Eisner

Walt Disney created much more than a company—he created a real part of the American Dream. Many of our values and goals have been shaped by the fantasy of Disney's stories. Those skillfully crafted tales made it possible to see an exciting future painted with the wonderful colors of imagination. After Disney's death in 1966, the entertainment empire he constructed missed its innovative leader. In an article in *Fortune* magazine, Myron Magnet sums up the Disney situation with a comparison: "University College, London, to memorialize its founder, Jeremy Bentham, keeps the nineteenth-century philosopher's embalmed body fully clothed in a cupboard. Walt Disney Co. had memorialized its august founder by embalming itself."

In 1984 there was somewhat of a shareholder revolt, which in turn led to an onslaught of potential corporate raiders. Walt's nephew Roy, along with the Bass brothers, put Michael Eisner in the chief executive's seat. Eisner, a former president of Paramount with a solid track record of successes, brought ideas back to Disney. Drawing on the vast treasury of Disney films and characters, Eisner revived Disney's television presence, which promoted the Disney theme parks, which in turn sold Disney merchandise, which helped the Disney movies. Under Eisner, the Disney company again discovered its ability to experiment in new areas of entertainment.

CONSIDER THIS: The exit of a strong founder may signal the beginning of the end. Smart companies will not languish for long but will find a new source of inspiration.

Bill Murto of Compaq

*"Happiness is in your mind and how you think
about yourself and what you're doing."*

— Bill Murto

Too often we have a view of success that is strictly monetary. Such a view can make one's life a disaster. Success in anyone's life is measured in terms of fulfillment, not money, and that fulfillment may come from a variety of accomplishments. Bill Murto made a dramatic decision about what he was going to accomplish in his life. After he had finished an M.B.A. in 1977, Murto accepted an entry-level position with Texas Instruments. In five years with TI he was able to involve himself in a variety of projects concerning computer technology. In 1982 he and two other TI employees, Rod Canion and Jim Harris, left to begin Compaq Computer Corporation. The IBM personal computer had already become a success, and the trio wanted to share in the growing market.

Within a year, Compaq had shipped its first PC, and that year's sales volume reached $111 million. Among the hundreds of PC clone makers, Compaq has been the most successful. Murto bought a top-of-the-line Mercedes, a Tudor mansion, and everything else he wanted. But as his personal wealth grew, he found had to clarify his life's priorities. Although he had acquired great material wealth, he felt a need to fulfill a service to mankind that was expressed through his religious faith. After five years with Compaq, Murto resigned to return to school to work on a degree in religion.

CONSIDER THIS: Circumstances should not make choices for us—we should know our own priorities and make our own active choice about which path to follow.

Grandy's Restaurants

"Our goal is to please the customer, and everything we do is designed for that purpose."
— Bill Shaw, president of Grandy's

Over forty years ago, two teenagers worked busing tables in a Dallas cafeteria. Their American Dream was to someday own their own restaurant. Ed Johnson and Rex Sanders paid attention to what worked and what didn't work in the food industry. In 1973 they believed they had devised the formula for a restaurant that would fit in a niche between fast-food hamburger outlets and expensive restaurants. Their Grandy's restaurant was based on their three-part goal of providing better food, better service, and a better dining experience. Instead of burgers and fries, they offered a plate lunch with meat and vegetables. Their "sinnamon" roll desserts were baked from scratch.

The Grandy's philosophy concentrated not only on matching fast-food restaurants' speed of service, but on being different. The owners originally targeted those in the twenty-five-and-older age group who were looking for a family restaurant. To provide that kind of ambience, Grandy's often used a friendly Grandy's hostess, dressed up like the grandmotherly Grandy, to make customers feel at home by giving them individual attention, refilling tea glasses, and chatting. The Grandy hostess is a part of the relaxed, neighborly atmosphere that makes eating a more enjoyable experience. The initial years of careful planning and plain hard work made Grandy's one of the fastest growing restaurant chains in America.

CONSIDER THIS: Even when it appears the big corporations have a market sewn up, there may still be successful niches that can be carved out.

Jack Telnack of Ford

"Whenever you see a successful business, someone once made a courageous decision."

— Peter Drucker

In 1980 Jack Telnack, chief designer for Ford Motor Company, was given the opportunity to create a new American automobile. It would be the car that would lead Ford into the 1990s. In the 1960s, before coming to Ford, Jack had designed powerboats for the Trojan Boat Company. Perhaps it was the sleek, stylish lines of a boat that crept into the design of the new Ford car. The new vehicle, as Jack saw it, had to be efficient and had to give the appearance of speed, even when standing still. Jack was also aware that good looks are not everything, that the car's appearance had to enhance its function; otherwise, it would be a sculpture and not a vehicle.

As head of a 550-person staff, Telnack no longer drew designs himself. Instead, he provided inspiration, leadership, and guidance. He sought out the best ideas in automobile design and promoted their use in the new car. Starting with a clean sheet of paper, the automobile that would become the Ford Taurus began to take shape. "It was a very well calculated risk," Telnack says. "We wanted the customers to feel a bit uncomfortable with the design." Such an approach enables a new design to last longer without becoming too commonplace. Being careful not to go too far in front of public taste, the design team created a new look for Ford that was so successful it was soon reflected in other models in the company's line. Indeed, the novel design of the Taurus set the standard for other automakers to follow into the twenty-first century.

CONSIDER THIS: Form must follow function. It is great to be good-looking, but it is awesome to be both good-looking and useful.

Stew Leonard

"If you want to attract attention, make an everyday chore exciting and fun."

— A. C. Elliott

Executives from major corporations have gone to Stew Leonard's store in Norwalk, Connecticut, to learn lessons from the master. In 1969, when the Leonard family farm was split by a new highway, they decided to take advantage of the traffic by setting up a small dairy store. Stew used ideas from two of his heroes, Dale Carnegie and Walt Disney, to develop his store into something special. From Disney, Leonard learned the virtues of "Cleanliness, quality, and fun." From Carnegie, he learned, "Successful people are the few / Who focus in and follow through" and "Lower the price / Sell the Best / Word of Mouth / Does the rest."

From a small start, his store expanded more than two dozen times. When it reached 100,000 square feet, it was the largest dairy store in the world. Carved into a three-ton granite bolder outside the store are "Leonard's Rules," which state, "Rule 1: The customer is always right! Rule 2: If the customer is wrong, reread Rule 1." Entertainment provided for customers has included a glass-enclosed dairy plant, a cow that moos at the press of a button, a petting zoo, and a singing eight-foot robot dog. The store's walls are covered with employee diplomas from Dale Carnegie and pictures of customers holding Stew Leonard bags. One picture shows a customer at the Kremlin, one is from atop the Great Wall of China, and one is from the floor of the Pacific Ocean. All of this hoopla has translated into a staggering success.

CONSIDER THIS: People want to have a good time, even when shopping. They want to feel like they are at Disneyland, and they want to be treated like royalty. Give them that, and they will come in droves.

The Flight of Voyager

*"Who never walks where he sees men's tracks,
makes no discoveries."*   — J. G. Holland

America is a land of invention. We are a people searching to go where no one has been, to do what no one has done, and to imagine what no one has imagined. Jeana Yeager and Dick Rutan imagined a pioneering aeronautical feat. Jeana grew up in Texas. She worked first as a draftsperson but decided to take up flying. It was at an air show that she met Rutan, who, along with his brother, owned the Rutan Aircraft Factory in Mojave, California. Jeana had been flying for ten years, and Rutan convinced her to come to Mojave as a test pilot. One day as Jeana, Dick, and brother Burt were having lunch, the conversation turned to the possibility of setting up an aircraft sales business. They had the background, but how could they develop a concept that would make people pay attention?

Jeana, Dick, and Burt began considering the long-distance flying record. The previous record for distance was 12,532 miles, set by a B-52 bomber in 1962. They would not only try to beat that record, they would double it on a non-stop flight around the world. With a little backing from some parts and material manufacturers, the Rutans and Yeager began to design the plane. The result was *Voyager*, which weighed only 1,860 pounds empty but would weigh 9,400 pounds when fueled and loaded for takeoff. The plane was slightly damaged on takeoff, and the round-the-world trip was complicated by a typhoon and unexpected storms. Yeager was badly bruised in the turbulence, and at times the pilots became disoriented due to exhaustion. Still, the record-breaking flight was a success. American ingenuity had done it again.

CONSIDER THIS: Progress is never made by doing the same old thing. Set out to accomplish something new.

Cybill Shepherd

"He who has not tasted bitter does not know what sweet is." — German maxim

If Cybill Shepherd appears "gutsy" in many roles, it is appropriate. Named after her grandfather Cy and her father, Bill, Cybill grew up in Tennessee, where she excelled in school and athletics. At age sixteen, she entered and won the Miss Teenager Memphis title, and at eighteen she won a contest for Fashion Model of the Year. Cybill suddenly became a hot property as the new cover-girl sensation. Director Peter Bogdanovich, who was looking for a lead for his movie *The Last Picture Show*, saw one of those covers. He went to New York and convinced Cybill to take the part. The pair collaborated on several movies, and Cybill's star was rising rapidly among the Hollywood crowd. Then came the crash as Cybill fell on hard times with the critics. *Rolling Stone* reported that "her fall from grace was steep and rocky."

Cybill became a liability and was shunned by producers. When Bogdanovich tried to get her a lead role in the 1976 movie *Nickelodeon*, he found that Cybill was unmarketable. Cybill left Hollywood and returned to Memphis, where she spent several years appearing in regional stage productions. She gained new acting experience and new confidence in her abilities. Cybill's star was relighted with the debut of the sassy television detective show *Moonlighting* in 1984. After a rather slow start, the show was ranked in the Nielson top twenty by the end of its first season. In 1986 the show received sixteen Emmy nominations, and in 1988 Cybill Shepherd's commemorative star was placed on Hollywood Boulevard.

CONSIDER THIS: When everyone is against you, it is easy to give up. It takes guts to fall back, improve your technique, and re-enter the fray.

Fred Smith of Federal Express

"You can tell how big a man is by observing how much it takes to discourage him."
— François Fenelon

Education is much more than simply learning facts. Facts do not provide insight. Facts do not promote risk-taking. Looking back on your life, have there been times when you had the gut feeling that something would work when everyone else thought it would not? Were you right? As a student at Yale, Fred Smith wrote a paper outlining the need for a nationwide delivery company that specialized in time-sensitive goods. According to Fred's research, such a company might have a substantial market. The paper got a C, but Fred did not forget the idea. After graduation and a stint in the Marine Corps, Fred bought into an aviation service in 1969. He commissioned two consulting firms to study the feasibility of overnight express delivery. What the companies told him confirmed Fred's earlier research.

Fred Smith raised $80 million, including some family funds, to start his new venture on June 1, 1971, in Little Rock, Arkansas. Large amounts were spent on advertising, which included full-page ads and television commercials. Operations began on April 17, 1973, serving twenty-four cities. The company almost went under several times and did not show a profit until 1976. By 1980, however, earnings totaled almost $60 million, and Federal Express had become the dominant force in the overnight courier business.

CONSIDER THIS: When your ideas are rejected or ridiculed, continue to investigate on your own until you know if those ideas were truly sound.

Mood Rings

"The business of life is to go forward."
— Ben Johnson

Innovation often comes when a person takes an idea from one area of science, business, or industry and applies it to another. Marvin Wernick constantly kept his eyes open for innovations in the jewelry business. He reasoned that although most of the jewelry designers were on the East Coast, people's tastes were different in California. Marvin knew that, just as some people preferred more color in their wardrobe, many also wanted jewelry that was more colorful than the classic styles then available on the market. As the operator of a jewelry store, Marvin saw firsthand the boring colors offered by the eastern designers. He felt they were not paying attention to what people wanted and were anything but "hip." That is when Marvin began making his own jewelry. His ideas of what people wanted proved to be correct and he soon became quite successful.

As Wernick searched for new materials to experiment with, he noticed a story in *Science Digest* about a new liquid crystal that was being used in cancer research. It changed color as the temperature changed. Wernick experimented with the crystal and fashioned it into jewelry that changed colors as the wearer's body temperature changed. The resulting "mood ring" became a huge success. Other manufacturers copied the idea, but Marvin was able to make his rings fast enough to stay ahead of the competition. Like most other fads, the mood ring lasted only a short time. Nevertheless, it stands as an excellent example of how innovation can quickly capture a market.

CONSIDER THIS: Be prepared to take advantage of fad ideas while they are hot, and also be ready for the bottom to fall out.

The Hula Hoop

*"Experience is not what happens to a man; it is
what a man does with what happens to him."*
— Aldous Huxley

Wham-O Manufacturing Co.'s original mega-hit product
was a financial failure. It began when a friend brought an Aus-
tralian exercise hoop to Rich Knerr and Spud Melin. The two
were already marketing several sports articles and thought the
hoop looked like fun. They called the item a Hula Hoop, trademarked the catchy name, and began promoting the hoop in
parks, where kids would gather around for a look and then run
to their local store to buy one. Wham-O gave away "seed"
hoops on beaches and college campuses to get the craze going.
The company's marketing plan was outstanding, and the Hula
Hoop took America by storm. However, there was a problem
with the success.

Although they had applied for a patent, more than forty
competitors entered the market, drawing on the promotion
that Wham-O had already begun (and paid for). It was too late
and too expensive to force the competitors out of business. Although millions of Hula Hoops were sold, the fad was short-
lived and, in the end, the company lost money on the toy.
However, the advertising placed Wham-O in the public eye.
The company became a household name. Also, the Hula Hoop
experience prepared the firm to better protect its next popular
product, the Frisbee flying disc. The Hula Hoop was brought
out again several years later, and although it was not as popular
as it was initially, Wham-O made money the second time
around.

CONSIDER THIS: A loss may really be a success in the long
run. It can give you experience and exposure, and prepare you
for the next challenge.

Dell Computers

"When fortune smiles, embrace her."
— Thomas Fuller

New ventures are often conceived on the leading edge of technology. Such has been the case for many companies in the microcomputer industry. Even with billion-dollar companies such as IBM and AT&T leading the way, the window of opportunity often opens wide enough for even an ill-financed college student to make it big. Michael Dell began preparing for his big opportunity as a teenager selling newspaper subscriptions. After working on a phone bank with fifty other callers and making few sales, Michael thought of a more direct approach. He began getting information about newlywed couples and contacting them directly. Sales soared. Later, when his family bought a computer, Michael took it apart in an effort to gain an understanding of the device all the way down to the chip level.

Michael believed his future was in computers, but his parents insisted that he enroll in the pre-medicine curriculum at the University of Texas in Austin. From his dormitory, he began to set up his business, placing ads in computer magazines, assembling the machines, and shipping them to customers. Michael's company, PC Limited, soon grew so large that he convinced his parents to let him run it full time. Within several years, his computer sales were over $100 million annually. Using the concepts of zero defects and just-in-time inventory, Michael's company, now Dell Computers, has kept costs down and quality high. Even though he is very sure of his business sense, Michael Dell has put together a senior management team from leading high-tech companies to ensure his firm's continued growth.

CONSIDER THIS: Watch for the window of opportunity to open. It is at that point that anyone with brains and determination can successfully compete against all the rest.

The Golden Rule Stores

"Do unto others as you would have them do unto you." — Jesus Christ

Today, when we enter a modern department store, we may think of how it is run by a gigantic and complex international conglomerate. Yet, every business was at one time a single person's idea. The giant corporation is an extension of that original idea. James Cash Penney was born in Hamilton, Missouri, in 1875, the son of a Baptist minister. During his early years, he raised pigs and watermelons and ran a butcher shop. He refused to supply meat to hotels that sold liquor, and his butcher shop failed. Next, he tried retail dry goods and in 1902 bought a one-third share in a dry goods store in Kemmerer, Wyoming. From that store he launched a chain called the Golden Rule stores, so named because they were based on the concept of treating all people with the kindness we ourselves expect, that is, the Golden Rule as taught by Jesus. Every store had a giant Golden Rule sign hanging on a prominent wall.

Penney believed that every person was a "human dynamo, capable of accomplishing anything to which he aspires." He despised debt, drinking, and smoking, and he demanded zeal, enthusiasm, and loyalty from every employee. Penney claimed that it was the application of the Golden Rule that made his stores (now named JCPenney) a success. By the time he died in 1971, Penney's stores had annual sales of over $4 billion and were the nation's sixth-largest merchandiser.

CONSIDER THIS: Do you apply the Golden Rule to your work? Do you demand zeal and enthusiasm from yourself and your employees?

C. E. Woolman and Delta

*"Honesty is the first chapter of the book
of wisdom."* — Thomas Jefferson

The airline on which many people travel for holiday visits and business trips traces its beginnings to the lowly boll weevil. It was the early 1900s and Collett Everman Woolman, an agriculture district agent, battled the destructive boll weevil in an 0X5 Jenny biplane that had been rigged as a crop duster. The dusting operation was a rousing success, and Woolman left the agricultural service in 1924 to join the newly formed Huff Daland Dusters company. He was made vice president and field manager. Since the dusting business was seasonal, Woolman worked to secure mail routes, and in 1929 he began to offer passenger airplane service. The company was renamed Delta Air Service for the Mississippi delta region it originally served.

In 1945 C. E. Woolman was named president and served Delta until his death in 1966. Under his leadership, the company became one of the largest and most respected airlines in the industry. Woolman's credo was found in his adaptation of the Golden Rule. He reworded it specifically for Delta Air Lines. "Let's put ourselves on the other side of the ticket counter," he would challenge. Woolman knew the value of each customer's loyalty, and he pressed Delta to provide a high standard of service. He believed that any business that was completely honest in all its dealings was likely to succeed. And Delta did succeed.

CONSIDER THIS: Never forget that businesses are made up of people with feelings, beliefs, and a hunger to belong to something that is good, honest, and worthwhile.

Bernie Kopell

"Every man is the architect of his own fortune."
— English proverb

Life can seem very tragic and unfair, even in the land of opportunity. You have a dream but find yourself in the dumps with no real prospects of recovery. You are depressed, and in your depression you cannot muster the energy to pull yourself up. You become too cynical to believe that there really is a "cure" for your failure. Bernie Kopell was a failure as a vacuum cleaner salesman. He had come to California to be an actor, but for even the few parts he was able to land, he received no pay. He thought that was what he deserved. Then, one day as Bernie was moping in the back room of the vacuum cleaner store, the owner put on a motivational record. "What a con job," Bernie thought. But as he was trying to ignore the record, he accidentally heard the statement, "Your mind is as the earth. Whatever you plant in it grows. If you plant potatoes you get potatoes. If you plant roses you get roses . . ." Bernie began to listen.

Soon he was paying attention to the record, and it wasn't long before he began reading and attending lectures. Bernie began to believe that God had given him talent, and he became proud to be who he was and considered himself worthy of success. Acting parts—paying roles!—began to come his way. He appeared on *Get Smart, That Girl,* and in tons of guest spots on other television comedy programs. His big break came was he was cast in the role of Dr. Adam Bricker on *Love Boat.* The popular show aired from 1977 until 1986 and made Bernie Koppel a well-known star.

CONSIDER THIS: There is no telling what we can accomplish in our lives if we will only begin to believe in ourselves.

Bill Moog

"Leadership is the capacity to translate vision into reality."   — Warren G. Bennis

Bill Moog was an engineer at Cornell Aeronautical Laboratories (later Calspan Corp.) when he invented a servovalve, a control mechanism used on a variety of machines. The company tried to market the device but received just one order for three of the valves. Since Cornell figured such a small order was not worth its effort, management let Moog personally handle the project. He cranked out the devices in his spare time. The company must have given up on the device too soon because orders kept coming in. Seeing an opportunity, Moog and his brother Arthur, along with Lewis Geyer, formed Moog Inc. The founders worked eighteen-hour days for over a year just to meet their orders. When new employees began coming on board, Bill made it his goal to make the company a good place to work.

The buildings at Moog Inc. were designed with plenty of windows, clean environments, and piped-in music in the cafeteria. Having felt intimidated by inspection policies at other places he had worked, Bill instituted a self-inspection that allowed each employee to act as his own inspector. The company instituted massive technical training to help its employees gain advanced skills, and it also offered grants for college tuition. Job security became a chief concern and provisions were made against layoffs. However, the exceptional work environment did create one major problem for Moog Inc.: Each year 12,000 people routinely applied for a handful of available positions.

CONSIDER THIS: A good environment provides a company with a loyal, dedicated, and productive work force.

The Leo Burnett Agency

*"I go at what I am about as if there was nothing
else in the world for the time being."*
— Charles Kingsley

For the past 50 years, the Leo Burnett advertising agency has created some of the best known and most remembered ad campaigns the world has ever seen, among them the Jolly Green Giant, Sunkist's Charlie the Tuna, The Pillsbury Dough Boy, The Maytag repairman, and countless others. The agency's personality mimics the personality of its founder, Leo Burnett, who demanded more than just creativity in ads. The ads had to sell the product, and to ensure that they would, Leo spent time getting to know his clients and spent hours concentrating on providing just the right "feel" for the product. He encouraged his representatives to become members of the client's family— to think like the client, to understand intimately the client's products, and to become consumed with desire to make the client successful.

Leo practiced what he taught. One of the corporate legends that illustrates just how deeply Leo would concentrate on a project involves his encounter with a custodian's closet. One day, with yellow pad in hand, Leo left his office and headed for the men's room. Being engrossed in thought, he opened a janitor's closet by mistake, went in, and locked the door behind him. After a period of time, people began to ask, "Where's Leo?" Finally, he carved a hole in the door with his penknife and got someone's attention. At the agency's Christmas breakfast that year, Leo was presented with the door as a gift. Although Leo Burnett died in 1971, his vision continues to drive the company.

CONSIDER THIS: Creativity just for creativity's sake is not as important as creativity that can solve a specific problem.

Coca-Cola

"Sometimes when I consider what tremendous consequences come from little things, I am tempted to think there are no little things."

— Bruce Barton

At the turn of the century, Five Points was *the* meeting place in Atlanta, Georgia. Anything new in town was talked about there, especially at Joe Jacobs's Drug Store. Therefore, Joe's pharmacy was a natural place for Dr. John Pemberton to test his new beverage formula. Willis Venable had a leased soda fountain in the store, and Pemberton asked him to mix one ounce of his syrup with five ounces of water and ice. Venable drank the concoction, smacked his lips, and suggested a second round. But as he began putting water in the glass, he accidentally pulled the lever for soda water. When he tasted the second mixture, his eyes lit up at the pleasing flavor and effervescence.

Pemberton explained that his concoction consisted of extracts from the coca plant and cola nuts, and that he was going to call it Coca-Cola. On May 8, 1886, Coca-Cola went on sale in Joe Jacobs's Drug Store. The first advertisement appearing in the local newspaper three weeks later described Coca-Cola as "Refreshing! Exhilarating! Invigorating!" Coca-Cola was not the first soft drink in the marketplace, but it offered a new and pleasing taste. Pemberton had a great product, but he did not possess the resources to make the beverage a success. He lost money on Coca-Cola its first two years, and just before he died, Pemberton sold his interest in the product for $1,750 to Asa Candler. It was Candler who took Coca-Cola from obscurity to success.

CONSIDER THIS: Even the best idea may take years and the right businessperson to crack the marketplace and become an industry leader.

Corporate Lore

*"I desire no future that will break the ties of
the past."* — George Eliot

In his book *Business as Unusual*, Hugh De Pree describes the
struggle that Herman Miller, Inc. faced in expanding from a
small family business in the 1940s into a major corporation
today. The office furniture manufacturer is a corporation based
on Christian religious values and traditions. When the company's rapid growth began to place a strain on those original values, Peter Drucker was asked to suggest methods to keep the
enterprise on track. What he recommended was that new employees be educated about the founders and their early struggles
and also about how the company's philosophy came into being.

When an enterprise is small and young, its employees know
its history because they were a part of it. They know the
founder and often relate to him on a first-name basis. As the operation grows, however, the impact of the company's beliefs
and mission may be lost on the average employee. Those companies which are able to maintain their corporate lore often do
so in the manner of such strong "evangelists" as Alfred Sloan,
Henry Ford, Thomas Watson, John Deere, Walt Disney, Tram-
mel Crow, and Bill and Dave Packard. While the leaders of a
large organization cannot know every employee, it is important
that the leaders' stories and experiences—in the form of corporate lore—be told frequently to workers to remind them of the
company's beliefs and goals.

CONSIDER THIS: Give people some tangible story, perhaps
a parable, on which to hang their corporate beliefs. One truly
inspirational story that describes the company's goals is worth
a thousand company rules.

Lane Cedar Chests

"Even the woodpecker owes his success to the fact that he uses his head and keeps pecking away until he finishes the job he starts." — Coleman Cox

In 1912 Edward Hudson's father told him to start making cedar chests in an old box plant that he had just purchased. The twenty-one-year-old youngster didn't even know what a cedar chest was, but he followed his father's instructions. Edward got help from his former high school woodworking teacher and ordered $50,000 worth of equipment. John Lane, Edward's father, went through the ceiling, but the terms for the machinery were good and the plant went into production. Sales of the chests were sluggish, so Edward started going on sales calls himself. After being turned down by several furniture stores, he came up with the idea of a fanciful cedar chest display. Then the stores bought Edward's idea and his furniture.

Lane used other promotional schemes for the chests. Finding that many women cherished the European tradition of the trousseau or marriage chest, Lane promoted a line of "hope chests." Dealers gave away millions of smaller Lane Love Chests to graduating high school girls. At one time, two-thirds of all girls graduating from high school received a miniature Lane Love Chest, which was promoted as "the gift that starts the home." After World War II, Lane added other furniture items to its product line and continues to be a successful marketer of fine furniture.

CONSIDER THIS: A product may not be profitable because it is not being sold correctly. Go into the marketplace and see how the product can most benefit people, then sell it with that information in mind.

Madeleine L'Engle

"Thy word is a lamp unto my feet, and a light unto my path." — The Bible

Born in 1918, the only child of strict parents, Madeleine L'Engle spent much of her childhood in the privacy of her room, where she often escaped into the world of books. Because of her father's health, the family moved to Switzerland when Madeleine was twelve. There she attended an impersonal boarding school, where she was known only as "Ninety-seven." At first, Madeleine had a negative view of herself, but after discovering the Bible, she began to relate to the "underdogs" that God seemed to use. In her isolation, Madeleine had begun to write, finishing her first story when she was five. She continued using that medium for expression and escape. Through her writing, she was able to have friends and work out problems that others had to solve in the flesh. As an adult, with more insight into the real world, Madeleine continued to experiment with writing and in 1959 sent a manuscript to a publishing house.

"This was a book I was sure of," she remembers. It was about a twelve-year-old girl who had problems in school. She saw herself as ugly, dull, and clumsy, but soon discovered spiritual powers in the universe that were on her side. The book was rather unusual and was rejected by forty-two publishers. But the forty-third accepted the manuscript, and *A Wrinkle in Time* went on to win the prestigious Newberry Medal, a top award for children's literature.

CONSIDER THIS: Every person has a talent to share with the rest of the world. Even those people who have a difficult childhood can grow up to be the best in their field.

Discovery Toys

"Things don't turn up in this world until somebody turns them up." — James Garfield

The home sales plan has been used with great success by Tupperware, Amway, Mary Kay Cosmetics, and a host of other businesses. Sometimes it may seem that there are no new ideas that could benefit from the marketing concept. However, Lane Nemeth found just the product. After working as a director of a day care center for three years, she became a housewife when her husband was transferred to another city. A friend asked her to go shopping with the idea of buying an educational toy for a one-year-old child. After checking store after store, they could not find even one toy that fit the bill. That night, Lane sat down on her living room floor and began developing a plan.

What she devised was Discovery Toys, educational toys that are sold through the home party concept. The toys are unique and appeal to the baby-boom generation of parents who want something more for their children than just the latest monster hero. Using well-known sales and marketing techniques like those employed by Mary Kay and Amway, Lane Nemeth was able to sell $280,000 worth of toys through her garage business in 1977. By 1985, her sales had grown to $40 million. Starting out had not been easy, but the combination of a good idea and a growing market of children from the baby-boom generation made the time right for Discovery Toys to succeed.

CONSIDER THIS: Old methods of marketing are waiting for a new product line. Who will be the next person to recognize the need and fill it?

Mail-order Copycats

"Learn from the mistakes of others. You can't live long enough to make them all yourself."
— Martin Vanbee

In his book *Getting Into the Mail-order Business*, Julian L. Simon reveals some insights that might be valuable in other businesses as well. Simon explains that, after he got a fine college education, he worked for major advertising agencies in New York and eventually went on to become an advertising consultant. Thinking that he would make it big in mail order, he started his own business and promptly found out how easily he could fail. After recovering from the shock, a humbled Simon decided to find out where he had gone wrong. He took the direct approach and visited successful mail-order dealers, asking them for their secrets. Ignoring much of his textbook learning, Simon listened to the voices of experience and studied their techniques until he found the reason for their success.

The answer was almost too simple to be true. As unlikely as it sounded, Simon found that the best way to achieve success was to be a copycat. He discovered that the mail-order business didn't require creativity, it just required that he sell items that were already making a profit. That is the approach Simon recommends for all beginners. It is true that larger companies in almost any line of business often experiment with new items in catalogs. Larger companies can afford to take such risks, but most newcomers need to get a profitable line established before trying anything innovative. The beginner can avoid many start-up risks by duplicating a currently successful plan.

CONSIDER THIS: Being innovative is risky. It is often wiser to establish a foundation of solid products and to experiment with innovation on a small scale rather than risking the whole business on a lark.

Mistakes

*"An error gracefully acknowledged is a
victory won."* — Caroline Gascoigne

Tom Watson Sr. was the guiding hand in the success of IBM
for forty years. He knew the risks associated with business and
the value of learning from mistakes. One year a young executive was given responsibility for a project that cost over $10
million. As it turned out, the idea failed, and when the young
man was called in, he offered his resignation. "You can't be serious," said Watson. "We've just spent $10 million educating
you!" When Thomas Edison was trying to invent the electric
light, he made thousands of "mistakes" before he had any success. The discovery of rubber vulcanization was made by accident. Gail Borden made countless business blunders before
achieving success with condensed milk. Levi Strauss made the
mistake of selling his entire supply of dry goods, leaving him
with only canvas to make pants from. Milton Hershey failed
more than once in the candy-making business before finding
success with the Hershey bar.

Almost every enterprise has experienced its share of mistakes. Mistakes are a tool of learning. Although repeating mistakes is foolish, a legitimate try that turns sour should be
accepted as part of the process of moving forward to a better
idea. Those who adhere to the old adage "If you are not making
mistakes, you are not making progress" are frequently the persons who make the biggest advancements in business. We have
a natural tendency to avoid trial and error, and often find risk-
taking to be unsettling. Yet, it is those who take calculated risks
who reap the benefits. As Edward J. Phelps so aptly stated, "The
man who makes no mistakes does not usually make anything."

CONSIDER THIS: Are you so afraid of making mistakes that
you are shielding yourself from success?

Kelly Services

*"It is no use saying we are doing our best. You
have got to succeed in doing what is necessary."*
— Winston Churchill

Many successful businesses have been spawned by persons who saw a new trend in an old industry and had the flexibility to change directions. Russell Kelly served as a fiscal management analyst in the Army's Quartermaster Corps during World War II. His job was to break through red tape and get food delivered wherever it was needed and on time. One person described Kelly as the General Patton of food delivery. When the war was over, Kelly formed a business to offer services to other companies that were in a boom period but often lacked the expertise to get paperwork done. Initially, Kelly offered to perform the work at his office, but his clients wanted the work done in their own offices.

Kelly began supplying skilled workers on an as-needed basis to get companies past a temporary manpower crisis. As demand for the service increased, Kelly realized that he was witnessing the wave of the future. Soon, all of the carefully selected talent he had recruited was busily employed. Then Kelly discovered there were vast numbers of women who wanted part-time or temporary work—particularly mothers with children in school and older women with secretarial experience. The term "Kelly Girl" soon became a household word. As times changed, Kelly Services expanded its temporary-help force to include marketing, labor, and technical services. From the very start, Russell Kelly offered an unconditional guarantee to his customers, and that commitment to satisfaction and quality put Kelly Services on top of the temporary-employment business for over fifty years.

CONSIDER THIS: Recognize what the market really needs and wants—give it to them, and you will develop a strong base of loyal customers.

Twinkies

*"Trust your hunches. They're usually based on
facts filed away just below the conscious level."*
— Dr. Joyce Brothers

Although they are seldom referred to as being as American as motherhood and apple pie, Twinkies are certainly recognized as an American tradition. Twinkies were invented by Jimmy Dewar during the Great Depression. (Isn't it amazing how many useful things were invented during that brief period of poor economic times?) As plant manager for Continental Bakeries, Jimmy, like almost everyone else during that era, was trying to think of ideas to keep his business profitable. One thing he noticed was that the shortcake pans used during the strawberry season remained idle the rest of the year. While considering how those pans could be used to make a low-priced snack, Jimmy also came up with an idea to inject the snack with a filling.

While thinking about the new snack, he went on a business trip to St. Louis, where he saw a billboard advertising Twinkle Toe Shoes. That is when Jimmy thought of the name "Twinkies." It had a neat "snack" sound, which meant that there would be two of the snacks in a package, just the right size to sell for a nickel. The snacks became popular and later received national publicity on *The Howdy Doody Show*, where Clarabell the Clown passed them out to the audience as Buffalo Bob Smith sang the Twinkies song. How big a part of the American culture has the Twinkie become? Archie Bunker took one for lunch on the classic sitcom *All in the Family*, people have made Twinkie wedding cakes, and even former first lady Rosalyn Carter was caught eating one in a candid photograph.

CONSIDER THIS: The best advertising available for any product is when it becomes a part of the culture.

Sherwin-Williams

"The world hates change, yet it is the only thing that has brought progress."

— Charles Kettering

At times, you must stick to your convictions. This can be particularly difficult when your convictions run counter to long-standing tradition. Paint has been around for thousands of years, having been used by the Egyptians prior to 1000 B.C. By the nineteenth century, paint was sold as a base color, with pigments available for custom mixing. However, the average nineteenth-century American rarely used paint. Most houses were left unpainted, but if a home was painted, the owner usually had to rely on a painter to mix the desired color or be content with white. It was almost impossible to purchase two batches of paint that matched exactly.

In 1870 a paint company named Sherwin, Dunham, and Griswold had to make a decision. One of the partners, Henry Sherwin, had come up with an idea to develop ready-mixed paints, but the other owners were against it. They were sure that people wanted to mix their colors at home—to get the tint just right. Sherwin disagreed, and as a result, the company was dissolved and Sherwin found another partner, Edward Williams. Their new firm, Sherwin-Williams, embarked on a lengthy research project to perfect a way to premix paint in a consistent and convenient manner. The company's ready-mixed paint was introduced in 1880 and signaled a revolution in do-it-yourself painting. Soon, few American houses were left unpainted, proving that Henry Sherwin was right after all—homeowners didn't like the hassle of mixing their own paint.

CONSIDER THIS: Some people cannot see advancement. Some will not consider change. Those who can see advancement and are willing to seek change can lead the way to the future.

Vicks VapoRub

"The doors we open and close each day decide the lives we live." — Flora Whittemore

Sometimes success comes from putting two and two together. It sounds simple enough. The problem is determining which two and two to combine. For years, treating the common cold has been a problem. It has long been known that some measure of relief could be gained from opening the nasal passages with various aromatic medications and vaporizations. From ancient times, poultices, plasters, herbal vapors, and the like have been touted as effective cold remedies. But most of those "cures" had unpleasant side effects. They smelled horrible and frequently irritated the skin, and using vapors in conjunction with steam often resulted in facial burns. By the turn of the twentieth century, druggists throughout the country were searching for an effective ointment with none of the drawbacks.

Sometime in the 1890s, Lunsford Richardson, a druggist in Selma, North Carolina, put together a salve for his "croupy" baby. He used menthol, a little known drug from Japan, in an ointment base. When the salve was applied to the chest or nose, the heat of the body would vaporize the menthol and permit the medicated vapors to be inhaled for hours. The ointment became one of several items sold under the name Vicks Family Remedies, and the product was eventually named Vicks VapoRub. The idea for the Vicks name came from a magazine advertisement for Vick's Seeds. Since Richardson's brother-in-law was named Vick, and because "Vicks" was short and easy to remember, Richardson selected it as the name for his product.

CONSIDER THIS: The ingredients for success may already be out there simply waiting for someone to put them together.

Rosie O'Donnell

*"Time and time again people told me to quit. . . . I
didn't listen to them."* — Rosie O'Donnell

Rosie O'Donnell is likable. Once you see her on television
or in a movie, you feel as if you could be best friends. She's a
wisecracking, funny, effervescent, down-to-earth comedian
with a New York accent. She's also very focused on her career.
The middle of five children, Rosie learned comedy from her
mother, a gifted amateur comedienne. Rosie was only ten when
her mother died of cancer. At about the same time, Rosie decided she would become a movie star—and her entry would be
through comedy. Watching TV "almost twenty-four hours a
day," she studied acting, delivery, and comedy. As a teenager,
Rosie excelled at mimicking popular comedians, and she eventually began performing her own material.

At age seventeen, after gaining experience at local comedy
clubs, Rosie began a five-year stint playing comedy clubs in
forty-nine states. As she gradually honed her material, Rosie
hoped someone would see her act and "discover" her. Although
she was well received by audiences, other actors told her to quit.
They called her too heavy, too tough, and "too New York," but
her dream kept her going. With money she won as a five-time
Star Search champion, Rosie moved to Los Angeles. Her dream of
being discovered came true when Brandon Tartikoff, then head
of NBC's entertainment division, saw Rosie perform at Igby's
comedy club and cast her in the sitcom *Gimme a Break*. Rosie's
childhood dream has come true. She has appeared in a number
of movies, starred in a Broadway revival of *Grease*, and established
herself as an award-winning TV and film actress and comedian.

CONSIDER THIS: Focus on your dream. Study and practice
to make yourself the best you can be. Don't believe the nay-
sayers. Keep taking steps toward your goal.

Reader's Digest

*"Don't dodge difficulties; meet them, greet them,
beat them. All great men have been through
the wringer."*   — Milne

Good ideas may meet with success initially, then hit a roadblock when everything looks good. In fact, many ideas are laid to rest at that point. DeWitt Wallace's dream would have been buried long ago if not for his determination to overcome obstacles. Wallace had an idea for a small publication that would be both entertaining and informative. At the time, there were many good magazines on the market, but a reader would have to spend a small fortune to buy them all. Wallace put together a dummy magazine that used condensations of previously published articles. He named his prototype *Reader's Digest*. Unable to secure backers for the venture, Wallace and his fiancée rented an office and set up their own small publishing concern.

On their wedding day, the couple sent out mimeographed circulars seeking subscriptions. When they returned from their honeymoon two weeks later, they had received 1,500 charter subscriptions. The first issue of *Reader's Digest* was dated February 1922. Everything went well for a while as other magazines readily gave them permission to reprint articles. But as subscriptions increased, the other magazines began to see *Reader's Digest* as competition, and sources for articles dried up. In 1933 Wallace began commissioning articles to be written for other magazines, securing the rights to reprint them later. He was widely criticized, but the concept kept his publication alive. The practice was discontinued in the 1950s, but by then, *Reader's Digest* had become a continuing success.

CONSIDER THIS: Even when your dream does not become a reality the first few times you reach for it, keep trying. Persistence is often your most powerful ally.

Life Savers

*"All progress, all achievement is the story
of imagination."* — A. B. Zu Tavern

McDonald's Restaurants may never have become so prolific without Ray Kroc. Elmer Doolin bought the recipe for Fritos corn chips from a man needing money to return to his home in Mexico. Although Christopher Sholes invented the modern typewriter, it was promoter James Desmore who made it sell. The Life Saver has a similar story. In 1912, Cleveland candy salesman Clarence Crane was looking for a summer substitute for his melting chocolate candies. He decided to produce a mint. To make his mints stand out among the competition, he designed them to be round and with a hole in the middle. He found a local pill maker who could produce the mints in quantity and wrapped them in a cardboard tube. Their shape made the name "Life Saver" a natural.

An advertising salesman named Edward Noble picked up a package of the mints at a New York candy store. He was so impressed with the candy, the shape, and the name that he immediately went to Cleveland to try to sell advertising for the product. Crane wasn't interested, since the mints were just a summer sideline. However, Crane suggested that if Noble liked the product so much, perhaps he should buy the rights to make the mints. A deal was struck, and Noble managed to raise the capital with a partner named Roy Arlen. A major problem with the candy was its inability to stay fresh in the cardboard tube. That was solved by enclosing the mints in a tinfoil wrapper. Placed next to cash registers as impulse buys, the mints sold quickly and soon became a national success.

CONSIDER THIS: You may not be an inventor, and that's okay. It is more often the inspired promotion of a good product that really makes the difference.

Bedtime Stories

"Train up a child in the way he should go. Even when he is old he will not depart from it."
— Proverbs 22:6

An important ritual that is performed in thousands of American homes each night is responsible for how many of us think and dream. That ritual is the bedtime story. After crawling under the covers, children listen to stories told to them, usually by a mother or father. Then, with the story fresh in their minds, they slip off into dreamland. Most of those popular bedtime stories are actually morality fables, which originally were developed to teach youngsters right from wrong or to inspire them to lead upright and productive lives. They served as a technique that enabled parents to pass along values to their children. The most ancient of these were taken from the Bible or were stories based on Aesop's fables. One particularly popular bedtime story is "The Little Red Hen."

In "The Little Red Hen," a wise hen decides that she wants to make some bread. However, before she can bake it, she must grow the grain. When she asks the other barnyard animals for help, each has something else to do. She asks for help in weeding the garden, harvesting, milling the grain, and baking the bread, but no one will help. Finally, after the hen has done all of the work herself, she asks "Who will help me eat my bread?" and all of the animals volunteer. She tells them that because they were too lazy to help her with any of the other tasks, she will not let them eat the bread. Through stories like these, American children for hundreds of years have been taught the importance of hard work and self-reliance.

CONSIDER THIS: People are not born with good character and integrity. They must be taught those attributes by example and through stories.

The Zipper

*"Everyone excels in something in which
another fails."* — Publius Syrus

Many inventions can be traced back to ancient Greece, Egypt, or Arabia. The toothbrush, cosmetics, the razor, and many other useful items were simply improved upon as technology advanced. The zipper is different, however. When Whitcomb Judson obtained a patent for his "clasp-locker" device in 1893, there was nothing to compare it to. Judson made boots and had invented a crude (by today's standard) zipper to take the place of the buttons and shoelaces on high-top boots. Judson and his partner, Lewis Walker, attempted to promote the clasp at the 1893 World's Fair, but no one was interested. The only substantial order they received was from the post office, but the bags equipped with the fastener jammed so often that they were soon discarded.

In 1913 an engineer named Gideon Sunback improved upon the original design and produced a fastener much like those in use today. First employed by the military, the device found its way to civilian clothing by the 1920s, but because of a rusting problem, the fastener had to be unstitched each time the garment was washed and then resewn. Zipper Boots, popular galoshes using the fastener, were introduced by Goodyear in 1923, and soon the fastener itself became known as a zipper. Steady improvements in the design and materials used to manufacture zippers made them a common part of clothing by the 1930s.

CONSIDER THIS: Any good idea can be improved on. Just because an idea fails the first time it is applied is no reason to give up. If you don't improve upon an idea, someone else probably will.

The Microwave Oven

"To maintain maximum attention, it's hard to beat a good, big mistake." — David D. Hewitt

Since World War II, the pace of American life has increased so dramatically that it appears we are trying to create an instant society. Consumers demand instant service. Many stores offer instant credit. There are instant potatoes, instant stock market quotes, and point-of-sale displays for instant buying decisions. A major component of our fast-paced society is the microwave oven, which essentially has provided man with the first new way to cook food since fire. Although it was bound to be discovered eventually, the microwave oven was invented "by accident" by Dr. Percy Spencer.

The apparatus that led to the development of the microwave oven was the magnetron, a device originally used in radars that was invented in England by Sir John Randall and Dr. H. A. Boot. Spencer, an engineer at Raytheon Company, was testing a magnetron after the war when he noticed that a candy bar in his pocket had melted. To find out what had taken place, Spencer exposed other foods to the magnetron's presence. Popcorn popped and an egg exploded, half-cooked from the inside out. Building on that research, Raytheon developed a commercial microwave oven, but because of the bulkiness of vacuum-tube technology, it was expensive and few were sold. Tappan introduced a much smaller home model in 1952, and the stage was set for a revolution in the way Americans cooked.

CONSIDER THIS: Many new ideas are developed "by accident," but it is those persons who possess the curiosity to follow up on unusual occurrences who often make the real discovery.

Thinking Good Health

"The joyfulness of a man prolongeth his days."
— The Apocrypha

Bacteria and viruses are not the only causes of disease in the human body. Many studies indicate that our own mind is frequently the real culprit behind many illnesses. In his book *The Healing of Persons*, Dr. Paul Tournier discusses how our physical health is often related to the way we think. It is well known that mental attitude and stress can have an impact on how our body reacts to the onset of infection and disease. A poor state of mind can lower our natural defenses against many kinds of illness. Laughter, on the other hand, can free people from pain and lift off the blanket of stress. Since stress is recognized as a contributing factor to illness in our fast-paced society, relief from its grip can help prevent or lessen the effects of countless maladies.

Although an increasing number of people seem to be seeking a pharmaceutical solution to stress, pills are not the answer. We must directly attack the specific problems that manifest themselves as physical disease, such as overwork and mental anguish. A return to good health requires a new perspective on life, one that changes our attitude and addresses the root causes of our problems. Dr. Tournier's approach is to attack the diseases of bitterness, hatred, gloom, and depression. If we can turn our mind to happiness, love, hope, and laughter, we often will be rewarded with good physical health.

CONSIDER THIS: Medicine is no substitute for a healthy attitude toward life. When is the last time you had a belly laugh? Really enjoyed an activity? Took a real vacation? Your life may depend on it.

Uncle Sam

"The memory of the just is blessed; but the name of the wicked shall rot." — Proverbs

There really was an Uncle Sam, and the person who was the model for that venerable character was a real American hero. Born in 1766, Samuel Wilson was a youthful patriot who served as a drummer boy during the American Revolution. After the war, Sam opened a meat-packing company in Troy, New York. He was a fair businessman and was known throughout the community as "Uncle Sam." When soldiers were stationed nearby during the War of 1812, Sam supplied them with meat. The crates that were to be sent to the army were stamped on the side with the initials "U.S." (This was before those initials were in common usage.) When asked what the initials stood for, one of Sam's employees said they were the initials of his boss, "Uncle Sam."

The designation gained popularity among the troops, and American soldiers soon began to refer to themselves as "Uncle Sam's men." A cartoon version of Uncle Sam first appeared in 1820 and depicted the character wearing a black top hat and tailcoat. Red pants were introduced during Andrew Jackson's presidency, and a beard was added during Abraham Lincoln's term in office. During the Civil War, artist Thomas Nast made Uncle Sam tall and thin, modeling the character after Lincoln. The modern version of Uncle Sam was created by artist James Montgomery Flagg for a World War I poster that bears the now-familiar caption "I Want You for the U.S. Army."

CONSIDER THIS: Uncle Sam was a real American who represented the American spirit of patriotism and fair play.

The Automobile Radio

"Now let's use our nutpickers on this problem, and then we'll decide what it is we have to do. Then let's do it." — Paul Galvin

Paul Galvin's radio business was doing pretty well in 1929 until "Black Friday" hit. After the devastating stock market crash, larger manufacturers began dumping radios on the market, and Galvin's retailers stopped orders and wanted to ship back products. Galvin found himself saddled with big shipments from suppliers for parts he could no longer use. Galvin traveled from Chicago to New York to work out a deal with one of his suppliers, and while there he heard about people who were putting radios in cars. They charged about $250, and each installation was a custom job. On his way back to Chicago, Galvin began to believe that his company could develop a lower-price automobile radio, one for the mass market.

The men at Galvin's shop gave it a try, but the automobiles of the day were not designed to accommodate the bulky tuner, battery, and speaker. The antenna had to be placed in the headliner, requiring the liner to be torn out and then replaced. Installation could take two days. After convincing a banker to give him a loan, Galvin's men installed a radio in the banker's car—but the vehicle caught fire thirty minutes later. Galvin went to a radio convention, and having no exhibit booth, he drove his car around the convention center as his wife convinced potential customers to take a demonstration ride. Little by little, the car radio was perfected, and one morning while shaving, Galvin came up with a new name for his product: "Motorola."

CONSIDER THIS: In the face of disaster, some people will quit. Others will seek new ideas and new ways of meeting the challenge. Which one are you?

Marva Collins

*"You can't weep or talk your way through a mess.
When you come up against a problem, you have
to work your way through it."*

— Marva Collins

There are many excuses why Johnny can't read. But to Marva Collins, Johnny can read—and if he is challenged, he can read far more than we would imagine. Educated in the South, Marva learned about teaching from caring and inspiring teachers and principals and from her own common sense. After moving to Chicago, she continued her teaching career. At first, she followed the recommended curriculum but came to believe that such stories as "Run, Spot, Run" had no meaning for children. She added Aesop's Fables and other classic children's stories to the classroom fare.

Marva told her students that they were the "brightest in the world." While children in other classes were struggling to learn thirteen words in a basal reader, her students wrote about the brontosaurus and tyrannosaurus. Colleagues belittled Marva's techniques, and she was eventually harassed out of the public school system. Convinced that her ideas about education were valid, Marva opened a private school, taking in problem children. She taught Shakespeare, Dickens, and other classics, and her students memorized quotations and poems, solved real mathematical word problems, and openly discussed the issues of life. Marva's students responded with a hunger for knowledge, and when her first class of "misfits" took standardized achievement tests, they ranked well above the national average.

CONSIDER THIS: What could we accomplish if we were truly inspired and pushed to meet our real potential?

Anne Sullivan

*"And now these three remain: faith, hope, and love.
But the greatest of these is love."*   — The Bible

The story of Helen Keller is well known. She was born a normal baby but as a young child was stricken with a disease that left her blind and deaf. Her parents were unable to communicate with her or control her, and Helen grew up like an animal. In desperation, the family called for help, which arrived in the form of Anne Sullivan. Anne had the understanding and love to bring Helen "back into the real world." How was it that she could perform such a miracle, when Helen's parents and countless doctors had failed to make any progress? Where did Anne find such love and patience?

It all began at a mental institution in Boston, Massachusetts, where a young girl who exhibited violent behavior and was thought to be hopelessly insane, had been consigned by doctors to a "living death" in a cage in the facility's basement. One elderly nurse, however, felt affection for the girl. She began to eat her lunch outside the youngster's cage and sometimes left brownies within her reach. The girl seemed to ignore the brownies, but they would disappear as soon as the nurse left. Gradually, the little girl in the cage began to respond to the nurse's love. She began to talk, became less violent, and started responding to other treatments. As her condition improved, the girl was removed from her cage and allowed to meet other patients, and quickly became a valued helper in the institution. She eventually was released from the facility and went on to lead a very productive life. That girl was Anne Sullivan.

CONSIDER THIS: Everyone needs care and love. Without them, there can be no worthwhile dreams. What personal mountains could be moved if people really showed a nurturing love for one another?

The Chicken Man

"Baldness. Handsome in a man, beautiful in a chicken." — Frank Perdue

Chickens are so common and plentiful that it seems they should be a commodity business. After all, one chicken looks like another. Or does it? There is one chicken business that has made a big name for itself by growing a chicken that is a cut above the rest. After saving money from his salary, Arthur W. Perdue entered the chicken business in 1920 with a small chicken house and fifty chickens. In that same year, Franklin Perdue was born. Arthur Perdue's chickens produced superior eggs, and young Frank learned a great deal by observing his father's careful attention to detail. Focusing on quality and cost gave Arthur a good profit in a low-profit-margin business. From the beginning, the Perdues always looked for ways to improve their business and their chickens. They learned that contented chickens produced more eggs. They learned how to developed better feeds. By 1970 they had learned the value of "quality-message" advertising, much of which featured Frank himself.

"It takes a tough man to make a tender chicken," said one Perdue ad. "I'm not about to compromise when it comes to my legs and breasts," quipped another. Frank declared, "If you can find a better chicken, buy it!" Perdue is one of the most successful chicken producers in the U.S., selling literally hundreds of chickens each minute of every day. Their branded chicken and turkey products sell from Maine to Florida and as far west as Chicago and St. Louis. Perdue's formula for quality and innovation has produced considerably more than chicken feed.

CONSIDER THIS: If the chicken business can be innovative, your business can be innovative. How can you improve the quality of your product? How can you shape your message so it is memorable?

Eastern Onion

*"Whatever you can do or dream, you can. Begin
it. Boldness has genius, power and magic in it."*

— Goethe

It doesn't take a college degree to be successful. Mary Flatt is testament to that. She had tried her hand at several businesses by the time she was thirty, but all had failed. Seeking new opportunities, she and her husband, Jim, and two kids moved to Las Vegas with no money and no jobs. Fortunately, Jim found permanent employment at a casino, but Mary skipped from one job to another. One day Mary was at a party when a Western Union singing telegram was delivered. Mary felt the presentation was flat. She believed that singing telegrams should be fun, exciting, and even outrageous. An idea was born.

Mary scraped together $1,200 to get her idea off the ground. At first Jim thought the idea was harebrained and gave Mary no support or encouragement. Still, Mary continued with her plans. Songs were written for almost every occasion, from birthdays to "Happy Divorce Day," and friends helped make costumes for the venture, which Mary cleverly named Eastern Onion. The first week, five "grams" were sold, and she was on her way. Although the business made virtually no profit during its first ten months, a big break came when stories about Eastern Onion's novel telegrams appeared in the local newspaper. With the free publicity, sales began to increase. When the company was featured in the national press, Mary Flatt began getting calls from people interested in obtaining franchises. Today, Eastern Onion is a franchised nationwide singing telegram company with locations in virtually every major U.S. city.

CONSIDER THIS: Many people have failed and failed again. If they keep trying, they increase their chances of finding that one idea that will make it big.

Wilma Rudolph, the Polio Victim Who Won the Gold

"He that is good at making excuses is seldom good at anything else." — Benjamin Franklin

How many times have you used excuses to rationalize your way out of success? Zig Ziegler calls the phenomenon "Stinkin' Thinkin' " and warns us about "hardening of the attitudes." Wilma Rudolph is an example of how an undying belief in oneself can be the catalyst to overcoming problems. Polio took a toll on Wilma as a child. For six years she wore braces and could not walk, but she believed the braces would someday come off. The doctor was doubtful Wilma would ever walk correctly, but he encouraged her to exercise. Wilma didn't understand that she might be permanently handicapped. She thought that if a little exercise was good, a lot must be very good. When her parents were away, Wilma would take off the braces and try again and again to walk unaided. When she was eleven, she told her doctor, "I have something to show you." Wilma removed her braces and walked across the room. She never put them on again.

Wilma wanted to play sports. After some false starts at basketball, she finally confronted her coach, saying, "If you give me ten minutes a day, I will give you in return a world-class athlete." The coach laughed uncontrollably but agreed to give Wilma the time. When basketball season was over, Wilma turned to track. By age fourteen she was on the track team, and by sixteen she was encouraged to prepare for the Olympics. Wilma Rudolph won a bronze medal at the 1956 Olympics and three gold medals at the 1960 Games.

CONSIDER THIS: Belief in yourself and hard work can make you a world-class individual in whatever area you choose. What will you have if you give up? What can you have if you keep on trying?

Henry Aaron

*"Unless you reach beyond what you already
know how to do, you will never grow."*
— A. C. Elliott

Few people garner recognition merely for being good at something. Recognition comes to people who are the best. Being the best means giving more of yourself, doing more than is expected, and producing more than everyone else. When most people believe it's time to quit, those who ultimately succeed go just a little farther. When young Henry Aaron suited up as a rookie for the Milwaukee Braves, he wanted to make a name for himself in major league baseball. However, so did every other rookie. To be remembered, Henry would have to do something spectacular. "Hammerin' Hank" Aaron did just that by eclipsing Babe Ruth's long-standing home run record of 714 in 1974 then tallying a major league record 755 homers by the time he retired in 1976.

Looking back on what gave him the ability to achieve those marks, Henry recalled a priest. Early in his career, as one of his twin babies lay very ill, Father Seblica came into his life. The priest was very caring and showed great concern for the family. The two became friends and handball rivals. Years later, when Henry was having trouble getting a child accepted into a private school, Father Seblica worked vigorously on the youngster's behalf. When Henry asked the priest what kept him going, Father Seblica replied, "I do what I can, and then some." Henry took that motto onto the playing field. He did all he could—and then some. That is when Henry Aaron began his climb to the top. History provides excellent examples of what you can accomplish when you seek to go farther than you believed you could.

CONSIDER THIS: Are you satisfied that you are doing all that you can do? Why not go even farther? Do all you can, and then some.

The Rest of the Story

*"A teacher affects eternity; he can never tell where
his influence stops."* — Henry Adams

Paul Harvey was born in 1918, in Tulsa, Oklahoma, and his
father died when he was just three years old. Since he showed
an interest in radio, Paul's high school English teacher pushed
him to take a job at KVOO, a local radio station. Occasionally, Paul would be allowed to do some announcing. Sometimes he read the news from the wire, and he even filled in a
few times by playing his guitar. Paul gradually moved up the
ranks, from station "go-fer" to spot announcer, newscaster, and
manager. "I hung around the studio every minute I wasn't in
school," he remembers. In 1944, Paul began two fifteen-minute
news commentaries from a Chicago-based radio station. He
added a segment in 1946 called "The Rest of the Story" in
which he told an anecdote that had a surprise ending. In 1976,
the ABC network decided to spin off that segment into its own
series.

Unlike the stereotype of many broadcasters as liberals, Paul
Harvey champions the old-fashioned values of God, country,
family, a strong work ethic, and rugged individualism. He
speaks with a homespun style that, to many, has made him the
spokesperson for middle America. No one sees him as a big city
journalist—he's just a guy telling a story. Paul's efforts have
earned him numerous honorary degrees and won him some of
the most prestigious awards in the communications industry.
With his distinctive style and instantly recognizable delivery,
Paul Harvey draws listeners into his stories, tells it like it is, and
then bids them to have a "Good Day!"

CONSIDER THIS: Be straightforward in your speech. Be clear
in your explanations. Say "yes" or "no" more often than you
say "maybe."

Milton Hershey

"The difference between mediocrity and greatness is extra effort." — George Allen

Some people see failure as a sign to give up. Those who eventually become successful see failure as a stepping-stone and another lesson in the business school of life. They just keep on trying. Milton Hershey's father was an itinerant speculator, moving from place to place and investing in every kind of business with little success. Milton, born in 1857, attended seven schools in eight years and never made it past the fourth grade. He first worked for a printer, was fired, and then was apprenticed to a confectioner. In 1876 Milton opened his own candy business in Philadelphia, but he couldn't make a profit. Next, he went to Denver and opened a candy store. It too failed. Milton made another attempt in New York City, and that business failed in 1886.

Finally, Milton Hershey returned to his hometown of Lancaster, Pennsylvania, and began making caramels. The candy came to the attention of an English importer, who placed a big order. The caramel business prospered, and Hershey built a modest factory on the site that eventually was to encompass sixty-five acres of candy manufacturing. In 1893, inspired by German chocolate makers at the World's Fair, Hershey began to produce his own chocolate. By 1900 he sold the caramel business and concentrated solely on producing chocolate. Hershey refused to advertise (a policy the company adhered to until 1970), believing that quality would sell his wares.

CONSIDER THIS: Failure can be a valuable part of learning. Some see it as a dead end, while others see it as an opportunity to learn a valuable lesson.

Peter McColough of Xerox

*"The secret of success in life is for a man to be
ready for his opportunity."* — Disraeli

C. Peter McColough attended Harvard Business School
after World War II and took a job as a salesman for a chemical
company. He loaned his resume to a friend, who wanted to
copy its format. The friend happened to show McColough's
resume to a corporate recruiter, who (as recruiters are apt to
do) kept the resume in mind. As a result of that tenuous con-
nection, McColough was offered and accepted a job at Lehigh
Coal and Navigation. After working at the company for several years, he was approached by another recruiter, who told
him of a position at the Haloid Company, a photographic and
camera concern.

McColough was not impressed as he toured Haloid's facilities. The vice president's bookshelf was actually an orange
crate painted green, he recalls. However, there was a Rube
Goldberg-like device called the "Model A" that made dry
copies using a photographic process. When McColough
talked to Haloid's president, Joseph Wilson, he was fascinated
by the prospect of making a product that would make high-
quality copies in large numbers using a new technique they
called xerography. It was a tough decision to move from a
good-paying job at a stable company to an enterprise in its infancy. In 1961 Haloid was renamed Xerox, and the company
introduced a copying machine that would forever change the
way business is performed.

CONSIDER THIS: Do you hear opportunity knocking? Do
you have the courage to open that door? Are you ready to take
advantage of what may be offered?

Federal Express

"When it absolutely, positively has to be there overnight."
— Federal Express advertisement

Once Federal Express popularized overnight air express in the mid-1970s, a host of other companies followed suit. By the mid-1980s the market had almost become saturated, and to maintain its lead, Federal Express provided improved efficiency and service to its customers. Each night at midnight, the FedEx hub in Memphis, Tennessee, takes on the appearance of a NASA launch site as hundreds of workers scamper to sort packages arriving on the company's large fleet of cargo aircraft and forward them to their destinations. Some nights over a million packages must be processed. Every minute counts. A single minute's delay can mean as many as 20,000 packages will miss the 10:30 a.m. delivery deadline, and each delay costs FedEx money as well as customer satisfaction.

Many Federal Express employees are college students. The company rewards those students by paying 75 percent of their college fees, if they keep their grades up. Even though it has tens of thousands of employees, FedEx's top officers meet weekly with workers who have complaints. The result is a very low turnover rate and a highly motivated work force. To enhance customer satisfaction, Federal Express has become one of the most computer-intensive companies in the overnight-delivery field, using more than 30,000 terminals worldwide to keep track of millions of packages. Even in an industry that is teeming with competitors, people notice the organization that successfully motivates its employees and keeps its customers happy.

CONSIDER THIS: Anyone can run "just another business," but companies that build employee loyalty and provide superior customer service are likely to have a stronger bottom line.

An Idea-nurturing Work Climate at 3M

" 'Tis wise to learn, 'tis Godlike to create."
— J. G. Saxe

Few businesses can remain prosperous on the strength of just one product. Most one-product companies have their heyday and then fade quickly from the marketplace. The companies that continue to be successful for decades are those that foster innovation. That is not easy for large companies, where the corporate bureaucracy often stifles creativity. Innovation is an issue that companies must address directly and from the highest levels of management. Many of the products produced by 3M are soon copied by competitors. To keep making profits, 3M needs new ideas; thus, it is essential that its corporate climate nurture ideas. To encourage its workers to participate in creative thinking, 3M has developed a series of policies aimed at creating an atmosphere conducive to the discovery of new product ideas.

Top management is encouraged to take a personal interest in the development of new products. They point with pride and great fanfare to each success and accept failure with constructive concern that encourages a "try again" attitude. Management allows new ventures to develop without the pressures associated with daily production. Researchers and marketing staff mingle to feed on each other's ideas. When a new product looks to be worthwhile, the person who developed it is given a great deal of responsibility in taking the product to the marketplace and giving it a chance to succeed.

CONSIDER THIS: There are innovative and creative individuals in almost every organization who are capable of developing profitable ideas. Management must be willing to take the risk of developing a business culture that allows experimentation and failure, and shares the rewards of success.

George Kress

*"Life is like riding a bicycle; you don't fall off
unless you stop peddling."* — Claude Pepper

Geoge Kress became a millionaire and then put his money to work helping other people. Inspired by a Norman Vincent Peale sermon, Kress established the Green Bay, Wisconsin, Chapter of the American Foundation of Religion and Psychiatry. Through that organization people of the region can receive help with such problems as alcoholism, family abuse, and marital conflicts. Kress sums up his belief in the following way: "Two characteristics are important to develop. The first is integrity. You'll need lots of help to make it; people have got to like and trust you or you won't get anywhere. The second is dedication; you have to be willing to make your work a priority."

George Kress earned his money by creating and selling boxes. In the early part of the century, the Green Bay Box & Lumber company made and sold wooden boxes. Kress was attending the University of Wisconsin, where he earned a B.A. in 1925, when his father's business took a turn for the worse. He had to put an accounting career on hold to rescue the family business, which Kress and his wife successfully nursed through the depression. The repeal of prohibition created a demand for boxes that could be used to ship beverages. Kress soon recognized that corrugated boxes would be ideal for that purpose and converted his business to meet the demand. By the late 1990s, Green Bay Packaging, Inc. employed more than 2,800 workers and had annual sales in excess of $600 million.

CONSIDER THIS: Those who hang on during tough times are often ready to meet the market when it arrives.

H & R Block

"Tomorrow's growth depends on the use we make of today's materials and experiences." — Unknown

Henry Bloch studied mathematics in college and completed his degree while in the Air Force. After serving as a first lieutenant and navigator on a B-17 Flying Fortress during World War II, he returned to his home in Kansas City, Missouri, and went to work for a brokerage firm. Seeking his American Dream after a year of working for others, Henry borrowed money from his aunt to join his brother Richard in forming United Business Company, which performed bookkeeping and other managerial services. As a service to their clients, the brothers provided free income tax preparation. As the clients began telling their friends about the Blochs, the brothers' tax preparation business grew. By 1954 the load was so great that the Blochs were working long hours seven days a week.

Henry saw that the income tax preparation business could support itself exclusively, and in 1955 he and Richard formed a new company called H & R Block, Inc. (an easier spelling of the family name). The enterprise expanded rapidly via a franchise arrangement, and H & R Block offices soon became familiar sights at shopping centers and Sears stores throughout the country. Many of the tax centers are also company-owned. A tax preparation school was established to train employees for the various offices. Today, H & R Block annually prepares millions of income tax returns at a price virtually every taxpayer can afford.

CONSIDER THIS: Rapid expansion and franchising work best for businesses with a single purpose and easily replicated formula.

Malcolm Forbes

> *"When what we are is what we want to be,*
> *that's happiness."* — Malcolm Forbes

Malcolm Forbes loved life, and he particularly loved the life of a capitalist. In fact, Malcolm was often called a "cheerleader for capitalism." Who else would name his Boeing 727 corporate jet *Capitalist Tool?* Who but a capitalist could afford a Boeing 727? Although he received a substantial inheritance from his father, Malcolm became a success in his own right. He was decorated during World War II, founded two weekly newspapers, and produced an award-winning history magazine before taking over the family enterprise. After he joined Forbes, Inc., the family empire grew much larger than Malcolm's father could ever have dreamed.

Malcolm Forbes claimed that a person can't be successful unless he loves what he is doing. In fact, if someone loves what he is doing, then he is succeeding, since that is really the meaning of success. The "income" a person derives from life is the opportunity to do those things that are the most fulfilling. One of Forbes's biggest breaks in life may actually have been a failure. In 1957, when he was running for governor of New Jersey, he was "nosed out in a landslide." That was the year he became editor-in-chief of *Forbes* magazine. Plunging into the life of a publisher, he became caught up in the joy of running the business, and his joy turned into a enormous success. During his life, Forbes was the leader of a New York motorcycle pack, became the first person to complete a hot-air balloon trip across the United States, and celebrated his seventieth birthday (in 1989) with a $2 million party in Morocco. Malcolm Forbes enjoyed life.

CONSIDER THIS: How can a person be successful if he or she is not happy? Success is fulfillment, which may or may not be related to any material goods.

Mary Kay

*"People and pride are the two foremost assets in
building a successful business."*
— Mary Kay Ash

In mid-1963, after a successful career in direct sales, Mary
Kay Ash retired—for a month. During that brief span, she decided to write a book to help women survive in the male-
dominated business world. At her kitchen table, she made two
lists—one contained the good things she had seen in companies; the other featured the things she thought could be improved. When she review the lists, she realized that she had
inadvertently created a marketing plan for a successful company. With her life savings of $5,000 and the help of her
twenty-year-old son, Richard Rogers, she launched Mary Kay
Cosmetics on Friday, September 13, 1963.

Mary Kay's goal was to provide women with an unlimited
opportunity for personal and financial success. She used the
Golden Rule as her guiding philosophy and encouraged employees and sales force members to prioritize their lives: God
first, family second, career third. Because of her steadfast commitment to her goals and principles, and her tremendous determination, dedication, and hard work, Mary Kay Inc. has grown
from a small direct-sales company into the largest direct seller
of skin care products in the U.S. with the nation's best-selling
brand of facial skin care and color cosmetics. By the late 1990s,
the company had more than 475,000 independent beauty consultants in twenty-six countries. A unique combination of enthusiastic people, quality products, an innovative marketing
concept, and an ambitious set of goals has turned Mary Kay
Inc. into an American business success story.

CONSIDER THIS: People who are respected and well com-
pensated will often be the best assets of a company.

Birds Eye's Frozen Foods

*"A determination to succeed is the only way to
succeed that I know anything about."*
— William Feather

Clarence Birdseye had a great idea for freezing food for
storage, but marketing the concept was not easy. After preparing over a million and a half pounds of frozen food in the summer of 1928, General Foods found it had no place to sell its
products. The company had no viable marketing plan and was
running out of money. After courting several established food
distributors, it finally joined with the Postum Cereal Company.
Postum took the name General Foods Corporation and began a
plan for marketing the Birds Eye-trademarked frozen foods.
First, it selected Springfield, Massachusetts, as a test site and installed free freezers in eighteen grocery stores.

For forty weeks, the General Foods marketing team gave
away free samples, conducted research in homes, and spoke at
clubs, schools, and nearly anywhere else they could gather a
crowd. Their research convinced the team members there was a
market for frozen foods, but in the first four years, the company
was able to make an impact only in the New England states.
Then, in 1934, General Foods changed its strategy and began
marketing its foods to institutions. Results were good, and by
1940 Birds Eye brand products were being distributed nationally. With the onset of World War II, the need to conserve metals resulted in increased consumer preference for frozen foods
over canned products. By the end of the war, most Americans
had become used to the convenience of frozen foods, and the
expansion of the market has continued ever since.

CONSIDER THIS: Finding the right way to market a good
idea often takes many trials—and sometimes years and a little
good luck.

Doing Business One-on-One

"No typewriter is as warm as the human voice, and no phone call can take the place of eyeball-to-eyeball contact." — J. B. Fuqua

J. B. Fuqua is one of the most successful businessmen in America. If you listen to him talk enough, he will tell you that part of his success is the result of doing business one-on-one. When he started in business, J. B. went to Augusta, Georgia, with a plan for a radio station. Without knowing a soul, he found several people interested in the idea and talked them into providing the funding. Once, when J. B. was attempting to buy some theaters from two brothers in Georgia, he heard that one sibling would be leaving town and would not be back soon. J. B. immediately took an airplane to see the brothers, and that evening the three men drew up a contract on a yellow writing tablet. It was a $20 million deal, and J. B. later said that if he had not met with the brothers that night, it might have never been done. When he heard about a bottler that wanted to sell but had tax problems, J. B. showed up at the man's office at eight o'clock the next morning and worked out a deal to buy the business using the other man's money.

Dealing directly with people means that J. B. Fuqua often answers his own phone. "It might be Santa Claus," he says. Being so accessible means that Fuqua seldom misses an opportunity. An idea that a secretary might think is nonsense could be worth a million dollars to a person who knows what to do with such an idea. After reaching his goal of becoming a millionaire in the 1950s, Fuqua continued making deals "for sport." He successfully led Fuqua Industries for over forty years and eventually "retired" to spend much of his time serving on the boards of various philanthropic organizations.

CONSIDER THIS: If you want information, go to the source. If you want a deal, talk directly to the owner.

Asa Candler

"The person who works diligently toward a dream, and keeps his focus on the goal, will wake up some fine morning and realize that he has achieved what he has dreamed." — A. C. Elliott

It took more than good taste to make Coca-Cola a beverage that is known throughout the world. When Asa Candler bought the company in 1889 from Dr. John Pemberton, he towed away all of the enterprise's assets in a single horse-drawn wagon. To market Coke beyond its Atlanta home, Candler instituted a far-reaching promotional campaign. The Coca-Cola trademark was promoted to soda fountains around the country on signs, serving trays, lamps, and every other item Candler could sell or give away. Until 1899 most Coca-Cola sold was in syrup form, but with encouragement from some Chattanooga businessmen, Candler agreed to set up an extensive network of bottling plants.

In 1899 Coca-Cola went to the Spanish-American War. Coke also became a familiar sight at baseball games, picnics, and nearly every other American pastime. In Candler's continual effort to get Coke's name before the public, he began promoting signs to small retail stores that promised "Ice Cold Coca-Cola Sold Here." For many of the stores, it was their first major sign, and they eagerly accepted it. Other promotional ideas included the creation of a distinctive soda fountain glass with the Coca-Cola label and the introduction of the classic-contour Coca-Cola bottle. Under Candler's leadership, Coca-Cola became one of the most successful products in American history. In 1919 Candler sold his interest in Coca-Cola for $25 million.

CONSIDER THIS: A good product still requires an inventive, effective, and long-term marketing campaign to become the leader in its field.

Dan Bricklin's Spreadsheet

"It's not what you take with you but what you leave behind that defines greatness."

— Edward Gardner

Dan Bricklin was playing with microcomputers before most of us had even heard of them. He entered MIT in 1969 to study mathematics but switched to computer science. While at MIT, Dan helped design an on-line computer calculator. After graduation, he went to work for DEC where he gained experience working on word-processing programs. In 1977 Dan entered Harvard to work toward an MBA. His familiarity with computers placed Dan in the right place to solve a nagging business problem: automating spreadsheet calculations. In his business courses, he had to calculate everything by hand, laboriously writing down hundreds of numbers and meticulously calculating sums, differences, and percentages. It was easy to make mistakes.

As a result of that frustration, Bricklin began to create a software program that would do for numbers what a word processor did for words. He linked up with a friend, Bob Frankston, to design a commercially functional program that would accomplish such a task. In 1979 they started Software Arts, Inc. and introduced their program under the name VisiCalc. Once VisiCalc became available on the Apple II computer, it caught on like wildfire. In many ways, VisiCalc was responsible for Apple's own success. Customers often would go to a computer store wanting VisiCalc, ask what type of machine the program ran on, and then buy an Apple computer. VisiCalc was the first "hit" microcomputer program, and it dominated the market until challenged by a new program, Lotus 1-2-3.

CONSIDER THIS: Cross-pollination among disciplines such as science and business may result in ideas that will advance them both.

The Super Bowl

*"Winning the Super Bowl the first time is an
unbelievable thrill."* — Roger Staubach

To virtually every professional football player and fan, winning the Super Bowl is the ultimate achievement. However, the annual Super Bowl game is a relative newcomer to a sport whose first professional contest was played in 1895 in Latrobe, Pennsylvania. The first Super Bowl was staged in January 1967 between the champions of the National Football League (founded in 1922) and the American Football League (founded in 1960) as a test to see which league's winner was better. The NFL's Green Bay Packers won that first game, and in subsequent years—especially after the two leagues merged in 1970—the Super Bowl has garnered more media coverage than any other professional sporting event. Why? Because it parallels our own ambitions to compete and succeed.

One of football's most heralded players, Hall of Fame quarterback Roger Staubach of the Dallas Cowboys, remembers the ups and downs that led to his second NFL championship ring, in Super Bowl XII. Dallas struggled against itself as well as the Denver Broncos in the early minutes of the game, fumbling the ball three times deep in its own territory. Somehow Dallas escaped without giving up any points, but the Cowboys also missed three field goals. Dallas was jittery and could have fallen under the weight of its mistakes, but the players refused to fold. Instead, the Cowboys capitalized on Denver's mistakes and held the Broncos scoreless until the third quarter. Keeping its collective cool, Dallas played with dogged determination and defeated Denver 27–10 to win its second Super Bowl.

CONSIDER THIS: Winners have their share of mistakes and bad breaks. Don't let mistakes make you stumble. Look for opportunities to move forward and "run toward the daylight."

Mary Crowley

"Real wisdom is looking at the world from God's point of view." — Mary Crowley

Her husband was too lazy to work, so Mary had to look for a job. She had never been employed before, and the country was in the throes of an economic depression. The day before beginning her quest, Mary stood in front of a mirror and practiced twelve ways of asking for a job. The next morning, dressed in her finest clothes, she went to town and entered what appeared to be the most prosperous department store. "I want to see the owner," Mary said. "Won't do you any good," came the reply, but Mary found the owner's office anyway. "I've picked this store to work in," she said. When told there were no jobs, Mary said, "Just let me work one Saturday. If I don't sell enough to more than pay my salary, you won't have to let me come back." The owner agreed, and that afternoon Mary outsold every other person in the store.

After her first marriage was dissolved, Mary met and married David Crowley. While raising her family, she continued her career and became a top producer for Stanley products. An importer asked Mary to help him sell home-decorating items, and Mary recruited a force of over 500 women. Using Proverbs as her "degree in business administration," she based her training program on Christian principles. A trip for top sellers was planned, and Mary learned that her boss had also included a cocktail party, an activity Mary didn't like. In the ensuing disagreement with her employer, Mary was shown the door. After a good cry, she picked herself up and began Home Interiors, which became one of America's most successful direct sales organizations.

CONSIDER THIS: You have to stick with what you believe in. If you compromise your beliefs, there is no way you can devote yourself fully to your goals.

Chuck House at Hewlett Packard

"Once a new idea springs into existence, it cannot be unthought. There is a sense of immortality in a new idea." — Edward de Bobo

I n his book *Intrapreneuring*, Gifford Pinchot profiles Chuck House of Hewlett Packard. Chuck worked in the oscilloscope division but had an inkling that there were other uses for Hewlett Packard's scopes than those for which they were sold. He got a crack at helping to find another application when Hewlett Packard was working on a project for the Federal Aviation Administration. The development team had hoped to build a better monitor for use in control towers, but what they came up with was a monitor that was half the size and weight and twenty times faster than existing equipment. However, the monitor didn't meet the FAA's requirements, and the project was scrapped. Chuck still had hope for the monitor and persuaded his boss to spend an additional $2,000 to show it to some potential customers.

Chuck thought he might have a winner and got permission to put several other people on the project. However, during H-P's annual review, the project received a thumbs-down from marketing and management. Dave Packard himself said, "When I come back next year, I don't want to see that project in the lab!" Nevertheless, Chuck's boss let him go "underground," and he was able to finish his two-year project in less than a year. When Packard returned to the lab the next year, the monitor had already shown that it would be successful in the marketplace. Chuck House was given a "Medal of Defiance" by H-P to celebrate his victory over the system.

CONSIDER THIS: All the corporate wisdom in the world cannot take the place of one person who believes in a project and will champion it to success.

Mrs. Fields Cookies

"Success is a ladder that cannot be climbed with your hands in your pockets."

— American proverb

Debbi Fields baked a very good chocolate chip cookie that everyone liked. With encouragement from her friends, she borrowed $50,000 and opened a small cookie store in Palo Alto, California. It took Debbi a while to discover the secret of making her business a success. Part of that discovery was that she was not selling cookies, but heart. To this day, Debbi believes that what people really want in her store is "caring." Debbi learned that she had to go into the mall and give away samples to bring people to her store. She had to use the finest ingredients to ensure the best cookies, and she had to price the cookies so that people could buy them for less than it would cost to make them at home. Debbi's company, Mrs. Fields Cookies, wants its customers to experience a warm feeling of quality and caring in every cookie. That is why all cookies are served warm. In many cases, cookies that are not sold within two hours are given to local charities.

Anyone who enters a Mrs. Fields store is greeted by a friendly salesperson who will help him or her have a brighter day. As her company expanded, Debbi Fields chose managers not only for their ability to run the store, but also for their ability to have fun. Believing that the cookie business should be more like a Disney spectacular than just a bakery counter, she is determined to give people a little of the fantasy that makes life fun.

CONSIDER THIS: Selling is more than just ringing up a sale. It is a Broadway production: Welcoming a customer with a warm hello, convincing him to believe in and enjoy your product, and sending him away with a smile.

New Coke vs. Classic Coke

*"Perhaps no other corporate leader in modern times
so beautifully exemplified the American dream."*
— Jimmy Carter on Roberto Goizueta

Roberto Goizueta was born in Cuba in 1931. He graduated from Yale and began working as a chemical engineer for Cuban Coca-Cola in 1954. When Fidel Castro's communist regime came into power, Roberto fled to the United States and went to work for Coke's Latin American operations. He built a reputation within the company as a relentless and meticulous worker. Roberto's accomplishments earned him advancements, and in 1979 he was elected Coke's vice chairman. In 1980 he became president and soon warned, "We're going to take risks."

Everyone wants to be remembered for their successes, but Roberto Goizueta had to live with one of the century's most-publicized marketing miscues: the introduction of New Coke. In response to the Pepsi Challenge taste tests, Coca-Cola conducted extensive research to develop a better-tasting cola. Researchers devised what many considered to be a more palatable formula, but the company failed to recognize the powerful consumer loyalty commanded by the original product. When New Coke was introduced, there was an immediate backlash from Coke's most loyal customers. Goizueta then made the bold move to backtrack and reintroduce the original formula as Classic Coke. Instead of letting the New Coke fiasco take him or his company down, Goizueta recovered from the mistake and took Coca-Cola to new markets and record sales. Over his sixteen years at Coke's helm, he was able to increase the company's value from $5 billion in 1981 to nearly $150 billion in 1997.

CONSIDER THIS: When you make a mistake, don't compound it with excuses. Change your direction and correct the mistake as quickly as possible.

Renovators Supply

"Genius is the very eye of intellect and the wing of thought; it is always in advance of its time."
— William Simms

In 1974 Claude and Donna Jeanloz began to restore an old home in Massachusetts when they discovered a problem common to most renovators: lack of authentic fixtures. In four years they tracked down source after source to get the items they needed. Once they had experienced this problem, it occurred to them that others would also have a hard time finding items for use in restoration. To address that need, Claude and Donna decided to start a small mail-order catalog business. Their catalog carried hard-to-find plumbing and electrical fixtures as well as doorknobs and hinges. Working with other suppliers, the couple was able to create a central clearinghouse for virtually everything that people involved in home renovation would need.

There is often a limited window of opportunity during which an idea can be successful. For Renovators Supply, the timing was right, as many baby boomers were moving into inner-city areas to reduce commuting time and costs. Houses were being renovated in virtually every major U.S. city. As their company grew, the Jeanlozes sold advertising in their catalogs to manufacturers and introduced supplemental catalogs specializing in accessories to add finishing touches to the restored houses. Business boomed, and the couple opened a series of retail stores called Renovators Supply where people could come in and quickly obtain the most common renovation materials.

CONSIDER THIS: What kinds of hard-to-get items do lots of people want? Keep an eye on the horizon for possible new trends, because if the timing is right and you can provide what others need, you could be the subject of the next success story.

Ken Olsen and DEC

*"We have committed the Golden Rule to memory;
now let us commit it to life."*
— Edwin Markham

Ken Olsen, founder of Digital Equipment Corporation (DEC), was a nuts-and-bolts engineer who maintained a down-home approach to product quality and ruled his empire with a well-defined set of beliefs and values. In an era when computers were gigantic machines, DEC created a relatively small computer that was rugged and well designed. When Olsen started his company, he struggled to define his own managerial style. For years Olsen began Tuesday mornings by attending a breakfast organized by Thompson Phillips, the CEO of Raytheon Corporation. The morning discussions often revolved around applying Christian principles to the business world. Olsen learned his management principles from Christian teachings, and he was sometimes known to quote hymns to make a point. Some may call his approach simplistic, but it was good enough to turn DEC from a small, obscure company into the second-largest (behind IBM) computer manufacturer in the world.

Olsen's heroes were the early American Puritans. To him, they were tough and well equipped to cope with failure. They never expected too much from sinful men and never blamed others for their mistakes. Olsen lived his beliefs. He often ate in the company cafeteria, welcomed advice, and encouraged employees to voice their opinions. When he felt his executives were too far removed from the end users of the company's products, he "invited" twenty-four managers to a warehouse where they put together computers from morning until dusk.

CONSIDER THIS: What are the basic values that drive you to succeed? Are your choices and decisions based on character and integrity or on whim and opportunism?

Quincy Jones

"I recommend that you take care of the minutes, for the hours will take care of themselves."
— Chesterfield

In 1974 doctors discovered that Quincy Jones had two brain aneurysms. "Please, God, not now," he cried. Quincy had played trumpet for years, and he still had too many dreams to let it all end now. One of America's top black jazz artists, he had worked with Lionel Hampton's band and eventually formed his own group. Quincy had worked on Broadway and still had a promising career ahead of him as a trumpeter when medical problems forced him to face the reality that he could not return to his beloved instrument. He would have to apply his musical talents elsewhere.

Quincy Jones is a perfectionist. He channeled his formidable musical ability into composing, directing, and producing, and soon began to attract the attention of some of the entertainment industry's most influential people. His attention to detail is legendary. He works and works to make the music just right, then works some more to see if he can make it perfect. Jones produced and conducted the "We are the World" recording, wrote the score for *Roots* and *The Color Purple*, and also produced *Thriller* with Michael Jackson, one of the most successful record albums of all time. He has been nominated for sixty-eight Grammy Awards and has won nineteen. Stephen Spielberg summed up Jones's intensity of life in a *Sixty Minutes* interview: "He takes a minute and finds two minutes of enrichment out of one minute of living."

CONSIDER THIS: Life is what you put into it. It is what you dream and how hard you work to make those dreams come true. What you make of your life is no one's responsibility but yours.

Estee Lauder

"If you put the product into the customer's hands it will speak for itself if it's something of quality."
— Estee Lauder

She had cracked the American market, but the European market, particularly Paris, seemed to belong to the Europeans. Estee Lauder was never one to accept defeat, so she "accidentally" spilled some of her Youth Dew fragrance at her display at Galeries Lafayette. The scent wafted throughout the store and enticed the women shoppers to discover its source. Lauder was conquering another continent. Estee Lauder's cosmetics empire had its roots in the stable behind the family home. During World War I, her uncle, John Schotz, had come from Hungary and set up a chemical laboratory, where he perfected a velvety skin cream. Young Estee Mentzer watched with awe and learned all there was to know about the process.

By the time she was in high school, Estee was making her own creams and testing them on every girl she could recruit. After marrying Leonard Alan Lauder in 1933, she continued her experiments in the kitchen and began selling her creams at beauty shops in New York. Estee insisted on creams of the highest quality. To expand her sales, she hounded the cosmetics buyers at the best department stores in the country—Saks, Neiman-Marcus, and others—and even visited each store to personally train the saleswomen. Estee Lauder placed her early advertising dollars into samples and giveaways, and pioneered the concept of gifts with purchases.

CONSIDER THIS: The product is only half the story. Success comes to those who market relentlessly, sell their story thousands of times, and continue to spread their message zealously even when others have stopped.

Charlie Chaplin, the "Little Tramp"

"Practice makes perfect." — Proverb

Charlie Chaplin will always be remembered for his creation of the "Little Tramp," a character he portrayed in dozens of movies. He is also remembered for his comedic insight and for the precision, cleverness, and seeming ease with which he performed on film. However, it is only recently that studies of Chaplin's life and work have brought his genius into focus. His was a genius of hard work, frustration and messy creation. Virtually all of his films were made with no script. Chaplin would have a germ of an idea and begin filming a scene, not knowing where it would lead. He would then build on that scene, ultimately developing a story line. Chaplin would often re-shoot entire scenes when he would think of one additional bit of information that was relevant to the story evolving in his head.

The scenes that seemed effortless to the viewers often were ground out bit by bit. Chaplin frequently filmed the same scene hundreds of times until he got it just the way he wanted. When his inspiration stopped, so did the entire production. The crew and actors would sit around for days with nothing to do until Chaplin thought of a new idea. As a result, he had many confrontations with studio chiefs and financial backers who felt he was using too much film and wasting the crew's time. In the long run, Charlie Chaplin's films were among the era's most successful. His genius was not in doing it right the first time, but doing it enough times to finally get it right.

CONSIDER THIS: Many times our society gives us one chance to get things right. If you have any control over your life, never be satisfied with the first "good" result. Keep going until the finished product is great.

Viking Freight

*"The greatest pleasure in life lies in doing that
which others say cannot be done."*
— Viking Freight's motto

Dick Bangham and friend Jim Haapoja were working for
Memorex when they were bitten by the need to follow their
own American Dream. In 1966, starting with a Chevy pickup
and an old Pontiac, the pair began a delivery service. Often
working sixteen hours a day, they survived on a few small delivery contracts. The business caught on, and they began to see
profits and the chance for additional growth. As they prepared
for expansion, Dick and Jim met with bankers and transportation experts, all of whom said it would be impossible for the
company become a successful common carrier due to tough
regulations, unions, and slim profit margins. But the two continued to pursue their American Dream.

Using loans, leases, and internally generated capital, Bangham and Haapoja steadily expanded Viking Freight. Bangham
insisted on extensive training for all employees, promotion
from within, and upward career planning. All new employees
spend a full day at the company's headquarters (known as
Viking University) where they learn the "Viking Way." Viking
has become one of the most envied common carriers in the
western United States and has received numerous awards of excellence from the trucking industry. To stay profitable, the
company often reminds its employees, "Viking doesn't pay your
wages, the customer does. Viking simply takes the money and
divides it up between the employee and the suppliers of equipment and services, and tries to keep enough to continue growing. Without customers, there would be no money to divide."

CONSIDER THIS: Do we often forget who is the most important person in our business? It is the customer.

Pillsbury Know-how

*"Whatsoever thy hand findeth to do, do it with
thy might."*   — Ecclesiastes

John Pillsbury came to Minnesota in 1855 and was soon joined by his nephew Charles. Since the new community of St. Anthony needed tools and supplies for building, Pillsbury opened a hardware store. By 1869 Pillsbury was successful but was looking for other opportunities. The area's milling industry was in poor condition and losing money. When the mill owners looked for a partner to save them, most investors turned them down as a hopeless cause. Charles Pillsbury bought a one-third interest and began to apply his know-how to bring the mills back to profitability. Although at the time he knew little about milling, he had a keen understanding of business. He bought new machinery to produce better flour and took a personal interest in improving the milling operation. By 1871 Pillsbury had bought out its partners, and the operation was named C. A. Pillsbury & Company.

Not happy to be just profitable, Pillsbury wanted to have the best and most modern mills available. The family purchased several other local mills and began increasing productivity with modern machinery. "Pillsbury's Best" flour began to establish a reputation as one of the best brands available. Charles traveled to Europe in 1888 and obtained special "secret" devices that made the new mill, named "A," the largest and most modern mill in the world. The foundation of the Pillsbury company was based on innovation and a constant desire to produce the world's best product.

CONSIDER THIS: An organization is not successful just because it provides a necessity. What makes an organization successful is leaders who have a vision and who work hard to make success happen.

Teradyne

"Concentrate your resources to win. You have a chance to lose because you might pick the wrong objective. On the other hand, if you don't concentrate, it's a sure loss." — Alex d'Arbeloff

Teradyne Inc. got off to a rough start. Nick DeWolf and Alex d'Arbeloff sat in DeWolf's living room in 1960 and began to draw up plans for a new company. Each was an engineer who had the itch to do something on his own. Together they successfully raised $250,000 and rented a space over a hot dog shop in Boston. Their first product, on which they had spent their whole bankroll, was a go/no-go diode tester. When the gadget was ready, they began showing it to potential customers. Everywhere they went, they were turned down. Friends even took them aside to express their sorrow that the new company wasn't working out. DeWolf and d'Arbeloff were discouraged but refused to give up.

The pair knew the tester was something their customers needed, but they had to convince the customers of that need. Sales slowly grew from nineteen units to fifty-nine in two years, and the company eventually began making a profit. Then, in 1969, the bottom dropped out of the semiconductor industry. Teradyne held on and used the slump to diversify into other kinds equipment. DeWolf eventually left the corporate life, but d'Arbeloff continued to head the firm and led it into a successful future. Tested in the corporate crucible, d'Arbeloff's successful "Three R's" management style consists of: Recruiting people from universities, Retaining them by giving them the freedom to operate, and putting them on the Right projects. The trick is to pick strategic projects and then devote sufficient resources to make them work.

CONSIDER THIS: Know your customers well enough to be able to provide them with precisely the products they need.

White Castle Hamburgers

*"Small opportunities are often the beginning of
great enterprises."* — Demosthenes

While many of the largest hamburger restaurants fight it out by redesigning their sandwiches over and over again, one company has been consistently successful by keeping its burgers the same for decades. In 1921 E. W. Ingram and Walt Anderson opened the first White Castle in Wichita, Kansas. Anderson was an experienced fry cook and Ingram knew real estate. They borrowed $700 to open their first restaurant and carefully selected the White Castle name to symbolize to customers the restaurant's commitment to purity and cleanliness. The entrepreneurs' innovative idea became the world's original fast-food hamburger restaurant chain. Unlike most fast-food chains, White Castle has remained a family business, with the Ingram family continuing to own all stores.

White Castle's success isn't based on a "big" burger. Its burgers, which are also known as "Sliders," are small and are served on buns about the size of a square dinner roll. The 100 percent USDA beef is punched with five holes and steam-grilled. Hardly anyone buys just one White Castle burger—most customers buy them by the bagful. White Castle customers are very loyal. One Chicago customer waited outside a new store for fifteen hours to buy the first hamburger sold at that location. Some couples have even been married at White Castle restaurants, and once two adventurers took a pair of Sliders to Antarctica and were photographed while enjoying the burgers at the South Pole.

CONSIDER THIS: You don't need to compete head-on with a company that dominates an industry if your have your own unique style, service, or product. Sometimes being different is good.

Carnegie's Cost Accounting

*"The biggest room in the world is the room
for improvement."* — Colton

Anyone who has made it through business school has taken a course in cost accounting. However, few people realize that the subject was a major reason why Andrew Carnegie became one of the wealthiest men the world has ever known. Carnegie learned about cost accounting during his twelve years with the Pennsylvania Railroad—considered by many to be America's "graduate school of business" in the mid-nineteenth century.

When he bought into the steel business, Carnegie found that most steel mills had no idea whether they were operating at a profit or a loss until their books were balanced at the end of the year. By instituting a weekly accounting of all functions, and by knowing precisely how much each activity cost, Carnegie was able to lower the cost of producing steel from $56 dollars per ton to $11.50 per ton. Other steel producers scoffed at his efficiency techniques, saying that running the mills twenty-four hours a day would wear out the equipment. That was true, but Carnegie had counted the costs and constantly bought better equipment, replacing older, inefficient equipment even when it was not worn out. Many called him wasteful, but Carnegie's mills made a profit while others barely survived. Even though Carnegie knew little about steel, he knew how to institute accounting techniques that would keep him in touch with costs and enable him to take advantage of economies of scale.

CONSIDER THIS: Do you really know where your bottom line stands on a weekly basis? Have you analyzed each part of your organization to determine precisely how much it contributes? Is your business always improving? How do you know?

Robert Goddard

"For every action there is an equal and opposite reaction." — Newton's third law of motion

When Robert Goddard began working on the problem of sending a rocket into space, he soon realized that the weight of such a vehicle's fuel would be tremendous. Further, the fuel would be expended quickly, leaving a heavy empty container attached to the spacecraft. Goddard's solution was to create a multi-stage rocket. As soon as the fuel in the initial stage was consumed, the fuel tanks and motor for that stage would be jettisoned, and the rocket would continue its climb with less weight to bear. It was a brilliant idea that ultimately enabled NASA to send men to the moon. But Goddard would never see his idea put to use. He patented the multi-stage rocket in 1914, nearly four decades before such a vehicle was constructed.

Robert Goddard's pioneering vision for rocketry is an example of American ingenuity that has placed the U.S. at the forefront of the technological age. In a 1907 article in *Scientific American*, Goddard explained how gyroscopes could be used to stabilize airplanes in flight. In 1919 he wrote a book entitled *A Method of Reaching Extreme Altitudes*. The press ridiculed Goddard, who was head of the physics department at Clark University, saying he didn't have even a high school understanding of physics. Goddard's research depended on occasional small grants, but even with such meager resources, he was able to construct the first liquid-fueled rocket in 1926. While the U.S. government generally ignored his work, Germany used Goddard's ideas to create the V2 rocket during World War II. Although Goddard died in 1945, his concepts for rockets and space travel are still used today.

CONSIDER THIS: If you are on the cutting edge of discovery, people may ridicule your ideas. Stick to what you know is right, and the truth will eventually be recognized.

Eli Whitney

*"I do the very best I know how, the very best I
can, and I mean to keep on doing so until the end."*
— Lincoln

Eli Whitney grew up on a small farm in Massachusetts before the American Revolution. Knowing that the acreage was not large enough to split between him and his brothers, he left home to seek his fortune. Although he had little formal education, Eli managed to learn enough to be able to enter and graduate from Yale. Later, after taking a tutoring job in Georgia, he used his farm background and mechanical aptitude to help a friend solve the problem of separating seeds, hulls, and foreign material from cotton. The invention helped the South rise from poverty to prosperity, but Eli's invention was quickly copied and he saw little profit.

Eli Whitney had learned that a product's success rests on the manufacturer's ability to make it better, faster, and cheaper than everyone else. He also realized that a product must be mass-produced if the manufacturer is to realize a profit on his investment. Knowing that the fledgling U.S. government needed a domestic supply of rifles, Whitney devised a plan to make the weapons with interchangeable parts. Standardization allowed production of the various components to be spread among several workers, rather than a single gunsmith, greatly reducing manufacturing time and costs. No bank would risk the capital, but the government was eager to back the rifle project. Whitney's idea became the pattern for American manufacturing that gave U.S. businesses a competitive edge over their entrenched European counterparts.

CONSIDER THIS: Learn and use the knowledge you have acquired to devise a better plan the next time around.

Rent-A-Wreck

*"Whenever you see a successful business, someone
once made a courageous decision."*

— Peter Drucker

When Dave Schwartz graduated from UCLA, he decided to go into the used car business. He had been buying and selling cars to work his way through college and enjoyed the work. After raising a little capital, he opened Bundy Used Cars in the Los Angeles area, near the Santa Monica Freeway. Times were tough, and the bills piled up faster than the sales slips. It wasn't long before Dave owed more than he was worth, almost a quarter of a million dollars. It seemed as though everyone's answer was to take it on the chin and declare bankruptcy. The thought was too much for Dave; he believed that he could turn his business around. If he could just hang on, maybe a break would occur.

A young woman bought a car from Dave, and it broke down the next day. Dave offered to refund the woman's money, but she suggested that Dave rent a car for her instead, since she needed a vehicle for just three months. Dave liked the idea, and used-car rentals soon became a sizable portion of his business. A local newspaper columnist gave Dave's car lot some publicity and coined the phrase "Rent-A-Wreck." People were impressed with Dave's honesty and the value of his vehicles. He rented cars to the rich, the famous, and anyone who wanted a bargain. One Volkswagen Beetle brought in over $30,000 in rental fees during its lifetime. Before long, Rent-A-Wreck franchises were popping up in major cities all over the United States.

CONSIDER THIS: Combining good value with a bit of mystique can produce good business and solid profits.

Collaring the Market

"Nothing in this world is so powerful as an idea whose time has come." — Victor Hugo

At the turn of the century, men's fashion clothing was more like a straitjacket than a comfort garment. Shirts in particular were an annoyance. Designers tortured men with shirts that buttoned up the back and had various kinds of stiff attachable collars. There had to be a way to devise a more comfortable dress shirt. In fact, there were potentially any number of ways to resolve the problem. However, the profits go to those who can turn a good idea into an actual solution. The collars we see men wearing in old photographs or period movies may look stylish and debonair, but in reality they caused rashes and contributed to headaches and stiff necks. Someone was bound to find a solution, and that someone turned out to be John Van Heusen. In 1919 Van Heusen developed a collar made of a semi-soft material that kept its shape without wrinkling. The detachable collar was a success, and Van Heusen, with partner John Bolton, sold the rights to the invention to the Phillips-Jones shirt company.

Van Heusen and Bolton became millionaires from the royalties generated by sales of the collar, but Van Heusen kept on inventing. Another of his inventions was the nonslip shoulder strap for women's lingerie. When one-piece shirts began to dominate the market, the name "Van Heusen" was transferred to the entire shirt. Now marketed by the Phillips-Van Heusen Corporation, the Van Heusen brand continues to be one of the most recognizable names associated with business and dress shirts.

CONSIDER THIS: Find out what's bothering people and come up with a way to make that problem go away. However, do more than just think of an answer. You must make it happen before you will be entitled to the benefits of its discovery.

Bissell Carpet Sweepers

> *"To give real service, you must add something
> which cannot be bought or measured with money,
> and that is sincerity and integrity."*
>
> — Donald A. Adams

In 1876 Melville Bissell and his wife, Anna, operated a crockery shop in Grand Rapids, Michigan. Each time they received shipments of glass or china, the contents had to be removed from the sawdust in which they were packed. The resulting mess required almost a day to clean up as the carpet sweepers of the day had little effect on the bouncy sawdust particles. Melville, who liked to tinker, put his talents to use and built a better sweeper. His customers and friends began asking where they could buy the invention, and finally Melville decided that there was a market for his device. At first, he hired residents of Grand Rapids to make parts at home, and Anna sold the sweepers to local retail stores. In 1883, the Bissells built their first factory, but it was completely destroyed by fire.

Melville and Anna had to mortgage all of their assets to build another plant. Then, it was learned that a particular Bissell model was defective. Melville recalled the entire output and destroyed the machines. However, that disaster and the Bissells' response to it solidified the company's reputation for integrity and reliability. Customers could be assured that The Bissell Company stood behind its products. Melville died in 1889, and Anna assumed overall management responsibilities, becoming one of the country's first woman corporate leaders. Under Anna's guidance, the company continued to grow, becoming one of the most recognized names in the carpet sweeper business, a distinction it still holds today.

CONSIDER THIS: A disaster can be turned into an asset if the response is right.

Maxwell House Coffee

"That coffee is good to the last drop."
— Theodore Roosevelt

Many Americans look forward to that first cup of coffee in the morning. They owe much of the satisfaction they derive from their daily ritual to the person who helped set the standard for consistently tasty coffee. Joel Creek was a salesman for a Tennessee wholesale grocer in the 1870s. One of the items he sold that never seemed to be up to par was coffee. Because of variations in coffee beans, roasting methods, and blending, the same brand of coffee would sometimes be too weak, too strong, or too bitter. Joel set out to make a better and more consistent coffee. He experimented with different types of beans and carefully monitored the blending process until he had developed his ideal coffee. George wanted a coffee that not only tasted good but would also taste the same each time it was brewed. He took his blend to Nashville's famous Maxwell House Hotel, where it proved to be so popular with customers that it soon became the specialty of the house.

The popularity of Maxwell House Coffee grew steadily, and in 1907 Creek served a cup of his blend to President Theodore Roosevelt. "That coffee is good to the last drop," was the President's reaction. The description stuck and has been used as the advertising catch phrase for Maxwell House Coffee ever since. Today, the selection of beans and the roasting and blending techniques are still an important part of the Maxwell House tradition. Rigorous taste-testing ensures that the company's coffee continues to live up to its reputation for good taste and consistency.

CONSIDER THIS: Give Americans a really good-tasting product, and they will eat—or drink—it up.

Castro Convertible

"Even a little child can do it."
— Castro Convertible advertisement

Bernard Castro arrived in New York from Italy in 1919. The fifteen-year-old could not speak English but managed to get a job with a travel agency. He took English courses at night and soon found a better job with an upholsterer. In 1931, when Bernard decided to go into the interior decorating business, he borrowed money to get started. When the Great Depression hit, Bernard owed everybody. He went to each of his creditors and promised to pay one or two dollars a week until his debts were settled. He explained that if he were closed down, the creditors would never get their money back.

Many of Castro's customers wanted heavy sofa beds re-upholstered and often asked if he could "slim them down." That always meant losing the bed. Castro began to experiment with ways to build a lighter sofa bed, but World War II was in progress and metal was scarce. Drawing his inspiration from bunks aboard ships, Castro believed that wooden slats could be used to make a sofa bed. When the war ended, he patented a lightweight metal version. An idea for marketing the new bed came one day when Castro went into his living room and found that his four-year-old daughter, Bernadette, had opened the sofa bed. In 1948 he filmed his daughter opening the bed and bought expensive commercials on television to promote the device's ease of operation. At first, the commercials seemed to have no impact, and Castro considered withdrawing the promotion. However, after the commercials had been airing for three months, orders began to pour in. That single commercial was aired more than 30,000 times.

CONSIDER THIS: Success seldom happens quickly. You often must be patient if you are to see positive results.

Liz Claiborne

*"Render a service if you would succeed. This is the
supreme law of life."* — Henry Miller

With an increasing number of women entering the work force during the 1970s, there was a growing need for better women's office apparel. Until the seventies, most women's clothing was considered either too conservative or too fashionable to be worn in an office setting. The growing gap in the women's apparel market did not escape the eye of Elisabeth Claiborne Ortenberg. She had been a designer at Youth Guild for 16 years when the company closed in February 1977. At about the same time, Elisabeth's husband began phasing out his consulting business. The couple advertised to find a production partner, Leonard Boxer, and a year later Jerry Chazen joined to complete the foursome that would found Liz Claiborne, Inc.

The Claiborne concept provided stylish, up-to-date women's apparel and added a unique service for retailers. A Claiborne representative would show individual retailers how to display, promote, and sell the Claiborne line as well as how to keep customers coming back for more. The Claiborne concept utilized sketches, photos, and printed materials to demonstrate exactly how to promote the company's products in the store. It taught the sales staff how to properly display clothing and how to explain to customers which blouse went with which skirt. The unique sales-training approach worked well, and the success of Liz Claiborne, Inc. was assured in its first year of operation.

CONSIDER THIS: If you provide your customer with a better way to make a profit and include a service that others do not provide, you will make a name for yourself.

Stew Leonard

"He has an advantage in any deal whose merchandise will stand inspection."

— Roy L. Smith

Does anyone really still believe that "the customer is always right"? Stew Leonard believes it, and that belief has served him well. At Stew's dairy store in Norwalk, Connecticut, the customer really is king. Stew goes out of his way to listen to his customers and study his competitors in order to provide a unique and fun store in which to shop. Stew invites customers to participate in evaluating the store and even holds meetings to allow people to complain or comment on store operations. He regularly loads his employees into a van to visit other stores in neighboring communities. Their task is to find out what the competitors do better and to decide how they can implement those ideas in Stew's store.

Kids will find a petting zoo at Stew Leonard's, and inside they will see "the world's fastest layer," a mechanical chicken that produces on demand. Stew encourages people to send in pictures of themselves with a Stew Leonard grocery bag, and he has over 5,000 such pictures mounted on the walls of his store. Some pictures are from as far away as the Great Wall of China. One lady requested that her most valuable belongings be buried with her in her Stew Leonard grocery bag. As a result of Stew's attention to his customers, his dairy store regularly records sales per square foot that are ten times higher than the national average.

CONSIDER THIS: People really do know when you put the customer first. It is often the little things that make the difference, and paying attention to a thousand little details will add up to one big success.

OCTOBER 12 **Bob Hope**

*"It has always seemed to me that hearty laughter
is a good way to jog internally without having to
go outdoors."* — Norman Cousins

The American Dream has not come without a price. Count-less thousands of young Americans have defended our freedom in wars on distant shores. They were often lonely, and many of those soldiers wondered if the people back home still remembered them. The USO remembered them, and so did Bob Hope. For more than half a century, the veteran comedian has entertained American troops around the world, keeping their hopes up and their dreams alive. In commemoration of his un-flagging efforts, Congress named Bob "America's Most-prized Ambassador of Good Will." Like any good businessman, Bob knows his fortune came from the people. Throughout his career, his job—much like a salesman's—has been to communicate with the audience. He makes people feel at home and makes them want to buy his "product." During his early days in radio, one show's producers didn't think Bob needed a live audience to perform. But Bob knew that it was people who made his act work, so he ushered in a sizable group from an Edgar Bergen show and never did another live broadcast without an audience.

Fans were Bob's customers, and he loved them. "When I open the refrigerator door and the little light goes on, I do ten minutes," he once quipped. At army bases and on college cam-puses, Bob Hope not only entertained, he sold America. He once told a group of university students, "America's greatest natural resource has always been her people. In times of crisis, this nation always finds the leaders to guide her through."

CONSIDER THIS: In tough times, laughter can help us put our lives back into perspective and help us hold on to our dreams.

Ya-hoo Cake

"Today's dream is tomorrow's reality. Success begins with a dream, but that is only the first step." — Unknown

Talk about an American Dream . . . Jim Read had been a good salesman, so good that his commissions were getting out of hand. As a result, he was fired by his company and at the age of forty-five was having trouble finding another job. To while away his idle time, Jim started experimenting with recipes in the kitchen and made a few cheesecakes. He thought briefly about going into the catering business but dismissed the idea. Then one night Jim had a dream that would change his life. In his dream, he saw himself assembling the precise ingredients for a special cake: cherries, chocolate chips, pecans, even the exact amount of baking soda needed. When Jim awoke the next morning, he promptly made the cake of his dreams.

A neighbor tried the concoction and yelled, "Ya-hoo, that's a terrific cake!" (That's how folks talk down in Texas.) The neighbor promised that if Jim would bake the cakes in the shape of the Lone Star State, he would buy 100. Jim thought that with that kind of first order, maybe the cake business had something to offer after all. Jim and his wife traveled to flea markets and gave away free samples of the cake, usually signing up new customers in the process. People soon began to pass along hints about baking and how to buy fresh ingredients and how to wrap the cakes to keep them fresh. During their first year in business, the Reads sold 5,400 cakes, and Ya-hoo cakes were on their way to success.

CONSIDER THIS: Your dreaming mechanism is smarter than you think. Maybe you should pay more attention to what you dream.

ROLM Corporation

*"A true friend is somebody who can make us do
what we can."* — Emerson

Eugene Richeson, Kenneth Oshman, Walter Lowen-Stern, and Robert Maxfield had several things in common. They were graduates of Rice University and graduate students at Stanford University, and they got together monthly for a poker game. In 1968 they began to dream about a computer company with a name derived from the first letters of each person's last name, ROLM. In 1969 they set up their business in a prune-drying shed in Santa Clara, California. Oshman wanted to be president, Lowen-Stern and Maxfield wanted to be in engineering, and Richeson became the marketer.

Their first product was a fail-safe computer for the military. After five years of moderate success, the entrepreneurs invested $1 million in developing a microcomputer-based PBX system. The ROLM CBX, a PBX system designed to accommodate from sixteen to 10,000 telephone extensions, became their major product. Knowing that a large corporate structure would tend to stifle the intimate atmosphere they had previously enjoyed, the principals spent considerable time and effort to ensure that their company would remain a "great place to work." They sponsored sports activities, provided wellness facilities, and offered employees incentives, career growth opportunities, and a chance to participate in business decisions. The employees responded with the innovation and productivity that helped ROLM become a large and successful corporation.

CONSIDER THIS: A few friends with a dream can make a big difference in the business world.

Merck and Co.

"Not greedy for money but eager to serve."
— The Bible

The E. Merck drug company originally came to America from Germany, where it was founded as a family business in 1668. To expand his operations, George Merck arrived in New York in 1891 and brought the already prestigious company to the United States. At first, George simply obtained drugs and chemicals from Europe, but in 1900 he built his own manufacturing facilities in Rahway, New Jersey. A second George Merck took over the firm in 1925, succeeding his father. A Harvard graduate, young George had first entered the family business in 1915. Under his leadership, the company expanded its sales from the 1924 level of $5.2 million to $94.1 million in 1950.

George often used the word "serendipity" to describe the firm's research efforts. Many times, the company's research into one chemical led to the discovery of other more valuable treasures. When pursuing a drug that could be used to treat a rare liver disease, Merck scientists found Vitamin B-12. Similarly, when working with cortisone as a treatment for the rare Addison's disease, researchers soon discovered the drug's anti-inflammatory properties. George Merck explained his philosophy of service: "We try to remember that medicine is for the patient. It is not for the profits. The profits follow, and if we have remembered that, they never fail to appear. The better we have remembered it, the larger they have been."

CONSIDER THIS: Profits are the by-products of providing a solution to human needs or desires. Spend lots of time looking for a good product before looking for profits to appear.

Reynolds Aluminum

" 'Tis the set of the sail that decides the goal, and not the storms of life."

— Ella Wheeler Wilcox

It seemed that no one could really see the potential of aluminum except R. S. Reynolds Sr. Reynolds's metal company had been producing packaging material and foils since 1919 but bought all of its aluminum from outside sources. In 1939, when Reynolds asked a French Aluminum Company official why Germany was buying so much aluminum, he was told that the lightweight metal was being used to make "door knobs, truck bodies, and other things." Reynolds suspected it was actually being used to build airplanes. With war looming on the horizon, he realized that aluminum would soon be in short supply. When Reynolds told Congress of his concerns, he was dismissed as an alarmist.

Reynolds finally convinced Sen. Lister Hill that the U.S. needed its own aluminum production capability and was able to obtain financing. Experts estimated it would take five years to produce the first ingot, but Reynolds built a plant and began producing aluminum in less than six months. A government commission initially predicted that aluminum production would be sufficient to meet America's needs for two years, but ninety days later, as its value to the war effort became apparent, aluminum became the first metal to be declared in shortage. After World War II, the government wanted to scrap several plants, but Reynolds, confident that aluminum was the metal of the future, purchased them. With aluminum foil as its keystone product, the Reynolds Metals Company soon was using aluminum metal to produce a host of commercially successful products.

CONSIDER THIS: At times, the experts don't know what they're talking about. If you know your industry better than anyone else, believe in yourself.

Digital Equipment Corporation

"The world wants leaders, thinkers, doers, men of power and action, men who can step out from the crowd and lead instead of follow." — Unknown

Ken Olsen liked electronics. As a teenager he fixed radios and built a homemade radio transmitter. He learned more about electronics during World War II and in 1947 enrolled at MIT, completing a degree in three years. Ken remained at MIT for graduate school and was involved in research with the then state-of-the-art concept of interactive computing. After working for two years on a project with IBM for Lincoln Labs, he became convinced that IBM was missing an important market, minicomputers. Working with an associate, Harlan Anderson, Ken began to look for backing to start a computer company. He began to study management and the financial records of major corporations. Ken practiced his management skills by taking on the job of superintendent of Boston's Park Street Church Sunday School.

In 1957 Ken Olsen and Harlan Anderson received $70,000 in venture capital to enter the computer field. At first, they built printed circuits in the corner of an old woolen mill. As they gained expertise in constructing circuit modules, they eventually put the modules together to create their first computer, the PDP-1, which sold for $120,000 in an era when most computers were priced above $1 million. Their computer was aimed at engineers and scientists, and as new computers were introduced, DEC became the computer of choice for most research institutions. It was not until 1976 that IBM began to introduce small computers, and by then DEC was already a thriving Fortune 500 company.

CONSIDER THIS: Look for those areas being ignored by other companies. There may be a substantial niche to be filled.

George Washington Carver

*"Let your intentions be good, embodied in good
thoughts, cheerful words, and unselfish deeds, and
the world will be to you a bright and happy place
in which you can work and play and serve."*
— Grenville Kleiser

Many selfish people have dreamed only of the betterment of their *own* lives. The real American Dream is one of improving the quality of life for everyone. Such was the desire of George Washington Carver. Born in Missouri at the end of the Civil War, George's poverty-stricken rural background gave him self-reliance and an understanding of the plight of poor farmers. His deep religious faith gave him a sense of purpose in giving of himself to benefit others. George fought a tough battle for an education and graduated from Iowa State College, where he became a member of the faculty. That feat alone would have placed him in a remarkable position for the son of slaves.

George Washington Carver earned a master's degree in 1896 and was appointed director of agricultural research at Tuskegee Institute in Alabama. Surrounded by poor farmers, he dedicated himself to making a better life for all southerners. When the boll weevil destroyed the South's primary cash crop, cotton, Carver encouraged the planting of other crops such as peanuts and sweet potatoes. He developed more than 400 products from those plants and introduced a new era of agriculture to the South. Disliking waste, Carver developed profitable uses for farmer's "trash," including dyes, soaps, and fertilizers. He never patented any of his discoveries but offered them freely to help improve the quality of life for his fellow man. To Carver, success meant helping people to succeed.

CONSIDER THIS: Real success is providing enrichment for all people.

Richard Sears

*"Our grand business is not to see what lies dimly
at the distance, but to do what is clearly at hand."*
— Thomas Carlyle

Like many young men in the late nineteenth century, Richard Sears believed that becoming a telegraph operator was the ticket to a prosperous career. It was, but not in the way he imagined. Richard was working as a station agent in North Redwood, Minnesota, in 1886 when a shipment of watches arrived. The timepieces were for a local jewelry store, but the store refused the shipment. Richard contacted the Chicago company that had sent the watches and offered to sell them himself. He telegraphed his fellow station agents up and down the line, and within weeks his inventory was sold out. Sensing the possibilities, he moved to Minneapolis and set up the R. W. Sears Watch Co. In 1887 Richard moved to Chicago and continued selling through station agents.

Everything was going fine until people began to return the watches for repair. Sears advertised for a watchmaker, and the ad was answered by Alvah C. Roebuck. In 1888 Sears opened his business to the public and published a catalog. Knowing that his primary target, the farmer, was a tough sell, Sears relied on three principles to bolster the reputation of his fledgling mail-order concern: (1) customers were given an absolute assurance of honesty, (2) all items sold were covered by a money-back guarantee, and (3) prices were kept low enough to justify ordering by mail. Even after Richard Sears retired in 1910, his original ideas have remained a key factor in the long-term success of Sears, Roebuck and Co.

CONSIDER THIS: Providing good service to the customer is not a new idea. It is a practice that has worked well in the past and will continue to work in the future.

Classic Driving School

"The force wherewith anything strikes the mind is generally in proportion to the degree of attention bestowed upon it." — James Beattie

There are many industries that seem to be dominated by billion-dollar multinational companies that spend untold sums on advertising. It is tough to compete against those behemoths, but enterprising Americans often can find a way. Such is the case of Jim Kirchmeier. After teaching driver's education for eight years, Jim was well aware that a mom-and-pop operation would have great difficulty competing with a nationally affiliated driving school. Nevertheless, he dreamed of owning his own school and began to seriously study the market. He found that while most of their customers were teenagers, the big driving schools used "family cars" as instructional vehicles. But what would a teenager really like to drive? The answer was a red Porsche 944.

Once Jim got the idea, there was a lot of work to do. His first problem was insurance. No company wanted to insure an expensive sports car for a driving school that taught teens how to drive. Jim spent days thumbing through the telephone yellow pages and talking to insurance agents without success. It could have been the killing blow to his dream, but Jim finally found one insuror that would cover the business. Since he could not afford television or radio advertising such as the big companies offered, he had to devise a highly targeted direct-mail marketing campaign. Classic Driving School made the right moves and earned a comfortable $180,000 in its first year of operation, and Jim Kirchmeier's dream was soon a lucrative reality.

CONSIDER THIS: To make a mark against entrenched competition, you must make people take notice of your product.

Mel Blanc

*"The Man who is born with a talent which
he is meant to use finds his greatest happiness in
using it."*
— Goethe

Entire generations have grown up listening to his famous voices. In fact, some of the world's most beloved cartoon characters speak with Mel Blanc's voice. Mel's virtual monopoly of Warner Bros. cartoon voices began in the 1930s, but getting to the top was tough. Growing up in a musical family, young Mel aspired to a career in the theater. But his first break came in radio, where he did "funny stuff," including the creation of various novelty voices. At that time the Warner studios were using spare actors to provide voices for cartoon characters, and Mel thought the performers' work was "god-awful." Every two weeks, he applied for the job but was turned down. Finally, the man who kept refusing to hire Mel died, and a new man was put in charge.

Treg Brown put Mel to work, and the chemistry started cooking. In 1938 "wascally wabbit" Bugs Bunny was introduced, followed by Daffy Duck, Elmer Fudd, Yosemite Sam, and numerous others. Mel had a versatile voice, but he still had to work at it. When a new character was being conceived, Mel would experiment with several voices, seeking to match the character's sound with its physical makeup. He paid close attention to diction in order to make the voice understandable. Warner Bros. stopped making cartoons in-house in 1963 and ceased all cartoon production in 1968. In the late 1970s many of Warner's most popular cartoon characters were revived. In his later years, Mel Blanc earned as much for speaking a single sentence as he did for making an entire cartoon years ago.

CONSIDER THIS: Don't use just anyone to do the job at hand. If you find someone really interested in doing it well, you may be creating a classic.

Brooks Brothers

*"Take great care to be dressed like the reasonable
people of our own age, in the place where you
are; whose dress is never spoken of one way or
the other."* — Lord Chesterfield

Perhaps the American business institution that speaks most
highly of quality and consistency is Brooks Brothers Clothiers.
The company's customers have included every American president from Abraham Lincoln to Bill Clinton, as well as military
leaders, business executives, Hollywood stars, and countless
persons around the globe who want the best in clothes. Many
customers have been served by their particular Brooks Brothers
salesman for decades. They are known by their first name and
can rest assured that whatever their salesman recommends will
be in the best of taste. One salesman, Frederick Webb, served
five generations of the wealthy Morgan family.

Henry Brooks had fine taste in clothes. He often traveled to
London and was frequently asked by friends to select clothes
for them while he was overseas. Sensing the need for a clothing shop, he opened H. & D. H. Brooks & Co. in 1818 on the
corner of Catherine and Cherry Streets in the center of New
York's mercantile district. Unique to the era, Brooks offered
both ready-made and tailored clothing in the same store. On
the morning he opened the business, his first bookkeeping
entry set the tone for the Brooks Brothers philosophy; it was a
$25 loan to a friend. The company has been making friends of
customers ever since. Its strong commitment to selling the very
best clothes and providing the very best service has set Brooks
Brothers apart from its competition for more than 180 years.

CONSIDER THIS: Commitment to the customer has been
and will continue to be the secret to any business's prosperity
and longevity.

DoveBar

*"The test of an enjoyment is the remembrance
which it leaves behind."* — Richter

When Leo Stefanos stepped onto the ground in New York after arriving from Greece, he must have wondered if he would ever be successful in his new country. Decades later, his son Mike stood in the same place and introduced Leo's answer to America's constant craving for chocolate and ice cream, the DoveBar. Over one million of the frozen treats were sold by street vendors that first year, which would have made Leo proud. The idea for the confection arose one day when Leo saw his young son racing recklessly down the street in pursuit of an ice cream truck. Leo knew that was dangerous and decided to make his own ice cream bar in hopes of keeping Mike closer to home. Since he owned a candy shop that also sold premium ice cream, Leo went into the store's back room and cut a few blocks of his best ice cream, which he then dipped into rich chocolate.

Leo intended the treat just for his family, but the bars eventually became a popular item at the Dove Candy shop. Mike grew up, earned a CPA degree, and then joined his father in the candy shop in 1977. After Leo died, Mike began to think of ways to expand the family business and introduced DoveBars to specialty stores and country clubs in the Chicago area. In 1984 he presented the DoveBar at the Fancy Food Show in Washington, D.C., and began to receive orders from around the country. Similar products have been sold for years, but Mike has continued to make DoveBars with the same care and high-quality ingredients that Leo used, even though that has resulted in the bars selling for two dollars or more each, nearly four times the price of most competing products.

CONSIDER THIS: Many people care about quality and will pay a premium price rather than accept a so-called bargain.

James Reid

> *"Let everyone engage in the business with which he*
> *is best acquainted."* — Propertius

All too often we are bombarded by stories in the media about high-tech heroes who are making the latest gizmos that astound us all. Such stories make good copy, but high-tech is not the only way to make money. In fact, many of America's most successful companies make mundane products. In 1960 fledgling attorney James Reid joined his father's company, Standard Products Co., to negotiate labor contracts. He proved good at it and soon became manager of a plant that was experiencing labor problems. In 1962 Standard was going into debt, but James's father was too absorbed in company politics to run the business effectively. The board called on James.

James Reid decided that Standard was trying to do too many things. He made a critical decision: "I decided that we were going to make only laminated extrusion products." If it wasn't made by sandwiching metal, rubber, and vinyl, the company would not make it. That decision eventually made Standard a national leader in laminated extrusions, and with automakers as its biggest customer, Standard even licensed its process to the Japanese. When the slumping automotive market of the early 1980s reduced the need for the company's door seals and automobile trim, Standard used the slack time to further improve its production techniques. By the late 1990s, the company had become one of the world's leading suppliers of sealing, trim, and vibration-control products, with production facilities in five countries.

CONSIDER THIS: Glamor is not the key to corporate success. If you are the best producer of any widget, you can become successful in your market.

S. O. S. Pads

"There are so many wonderful things in your everyday experience, lucrative opportunities, glorious occasions, that do not exist for you because you do not have the vision for discerning them." — Edward Kramer

Sometimes the things that can catapult us to success are the things that begin as sidelines. We devise a solution to a problem we have and then discover that many other people could use the same solution to solve their problems. That is what Edwin W. Cox experienced in 1917. As a salesman of aluminum cookware, he was mediocre. He just couldn't get housewives to listen to his presentation. That's when Edwin thought of using a gimmick. He decided to offer each potential client a free gift as a reward for letting him do his sales pitch. The gift had to be useful for the housewife and had to solve some cooking-related problem.

What Edwin Cox conceived was an abrasive pad containing soap that could be used to clean pots and pans. In his kitchen, he took small steel wool pads and repeatedly dipped them into a soapy solution. He let them dry and dipped them again, and continued the process until the pads were full of dried soap. When he began offering the pads as gifts, his cookware sales increased. Cox also found that housewives began calling him to obtain more of the pads. Soon, demand for the cleaning pads surpassed Cox's ability to make them in his kitchen. Eventually, he had to stop selling cookware to take care of the growing demand for his new product. Cox's wife called the pads S. O .S. for "Save Our Saucepans," and the name stuck.

CONSIDER THIS: Keep an eye on those sidelines that may point to something that has great potential.

The Statue of Liberty

"Give me your tired, your poor, your huddled masses yearning to breathe free."
— Emma Lazarus

Many Americans didn't want the Statue of Liberty. The giant copper figure, originally known as *Liberty Enlightening the World*, was a gift from the people of France and came with the stipulation that Americans must provide the foundation on which the statue would stand. Donations were first solicited in 1877 but came in slowly. The rich said the statue would ruin the view of New York harbor, and most ordinary citizens could see no reason why they should contribute to a monument that would stand in New York. Finally, Joseph Pulitzer, publisher of the *New York World*, took up the cause. His publications praised the symbolic importance of the statue and encouraged contributions.

Today, the Statue of Liberty is a symbol of freedom that is recognized around the world. During Chinese freedom rallies in the 1990s, students made a version of the statue and paraded it through Beijing. That was a fitting role for Lady Liberty, since she was conceived during a time of political turmoil. In Paris, Edouard Rebe Lefebvre first discussed the idea for the monument in 1865 as a way to keep alive the ideals of French liberty. Lefebvre discussed the concept with sculptor Auguste Bartholdi, who created a 1.25-meter likeness of the statue. For the full-size version, which was constructed in Paris in 1884, Gustave Eiffel created an inner support structure onto which Liberty's copper skin was affixed. By 1885, sufficient money had been raised to complete the foundation, and the Statue of Liberty was dedicated on October 26, 1886.

CONSIDER THIS: Other countries look to America for freedom and hope. Be thankful for the liberty that allows us to choose the dreams we follow.

Lane Bryant

*"Put your knowledge to practical experience and
reap the harvest."*   — Milne

Lena Himmelstein left Lithuania in 1885 at the invitation of distant relatives in America. When she learned a marriage was being arranged, she refused and joined her sister Anna, who worked as a seamstress for $1 per week in a New York lingerie sweatshop. Lena was adept at operating a sewing machine and eventually was earning $15 per week. Several years later, Lena quit her job to marry David Bryant. Shortly after their first son was born, David died, and the young widow moved in with her sister and began sewing at home for a few customers. Despite tough financial times, Lena's business slowly grew. One day a customer asked Lena to design a maternity dress, an article of clothing that was not available at the time. The result was the popular No. 5 Maternity Gown, named for its place on a price list.

When Anna married, her husband loaned Lena $300 to help her open a bank account. When the nervous Lena went to the grand Oriental Bank to open her account, she filled out the deposit slip as "Lane Bryant." The name stuck. In 1909 Lena married Albert Malsin, an engineer. By 1910 Albert saw more potential in his wife's business than he did in his career, and he became her finance manager. Lane Bryant's business grew, and Lena opened a store in New York that pioneered the acceptance of maternity wear. Albert began to recognize that customers, no matter how loyal they might be, needed maternity clothes only for relatively short periods in their lives. After researching other women's apparel needs, Lane Bryant began designing attractive clothes for full-figured women.

CONSIDER THIS: Most men and women do not look like the models in magazine advertisements. Who is going make everybody else look good?

The Teddy Bear

"Only that day dawns to which we are awake."
— Thoreau

Teddy Roosevelt was a popular president, and his exploits were well covered in the nation's newspapers. One of his adventures took place in 1902 when he went to the South to help resolve a border dispute between Louisiana and Mississippi. While he was in the area, he decided to go hunting. The friendly southerners wanted the president to take home a nice trophy, so they trapped a bear cub with the intention of releasing it at just the right moment to allow Roosevelt a clear shot at the animal. At the hunt, the president found out about the plan and refused to shoot the bear. The incident made a great newspaper story and also inspired a memorable cartoon. *The Washington Star* carried a cartoon by Clifford Berryman that showed Teddy Roosevelt, gun in hand, standing with his back turned to the bear cub.

Russian immigrant Morris Michtom was the owner of a small candy shop in Brooklyn when he first noticed the poignant cartoon in the paper. Thinking that he could use the incident to attract the attention of potential customers, Michtom placed a small stuffed bear in the window of his store with a sign saying "Teddy's Bear." The bear did attract attention, but Michtom had not expected that people would actually want to buy it. Michtom asked Roosevelt's permission to call his bear "Teddy's Bear," to which the president responded that he "couldn't see what use my name would be in the stuffed animal trade." As demand for the Teddy bear grew, Michtom turned his attention to the toy market and founded the Ideal Toy Company, which has now sold millions of the stuffed critters.

CONSIDER THIS: You never know what idea may turn into the next national sensation.

The Need for Direction

"I hold it more important to have the players'
confidence than their affection."

— Vince Lombardi

What teacher do you remember most from school? The majority of people say it is a teacher they considered hard, demanding, and challenging. While in school, they may have "hated" that teacher, but looking back, they often see how he or she taught them more than any other instructor—usually by forcing them to push themselves beyond their expectations. Many adults look back on their childhood and wish they had listened more to their elders. Most people need challenges and direction. They need leaders to show by example how to do things correctly or how to succeed during difficult times. By trying to be too popular or by striving to be liked, many managers (and parents) are too namby-pamby when it comes to leading. Leaders must give direction or they are not leading. They must demand results or they will get excuses. They must expect the best out of people or they will get mediocrity.

William James said, "Need and struggle are what excite and inspire us." New recruits at Mother Theresa's Sisters of Charity in Calcutta were routinely sent the next day to serve in the Home for the Dying. Mother Theresa never made it easy to join the religious order. That type of "tough love" often means that a leader who cares about people must take a stand. If you are that leader, you must set the example for excellence. A leader must be willing to forgo popularity in order to demand the best from someone else.

CONSIDER THIS: People who care about other people will call on them to reach a higher plane of knowledge, service, or performance.

The Brown Paper Bag

"The human race is divided into two classes, those who go ahead and do something, and those who sit and inquire, Why wasn't it done the other way?"
— Oliver Wendell Holmes

We tend to take simple things for granted. When we think "invention," what often comes to mind are complicated things like the telephone or automobile. In fact, we are literally surrounded by mundane inventions. Millions of people "brown bag it" each day, taking their lunch to school or work in a small brown bag. A larger version of the bag is a necessity in the grocery business, and the sacks are commonly used for trash bags, Halloween masks, and for storage. We take them for granted now, but prior to 1883, the square-bottom paper bag did not exist. For that invention, we owe a debt of thanks to Charles Stillwell, who was born in Ohio in 1845. After service in the Union Army, Stillwell began to invent things. Most of what he devised was forgotten, but in 1883 he came up with a new type of paper bag.

Unlike the V-shaped bags that had been produced by hand for years, Stillwell's bag had a square bottom and pleated sides, and could be opened with a flick of the wrist. The square bottom allowed the bag to stand on its own, allowing the user to fill it easily without having to hold it open at the same time. The design was not the only important part of Stillwell's invention. His bag was produced by machine, whereas other bags of the period were all hand-pasted. The "self-opening sack" became immediately popular, but its real leap to success did not come until the 1930s, when the American supermarket was born. Today, millions of brown paper bags are sold every year.

CONSIDER THIS: Simple things that solve simple problems are important advancements in our lives.

Carrier Air Conditioning

"Are you in earnest? Seize this very minute. What you can do or think you can, begin it."

— Goethe

Early in the twentieth century, mechanical cooling devices began to come into use; however, they used an ammonia refrigerant that was highly volatile. Many cities would not allow the operation of devices using ammonia coolant. That was the reason that Dr. Willis Carrier was looking forward to a presentation he had scheduled for May 22, 1922. He was excited about a new cooling device he had developed that was smaller, more efficient, and used a safer coolant called dilene. Carrier wasn't so sure that his 500 invited guests would be excited enough to come, so he offered a free dinner and a six-round boxing match.

After the meal, a large curtain was pulled aside to reveal a refrigeration machine like nothing anyone had previously seen. Some of the guests placed orders for the invention on the spot, but there were problems. The New York City building safety chief would not approve the device, calling its coolant untested and unlisted. Carrier decided to take the matter into his own hands. He went to the chief's office, poured some dilene into an open container, then struck a match and threw it into the can. The chief almost leaped out of the window until it became evident that the substance was simply burning gently. There was no explosion. The safety chief lifted his ban, and the Carrier air-conditioning system was on its way to changing the way Americans lived and worked.

CONSIDER THIS: Some people won't believe published facts. You must show them by example—and sometimes in dramatic fashion—that what is purported to be true is actually true.

Andrew Carnegie

*"The way to gain a good reputation is to endeavor
to be what you desire to appear."*   — Socrates

Everyone has heard the phrase "It's not what you know but who you know." Although that may not be the whole truth, there is much to be said for having a network of friends to help you get the breaks. In fact, there are a number of groups such as university alumni associations, Chambers of Commerce, and clubs whose purpose includes giving members an opportunity to network with others. There is no doubt that, on his way to becoming one of the richest men in the world, Andrew Carnegie got a few breaks through networking. He was also a hard worker. After coming from Dunfermline, Scotland, in 1848 at age thirteen, Andy took a dirty and dangerous job at a bobbin factory that was owned by a fellow Scot from Dunfermline. Andy's hard work earned him a better position in the accounting department. He was soon hired by another Scot to work in a telegraph office. In that job, young Andy met all of the important business people in Pittsburgh and came to know all about who sold what merchandise for how much and on what terms. He was soon promoted to a full-time position as a telegraph operator.

Andrew Carnegie's biggest break came when he was offered a job as a personal telegraph operator for the Pennsylvania Railroad, the most prestigious corporation of its day. In that position he learned the best management techniques and also was taken into the confidence of men who gave sound advice about investing in the nation's best companies. Carnegie learned from his mentors and in 1865, in a letter to a friend back home in Scotland, was able to proclaim "I'm rich! I'm rich!"

CONSIDER THIS: Three things can help you move forward in your career: Hard work, a good reputation, and a network of friends.

The Frisbee

"Advertising is the mouthpiece of business."
— James R. Adams

It may not be necessary to come up with a brand-new idea to make it big. There are plenty of examples of businesspeople who have "discovered" something that may have been around for years. The trick is to recognize that an idea has potential and then to find a way to bring the potential to market. When Rich Knerr and Spud Melin started Wham-O Manufacturing Co., their main product was a slingshot (hence the name Wham-O) that they sold primarily through mail order. One day at the beach, the partners ran into Fred Morrison, who was selling discs that would fly through the air when thrown. Wham-O bought the rights to the disc but it didn't sell very well. Over the next several years, the company promoted the hula hoop and several other sports toys. After four years of little success with the "Pluto Platter," the principals decided to take another look at the flying disc.

Remembering a lesson from the easily copied hula hoop, they had the disc re-engineered so that it would be easy to fly but hard to duplicate. In 1959 they renamed it the "Frisbee." The name originated from a tin pie plate imprinted with the name of the Frisbie Pie Company and used by Yale students as a flying disc as early as 1920. To target advertising for the device, Wham-O recruited youngsters to play with the toy on college campuses and playgrounds. That promotion worked, and the Frisbee soon caught on, becoming a staple on college campuses and at beach parties and picnics, and spawning such popular sports as Frisbee golf.

CONSIDER THIS: Your idea may be good, but you may have to learn the right way to promote it. It is surprising how much a name can do for success.

Walgreens

"A good appearance is at a premium everywhere."
— Jean La Fontaine

Charles Walgreen worked in a Dixon, Illinois, shoe factory until he lost part of a finger in an accident. The doctor who treated Charles took a liking to him and persuaded him to become a druggist's apprentice. In 1893 Charles went to Chicago, where he worked in a drug store during the day and studied pharmacy at night. After fulfilling the requirements to become a registered pharmacist, Charles enlisted to fight in the Spanish-American War, during which time he contracted malaria. Although the disease left Charles in poor health for many years, he continued to work as a druggist and in 1902 was able to buy an interest in the pharmacy from a retiring owner for $2,000. The other owner retired in 1909, and Charles acquired the remaining interest in the store, which he renamed the C. R. Walgreen Company.

Walgreen trained managers and slowly added more stores. By 1927 the Walgreen Company had 110 stores, and when Charles died in 1939, there were 493 stores. Known as the "father of the modern drug store," Walgreen generated much of his success from innovations he made in the areas of the lunch counter, the soda fountain, and the open display of merchandise. His stores were well lighted and clean, and Walgreen paid keen attention to small details. He made products that were of better quality but less expensive than those offered by his competition. In 1934 Walgreen introduced display counters that enabled customers to pick out merchandise for themselves. Today, such things seem simple and obvious, but it took Charles Walgreen to introduce them to the world.

CONSIDER THIS: Walgreen's concept of bringing products to the customer in a clean, attractive, and cost-effective way is an idea that still has merit today.

How Lucky We Are!

"Three grand essentials to happiness in this life are something to do, something to love and something to hope for." — Joseph Addison

Growing up in America, we often have a tendency to discount the notion that ours is the "greatest country in the world," because we have nothing to compare it to. We may see the plight of those in other countries, but somehow it doesn't sink in that America really is different. If we listen to immigrants who have discovered the American Dream, we may gain a new appreciation for what we frequently take for granted. When veteran baseball manager Tommy Lasorda feels depressed about something, he just remembers his dad. "I'm the luckiest man in the world," his dad would say. But when Tommy was a child, he didn't see things that way at all. Tommy asked his dad how he could be happy driving a truck for a stone quarry. How could he be happy about getting so cold that he had to massage his feet to get any comfort? How could he be happy when his wife had arthritis? How could he be happy about trying to feed five kids and pay all the doctor bills with hardly any money? How could be happy?

His dad told Tommy about coming from the old country. He told the boy how lucky he felt to have a job, to have a wife, and to have five wonderful kids. He was lucky to live in a house, to have a car to drive, to live in a great country. "I'm the luckiest man in the world." Later in life, whenever Tommy Lasorda found himself complaining, or when things just didn't seem to be working out, he remembered his dad's words and his attitude improved dramatically. Happiness is all a matter of perspective.

CONSIDER THIS: Why dwell on the things that are wrong in your life, when there are so many things that are right? Count your blessings; they will probably far outnumber any complaints you have.

Following Your Dream

*"Put your life's plan into determined action and go
after what you want with all that's in you."*
— Henry J. Kaiser

What good is the American Dream if you never follow it?
Many people dream and dream, but they never act. For dreams
to become reality there must be a conscious plan of action. In
a 1986 *Reader's Digest* article, Barbara Bartocci listed six points
to consider while searching to find your dream. It seems that
many people have a dream but are content to accept whatever
comes along. Bartocci says that we must take our dreams seriously. Age and lack of education or experience can all be overcome. Never believe that you are too old to accomplish
something. Col. Harland Sanders began selling his chicken
recipe at age sixty-five, and his "new" career lasted twenty-five
years. Take on your dream in stages. Make plans to move
closer to its reality, one step at a time, breaking each step into
small, attainable goals.

Some people try do a little bit of everything in the hope that
something will hit pay dirt. Such a lack of focus can hold up
your progress. You must pick and choose; you cannot have
everything or do everything at once. Do only those things that
are really important. Drop all non-productive chores. Be willing
not only to change your circumstances, but also to change your
thinking and personality. Develop yourself into the individual
who can actually be a success in your dream. Finally, refuse to
accept "no" for an answer, even from yourself. Yes, you can
change. Yes, you can follow your dream.

CONSIDER THIS: You must dream your own dream and then
follow it. No one else can do it for you. If you do not make your
own life decisions, you will never experience the best that life
can offer.

Reg Brack

"I can only say that I have acted upon my best convictions, without selfishness or malice, and by the help of God I shall continue to do so."

— Lincoln

Reg Brack learned the basics of business from his father. Only an average student in high school, Reg's grades improved when he entered business school. He first considered marketing as a career, but an early job with Curtis Publishing turned him on to the world of magazines and publishing. In 1962 Reg moved to Time, Inc. and began working his way to the top. In more than thirty-five years with that company, he has held nearly twenty different positions and has learned a lot about what it takes to make a product a success.

Reg Brack has been described as one of those unique individuals who can be both a leader and a manager. As a manager, he can cut costs to the bone. His credo is "Can my kids eat it?" If something doesn't produce a meaningful profit, don't bother doing it. On the other hand, Brack is not afraid to innovate and take risks. To bolster Time's travel department, he suggested chartering a jetliner and mingling advertisers with correspondents in a one-day blitz of the Paris Air Show. Everyone thought it was a bad idea, but Brack went through with the plan anyway, and it proved to be a great success. Once appointed Time, Inc.'s chief executive officer, a position he held until 1995, Brack used his talents, determination, and discipline to turn many formerly marginal Time departments into profit centers. He claims that his secret is to keep only those people who are the best and to give them the power and responsibility to get things done.

CONSIDER THIS: There are many options in life from which to choose. You have to decide which is the best one to help you reach your goals.

Pianos to Computers

"Aim above morality. Be not simply good, be good for something." — Thoreau

Tom Watson was born in 1874, the son of a lumber dealer. After a stint at a school of commerce, he worked as a bookkeeper and as a salesman of organs, pianos, and sewing machines. For a while, Tom also worked in an ill-fated job selling stocks. He later found out the company's dealings were less than completely honest, and the episode resulted in a close brush with the law. After that experience, Tom applied for a job with National Cash Register. The company turned him down, but Tom kept showing up and was finally hired as a salesman. As a new employee, Watson often went weeks without making a sale. But he was determined and soon rose to the top of the sales force.

In 1913 Tom Watson was fired from NCR and became the head of the Computing-Tabulating-Recording Company, which eventually was renamed International Business Machines. The company was in poor financial shape, and Watson invested money in new products and in training for the sales force. He was very picky about who IBM hired, and paid his employees more than the going rate and rarely fired anyone. During World War II, Watson sent parcels to employees serving in the armed forces to let them know that they were still part of the IBM team. He educated everyone, even customers, and encouraged them with slogans such as "Think" and "Aim High." Under the Watson's watchful eyes, IBM grew to become one of the most profitable and respected companies in the world.

CONSIDER THIS: To be the best, you must recruit the best, pay the best, and expect the best. To encourage loyalty in your employees, first show your loyalty to them.

Herman Miller's Model

*"A principle is never useful or living or vital until
it is embodied in action."* — Manley Hall

Office furniture manufacturer Herman Miller, Inc. is a very successful corporation. It is also known as one of the best companies to work for and attracts some the best designers and managers in the industry. Why is it successful? Probably because of it offers a superior working climate. Miller has defined a series of statements that outline the values by which the corporation strives to operate. These values are not only written, they are ingrained into the fabric of the corporate culture.

Miller's first value of business is Innovation. The company's stated goal includes the desire to create innovative business solutions for its customers. Next, Miller strives to provide Quality and Excellence in every task it undertakes. The principle of Participation means that the firm's employees work together in teams, with each person contributing to the level of his or her capability. Each team is held accountable for its own performance and for the integrity of the relationships within the team. Miller employees also have a stake in the company's Ownership, with each person sharing in the risks as well as the rewards that ownership brings. Finally, Miller's managers believe that the overall corporate vision is achieved by practicing Leadership, by being dedicated examples, and by enabling others to reach their own level of excellence. Such lofty ideals may be written down and made "official," but they will have no meaning until they are supported at the highest levels of company management.

CONSIDER THIS: What are the principles by which you operate? Are they adhered to, or do they change from circumstance to circumstance? Who holds your organization accountable to those principles?

Van Camp's Baked Beans

"Ideas are the beginning points of all fortunes."
— Napoleon Hill

The recipe for success may be right in front of you. In fact, it may be staring you in the face. Sometimes people move too fast to see the obvious. They are too busy to put two and two together, and often can't see the forest for the trees. In 1890 young Frank Van Camp was taking a little time out, eating lunch at the family cannery in Indianapolis. He may have been daydreaming or relaxing, but his frame of mind allowed him to be susceptible to a new idea. There were cans of pork and beans stacked up all around him, so when he pulled a tomato out of his lunch pail, he sat it down on a can of the beans. At that time, tomatoes were not used in many canned products. Frank stared intently at the tomato and the beans and imagined them being together. What a novel idea! Why not cook beans and tomatoes together? Frank wondered if the idea had any merit. He could have stopped wondering, but he followed through on the thought.

Frank and his father, Gilbert, tested the idea and discovered that beans baked with tomatoes made a nice combination. They began canning the "baked beans" and promoted the product in national magazines. The idea was so good that almost every canner began making beans in tomato sauce. Frank eventually became the president of the Van Camp company, which became the largest producer of pork and beans in the United States.

CONSIDER THIS: Daydreaming can turn into ideas and ideas can turn into reality, if you follow through. Step back and see what new ideas you can imagine.

Joseph Welch Goes Fishing

"I will study and get ready, and perhaps my chance will come." — Lincoln

Few people will catch many fish by waiting until one swims by and then dropping their bait into the water. Successful fishermen are prepared; they have their bait in the water, ready for the fish to arrive. Often, they have to be patient and wait for the right moment. Finding a good business may take the same kind of patience and planning. It also requires the ability to snap into action when the "fish" bites. Joseph Welch was fishing for a company. His preparation was to approach a local banker and describe his wants, thereby laying the groundwork for a deal. When Joseph's "fish" was ready to bite, there would be little time to go out and get more bait. On December 17, 1979, the banker called Joseph and told him that Culbro Corporation was ready to sell the Bachman Company, but the deal had to be completed within five days.

Culbro had bought the profitable Bachman snack company five years earlier, but the unit was now swimming in red ink and Culbro was willing to sell it at a liquidation price. Since Welch had already laid the groundwork with the banker, he was prepared to move quickly. With the banker's help, Welch managed to put together a deal and purchase the company. Capitalizing on the snack company's 100-year-old reputation and name, Welch was able to turn Bachman around and expand it into a very profitable enterprise. Joseph Welch's fishing expedition netted a catch that he can tell tall and true stories about.

CONSIDER THIS: If you want to enter a new enterprise, what preparations have you made? If opportunity knocks, are you ready to go?

Doctor Mary

"Expect problems and meet them as a friend."
— Milne

Mary Groda had never been a very good student. At first, no one was aware that the primary cause of her learning problems was dyslexia. To hide behind a handicap she did not understand, Mary became a problem student. Making the situation worse, Mary's family became impoverished, and she spent her teenage years picking berries and living in a house made of cast-off materials. When her family moved to Portland, Oregon, Mary took up with street kids and became involved with alcohol and theft. A counselor recognized that Mary had dyslexia and discovered that she was actually quite intelligent. Mary entered the Upward Bound program and earned a high school equivalency diploma. At age seventeen, Mary decided she wanted to become a doctor.

Complicating matters, however, Mary became pregnant twice during the next few years and had no husband to help support her. The second delivery almost killed her, leaving her unable to walk or speak. Recovery was slow, but with the help of her parents, Mary made a comeback. She got a job and began attending college while taking care of her two children. In 1974 she married David Lewis. After being rejected by fifteen medical schools, Mary wrote personal letters to each, explaining more fully her circumstances. Albany Medical College gave her a chance. At first, the courses were too difficult and Mary had to enroll in remedial courses, but she eventually was able to complete her medical degree. "Dr. Mary" ultimately became one of the school's most trusted and capable physicians.

CONSIDER THIS: Tough times can be overcome if you are willing to set your mind on the goal and persevere when the going is rough.

The Business "Family" at Publix

> *"The greatest need in the world today is for people of sweet disposition, good character, and harmonious nature."*
> — Pearl Buck

Publix Supermarkets are found only in the Southeastern United States, yet they comprise one of the largest supermarket chains in the country. George Washington Jenkins had grown up in a Georgia retail family and was seeking his fortune in booming Florida when he founded the company in 1930 with a single small store in Winter Haven. From the very beginning, one of the things that set Publix apart from the competition was the pride employees took in keeping the store immaculate and inviting to customers. Jenkins taught his principles by example and sought to make every detail of his store appealing. As Jenkins began opening new locations and refurbishing acquired stores, a tradition began.

The weekend before opening day was key in getting a Publix store ready. Everything had to be perfect. Without notice, 100 to 150 employees would appear at the store and work without pay to help the crew get ready. After work, the employees would stage a cookout. On opening day, the employees would return to hand out brochures about Publix and help customers find their way around. Even the company's top executives would take a turn bagging groceries. If a store suffered a fire, workers from other Publix supermarkets would turn out in force to help repair the damage. Usually, the stricken store could re-open within a week. Publix, with a tradition of exceptional service, has instilled a sense of familial pride in its employees. The result is a profitable chain of stores that makes shopping a pleasure.

CONSIDER THIS: Everyone likes to be a member of a "family" whose standards are high, whose reputation is respected, and whose accomplishments generate pride.

I Dare You!

> *"Catch a passion for helping others and a richer*
> *life will come back to you!"*
>
> — William H. Danforth

William H. Danforth was the founder of Ralston Purina Company, but the people who knew him best remember his little book *I Dare You*. William was a sickly child growing up the swamp country of Missouri when a schoolteacher "dared" him to become the healthiest boy in the class. The dare embarrassed young William, but it also made him angry enough to do something about his life. From that moment on, he based his life on the proposition that to live is to dare. William spent most of his life on a quest to help young people develop the qualities of leadership and responsibility. His book is based on four actions: "Think Tall," "Stand Tall," "Smile Tall," and "Live Tall."

I Dare You begins with a series of stories about people who were dared to "sell more today than you have ever sold in your life" and "quit your job, and go back and get the education you have always wanted." Danforth talks about becoming a "crusader," finding a quest and working with vigor to see it achieved. Much as Ben Franklin did in his autobiography, Danforth encourages readers to make a list of items to improve themselves. For instance, good posture will make a person look and feel like a winner. Be a dreamer, but turn those dreams into reality by ordering yourself into action. Develop a magnetic personality with a warm handshake, a smile, and a genuine desire to help other people become winners also. Finally, Danforth dares readers to build character and demand the best from themselves at all times.

CONSIDER THIS: Everything can stand improvement, including ourselves. What are you doing to improve yourself right now?

Erie Insurance Exchange

"Fortitude and the power of fixing attention are the two marks of a great mind." — Francis Bacon

Businesses, especially in their formative stage, must often survive crisis after crisis. Usually, it is the founders' creativity, hard work, and determination that will bring a company successfully through that early stage. The difficulties experienced by Erie Insurance during its initial days are examples of the kinds of problems that must be overcome. It all started when two agents who were disgruntled with their boss at Philadelphia Reciprocal decided to form their own insurance agency in Erie, Pennsylvania. They needed a $25,000 guarantee fund to obtain licensure and were able to raise the sum primarily by selling $100 shares in the company. Just as things were looking very promising, their former insurance company began promoting a piece of legislation that would raise the ante to $100,000.

Upon hearing of the proposal, the newly formed board voted eleven to four to stop organizing the company at once. The four directors who voted to continue with the company got together and created a special fund that would pay all of the licensing expenses in case the company had to fold if the new law were enacted. With that offer, the rest of the board reversed its vote. While trying to delay the law by lobbying, the two salesmen-founders scurried to obtain the minimum number of applications necessary to qualify for licensure. In two days, they gathered 150 applications, fifty more than needed. The license was approved on April 1, 1925, just days before the new law went into effect. Today, Erie is one of the top property and liability insurance companies in the U.S.

CONSIDER THIS: When a crisis occurs, a cool head (or several cool heads), creativity, and guts can often lead to a solution.

John Deere

*"If we don't improve our product, somebody else
will and we will lose our trade."* — John Deere

John Deere was born in 1804 and apprenticed as a blacksmith
in Vermont. During the 1830s, the state's economy was poor,
and like many Americans, John headed west to seek his fortune.
Settling in Illinois, he found that his skills were in great demand. The dense midwestern soil often clung to plows that
were designed for eastern dirt, requiring that farmers stop every
few feet to clean their plow blades. John studied the problem
and came up with had an idea to produce a self-polished plow.
Using a broken steel saw, he fashioned a plow blade that would
turn a clean furrow.

John Deere knew his invention was a good one and began
producing the plows before he received orders. When he had
sufficient stock on hand, he went into the countryside and sold
the implements from farm to farm. At first, he had to make the
plows from whatever steel he could find. Then, in an ambitious
move, he ordered steel from England and paid the high cost of
having it shipped up the Mississippi and over forty miles of
land. His business continued to grow, and Deere moved his operation to Moline, Illinois, where he opened a factory and convinced an American steel manufacturer to provide rolled steel.
Deere prided himself on experimentation and innovation, and
constantly tried to improve his designs. He knew that competitors would be breathing down his neck. Deere frequently
stated, "I will never put my name on a plow that does not have
in it the best that is in me."

CONSIDER THIS: A good idea and a persistent obsession for
quality are two of the most important factors in the creation of
a successful product or service.

Everyday Millionaires

"It is not what comes into a man's hands that enriches him but what he saves from slipping through them."
— H. F. Kletzing

There are many myths concerning what it takes to be a millionaire, and many people have a misguided conception of what the "average" millionaire is like. A study by Professor Thomas Stanley of Georgia State University dispels some of those images. Although many millionaires inherit wealth, the study found that most were born into middle-class or working-class families. Millionaires do not have to be wheeler-dealers, movie stars, or high-powered corporate executives. The average American millionaire owns a rather mundane business such as a fast food restaurant or an auto parts store, and may have made his or her money in sales or marketing. The average millionaire usually drives a slightly out-of-date American car, leads a stable family life, is often married to his or her high school sweetheart, and avoids status symbols.

A millionaire does not necessarily have a million dollars in the bank. In 1996, according to Stanley, the median annual income for an American millionaire was about $131,000. Potential millionaires save their money, and that is often the key to their financial stability. But even those millionaires with considerable savings often find themselves strapped for cash, since much of their worth is frequently tied up in their business or in real estate. As unglamorous as it may seem, today's millionaires tend to be the people who live next door. They work hard, save their money, and invest wisely.

CONSIDER THIS: Glamour is what we often associate with success. Many people who have achieved success have done so through hard work and the wise use of their time and talents.

Charles Lindbergh

*"It is the surmounting of difficulties that
makes heroes."* — Lajos Kossuth

Few names are so associated with American heroics as Charles A. Lindbergh. His 3,600-mile solo flight across the Atlantic caught the imagination of people on two continents, and his accomplishment has been the model for many young American dreamers. In 1919 Raymond Orteig had offered a $25,000 prize to the first person to make such a flight. No attempt was made for eight years, but by 1927, a number of pilots wanted to accept the challenge. Lindbergh was one such pilot, and he worked with a group of St. Louis businessmen to raise $15,000 to build a plane with specially designed fuel tanks and engine.

The plane was ready on May 12, 1927, the same week two Frenchmen were lost during an attempted crossing. Weather delayed Lindbergh's departure, but as the rain finally began to abate, pilot and crew began to make final preparations. By the time Lindbergh crawled into the cockpit, he had been awake for twenty-four hours. The *Spirit of St. Louis* was so heavily loaded with fuel that getting it off the ground proved very tricky. With every rivet straining, the small plane clawed its way into the air, barely clearing utility wires at the end of the airstrip. The former mail pilot battled storms, icing wings, and long hours without sleep. Newspapers had covered his takeoff, and Americans held their breath awaiting word of Lindbergh's fate. Then, after thirty-three and a half hours, the *Spirit of St. Louis* arrived over Paris. Lindbergh circled the Eiffel Tower and landed at a nearby airfield, where he was greeted by throngs of excited Frenchmen. Newspapers the world over proclaimed "Lindbergh Does It!"

CONSIDER THIS: Many people try to be a hero, but those who actually enter that select fraternity often do so by planning, hard work, guts, and luck.

What's in a Name?

"Problems are only opportunities in work clothes."
— Henry J. Kaiser

John Cullinane founded Cullinane Database Systems in 1968 with $500,000 in venture capital. The company name was soon changed to Cullinet Software, Inc., and the first product released was a report generator for programmers, called Culprit. The program was good but sales did not meet expectations. Some people thought the program's name had a negative connotation. At one point in 1972, Cullinet's checking account was down to $500, and its $8,500 payroll was due that day. But when the mail was opened, it included a life-giving payment in the amount of $8,500. A radical change was called for if the company was to survive. Cullinet's technical management agreed that the company had to develop software according to customers' perceptions of their needs, not Cullinet's. A new product similar to Culprit was developed, but Cullinane decided to call the program by a more sophisticated-sounding name, EDP Auditor.

The marketing staff began to promote the software, and a special EDP Auditor's training program was developed. The strategy pumped new life into the company. Auditors liked the new program, sales took off, and for the first time, Cullinet was making money. With that initial success under its belt, the company went public in 1978, becoming the first software company to be listed on the New York Stock Exchange. For thirteen consecutive years Cullinet produced annual profits of 50 percent or more. By redirecting its technical development and marketing focus, Cullinet was able to stop losing money and become a very successful enterprise.

CONSIDER THIS: You can't sell a product if is not marketed correctly or to the right audience.

Whitewashing the Fence

"One man's work is another man's fun."

— Anonymous

It was the 1830s and young Sam Clemens had disobeyed his mother and taken a dip in the swimming hole near his hometown of Hannibal, Missouri. When his mother discovered the misdeed, she sent the boy out to whitewash the fence as punishment. Sam looked down the thirty-foot-long fence and slowly began to paint, all the while trying to think up an excuse to get out of the work. Sam had painted just half a board when his friend John Robards happened by. "I guess you can't go with me, 'cause you gotta work," said John. "You call this work?" replied Sam. "A boy doesn't get to whitewash every day." Sam continued painting, pretending that he was really enjoying the chore. John watched for a minute, then said, "Let me whitewash for a minute." Sam smiled and said the job couldn't be entrusted to just anyone.

"I'll give you the core of my apple," offered John. Sam "reluctantly" accepted and for the better part of the afternoon continued to convince boy after boy to pay for the privilege of whitewashing a portion of the fence. By the time the fence was completely painted, Sam had collected a brass doorknob, a dead cat, a dozen marbles, the handle of a knife, and a kitten with one eye. Years later, after he had taken the pen name Mark Twain, Sam Clemens recounted the episode in his classic book *The Adventures of Tom Sawyer*. The story has since come to epitomize the inventiveness of the American spirit to make the best of a situation and to turn one person's chore into another person's play.

CONSIDER THIS: Work can be unpleasant or fun, depending on the way you look at it or the spirit in which it is performed.

The Journey of Success

"The blessings we evoke for another descend
upon ourselves." — Edmund Gibson

Success is difficult to define. Some people think that success is the accumulation of a certain amount of wealth—a million dollars, for instance. Some people view success as having power over the lives of other people, perhaps as an elected official, the owner of a large business, or a high-ranking bureaucrat. Some people envision success as the attainment of a certain station in life. While some people may define success in terms of themselves, other individuals measure success in terms of their contributions to others. To some, Howard Hughes represented the pinnacle of success. Others believed that Mother Theresa was a model of success. Many people who have experienced success claim that they derived excitement not from reaching their ultimate goal, but from the journey itself. The road you take toward a particular goal will lead to either success or failure. Both are stepping-stones to another task, a new adventure in life.

One of America's greatest philosophers, Ralph Waldo Emerson, described success this way: "To laugh often and much; to win the respect of intelligent people and the affection of children; to earn the appreciation of honest critics and endure the betrayal of false friends; to appreciate beauty; to find the best in others; to leave the world a bit better, whether by a healthy child, a garden patch, or a redeemed social condition; to know even one life has breathed easier because you lived; this is to have succeeded."

CONSIDER THIS: What is your definition of success? If you do not know what success is, it is unlikely that you will ever attain it.

H. B. Fuller Company

"In life, as in a football game, the principle to follow is: hit the line hard."

— Theodore Roosevelt

Harvey Benjamin Fuller was repackaging glues in 1887 when he decided to create his own formulas and start his own business. With $600 he obtained from three lawyers, Benjamin began marketing premixed wallpaper paste, an innovation in an era when wallpaper hangers had to mix their own paste on the job. He went on to develop other new adhesive products, such as a dry wall cleaner that could be mixed with cold water and a dry wall paste. However, even with the new inventions, Benjamin's business was up and down. Key people left to start their own ventures, and the Great Depression almost pulled the company under.

When innovations in glue proved unable to revive the company, management tried other methods. A new sales manager, Elmer Andersen, suggested incentive plans for the salesmen. Although other managers balked, a one-year experiment was agreed upon—and sales for that year increased by 25 percent. In 1941, Andersen bought a majority share of stock in the company. He instituted a philosophy that gave employees incentives for success and also established a minimum wage at the company. H. B. Fuller was one of the first companies to give each employee a "holiday" for his or her birthday. The business was set up as small "companies," with "presidents" acting as entrepreneurs, owning stock in the company, and earning a percentage of sales. In more than half a century under Andersen's leadership, H. B. Fuller not only became a Fortune 500 company, it was also named one of the best 100 companies to work for in America.

CONSIDER THIS: Innovations and incentives work hand in hand. Success takes both a good product and motivated marketers.

Harry Mullikin at Westin Hotels

"Be an earnest student of yourself. Study your leading desires and tendencies."
— Grenville Kleiser

At age fourteen, Harry Mullikin was just out looking for a job and had no particular career in mind. The job he found was at the Cascadian Hotel in Wenatchee, Washington, where he worked as an elevator operator, bellboy, porter, night janitor, and room clerk. Later, after serving in the Air Force, Harry tried to get into Washington State College. When his application was rejected, he went back to work at the hotel. One Sunday while helping a customer check out, Harry noticed that the man's business card said he worked for Washington State College. "You didn't let me into your college, why should I let you out of my hotel?" Harry quipped. The customer promised to look into the matter, and a few weeks later, Harry received a letter. The man turned out to be the school's director of admissions.

Not knowing that Washington State had a school of hotel management, Harry decided to become an architect. One day, he ran into the man who had helped him get into school. The man asked why Harry wasn't enrolled in the hotel school. "What hotel school?" Harry replied. Later, Harry confessed that he "never knew you could do something you liked." Harry liked the hotel business and became manager of one of the Western (later Westin) hotels. Harry Mullikin became known for his good judgment and attention to detail. He was given the task of building the Century Plaza Hotel in Los Angeles and was later named chairman and CEO of Westin Hotels and Resorts.

CONSIDER THIS: You really can be in a profession you like. In fact, that is probably the profession in which you will have the most success.

Celestial Spin-offs

"With some people, even their roosters seem to lay eggs." — Russian proverb

"Two hippies walking around in the mountains picking herbs" started it all. At the time, no corporation was interested in the antics of a couple of flower children, but the company John Hay and Mo Siegel started in 1972 took the tea business by storm and carved out a new niche in an herbal tea market that the firm itself defined. They successfully brought together a team comprised of employees from other corporations and personal friends to create an electric atmosphere at Celestial Seasonings. Former marketing vice president Keith Brenner reflected on the firm's formula for success, saying, "The company always went for the best—the best art, the best people, the best machinery." Celestial's hard-working, uncompromising desire to be the best brewed a formula for success.

For ten years the company was immersed in a veritable garden of entrepreneurship. However, by the mid-1980s, Celestial Seasonings was becoming a corporation that could no longer maintain its original barefoot culture. It was simply becoming too big to be ignored by the major corporations and was soon gobbled up. When Kraft Foods Inc. bought it, Celestial left its imprint on the Colorado business scene by birthing over a dozen other entrepreneurial start-ups that were organized by Celestial's founders and early employees. Those individuals had gained considerable experience in creating one of the most viable companies of the decade and, financed by their stock ownership plan, were itching to try their own hand at success.

CONSIDER THIS: Success breeds success. A company must provide its employees with opportunities for entrepreneurship, or its brightest stars will start a new business somewhere else.

Quad/Graphics

"It's not the big that beat the small, it's the fast that beat the slow." — Harry Quadracci

Quad/Graphics is tucked away in Pewaukee, Wisconsin, but the magazine printing company has often maintained a 30 to 40 percent growth rate in an industry in which the average annual growth rate is less than 10 percent. Founded in 1971 by Harry V. Quadracci and a covey of managers from a strike-ridden printing company, Quad/Graphics had little time to establish a formal management style. The founders instead based their new company philosophy on bits and pieces of management theory culled from the works of Kenneth Blanchard, Tom Peters, and a host of other managerial theorists. At Quad/Graphics, a major part of the management strategy is to give each employee the responsibility to make his or her particular department productive and profitable. The plant itself is a textbook example of participative management.

In the transportation department, the truckers themselves were given the responsibility to make a profit on their runs. With only an occasional "course correction" from management, the truckers worked with the Interstate Commerce Commission to get common-carrier status and then marketed their services to brokers. Similarly, other departments are charged with the responsibility to generate profits. To get the most productive work from employees and allow them more free time to pursue leisure activities, the company instituted a three-day, thirty-six-hour work week, a stock ownership plan, and a training program that offers college credit. Quad/Graphics also constructed a $3 million sports facility for its employees, and the entire plant, even the restrooms, was luxuriously appointed.

CONSIDER THIS: People will respond to the trust given to them to collectively manage for the good of all.

Will Rogers

*"Some folks figure it's a compliment to be called
broad-minded. Back home, broad-minded is just
another way of sayin' a feller's too lazy to form
an opinion."* — Will Rogers

In many ways Will Rogers epitomizes the character of Americans—at least how we would like to be. Born in Oologah, Indian Territory (Oklahoma), he was five-sixteenths Native American. He would often quip, "My ancestors didn't come over on the *Mayflower*; they met the boat." Will was a real-life adventurer. Before becoming a star rodeo performer, he learned his cowboy skills roping cattle in Argentina and Africa during the 1920s. It was in Texas Jack's Wild West Show that Will got his start on stage with a trick roping act. One night during the act, he made a mistake and found himself ensnared in his lariat. Thinking quickly, Will told the audience, "A rope ain't bad to get tangled up in if it ain't around your neck." The ad-lib got a big laugh, and that was the beginning of his famous off-the-cuff roping routine.

Americans heard Will Rogers talk about the very things they would like say, if only they could have thought of the right words: "Our foreign policy dealings are an open book—a checkbook." "Too many people spend money they haven't earned to buy things they don't want, to impress people they don't like." Rogers was himself a risk-taker, trying new ideas and telling his audiences, "Why not go out on a limb? That's where the fruit is." After his death in a plane crash in 1935, a statue was erected to his memory and bears an inscription that perhaps tells us more about that insightful American than any other legacy: "I never met a man I didn't like."

CONSIDER THIS: Americans respond to common sense. Humor is better than hype, and possessing good character is better than being clever.

Billy Graham

> *"Although hotels, night clubs, and bars in the city*
> *were crowded last night, the largest gathering . . .*
> *packed Mechanics Building to hear Rev. Billy*
> *Graham."* — Boston Sunday Globe

Billy Graham is known as "America's Pastor." In an age when some evangelists are mistrusted and considered charlatans, Graham has maintained his integrity. He has met, encouraged, and advised every president since Harry Truman. He has brought a message of God's love and the need for repentance to millions of people throughout the world. When the nation grieved after the Oklahoma City bombing, Billy Graham was called to lead the nation in mourning and recovery.

Power and prominence often destroy men whose original intentions were pure. Perhaps one reason Graham never succumbed to such forces stems from a 1948 meeting of Graham's team of evangelists in Modesto, California. Graham, Cliff Barrows, Bev Shea, and Grady Wilson were all concerned about the poor image of evangelists. The team prayed, discussed the problem, and came up with a list of actions they would take to avoid falling into moral problems. They would be paid by salary instead of depending on offerings. They would work through local churches and not independently. They also committed themselves to maintaining integrity in publicity and in the reporting of attendance figures for various religious services. Finally, they pledged to avoid any appearance of sexual impropriety. From that day forward, Graham never traveled with, met, or dined alone with any woman except his wife.

CONSIDER THIS: Integrity doesn't just happen. You must pledge yourself to it and call on your closest associates to hold you to its standards.

Joe Camp and Benji

> *"To a child, this world is brand-new and gift-wrapped; Disney tried to keep it that way for adults . . ."* — Eric Sevareid

In 1968 Joe Camp was an advertising copywriter, but his childhood dream was to make films. In his spare time, he wrote scripts, hoping someday to break into the big time. His hero throughout his life has been Walt Disney. One Sunday evening while watching Disney's *Lady and the Tramp*, Joe asked himself, "I wonder if it would be possible to do [the story] . . . using a real dog?" The next morning he got up at four o'clock to do his usual writing, but he instead wrote the entire story of *Benji* in just two hours. Joe woke his wife and read her the story. "She cried in bed," he recalls.

Camp turned the story over to his agent, but the only response he received was, "Disney has already done it." For a while, Joe shelved the story and began making short films. Within two years, he formed Mulberry productions, primarily for making television commercials. By 1973, Camp had enough experience and backing to make the motion picture *Benji*. His first task was to find the right dog to play the lead. After hundreds of auditions, Camp finally found Higgins, a thirteen-year-old canine that had appeared regularly on the *Petticoat Junction* television series. The going was tough at first, with Camp being very particular about every shot. The opening sequence was filmed eighty-four times. When the film was completed, he took it to Disney Studios for distribution but was turned down. Camp had to form his own distribution company and write his own ads to promote *Benji*. In the end, the film was a success, and Camp was able to realize his fondest childhood dream.

CONSIDER THIS: Your dream can become a reality, but you may have a long road to trod, and you may have to pull the bulk of the weight yourself.

George Eastman

"It is indeed astonishing how many great men have been poor." — John Lubbock

Poverty is a prison to many Americans. But to some, the fear of permanent poverty has led to Herculean efforts of inventiveness. Such was the case of George Eastman. In 1868, when George was fourteen, his father died, leaving the family penniless. Quitting school, George became a messenger boy for an insurance firm. He was a good worker and studied at night to advance in his career. At age twenty he was hired as a junior clerk at the Rochester Savings Bank. Finally able to save money, he intended to take a long-needed vacation trip to Santo Domingo. Someone mentioned that he should photograph his trip, which led George to buy a photographic outfit.

Wet plate photography was difficult and tedious, and Eastman soon read in a British magazine about how to make a dry plate. Working at the bank in the daytime, he labored at night to formulate his own photographic plates. Often Eastman would work late into the night and not go to bed. He experimented for three years and in April 1880 leased a room and began to produce dry plates for sale. Eastman quickly learned that his process had flaws; once he almost lost all of his business due to a poor batch of plates. By 1888 he had perfected a process that enabled the necessary photographic chemicals to be placed onto a roll of paper, which was then inserted into the camera. Known as the first Kodak camera, the device was preloaded and required only that the user press a button to take a picture. Eastman's revolutionary camera brought photography to the general public.

CONSIDER THIS: If you are seeking to improve your life, open your mind to new ideas. Try a new hobby. Improve on someone else's idea. Go exploring. You may find the adventure of a lifetime.

New Beginnings for Borden

*"Many strokes, though with a little axe, hew
down and fell the hardest-timbered oak."*
— Shakespeare

The tombstone above Gail Borden's grave reads, "I tried and failed, I tried again and again and succeeded." Borden did not have success early in life. Yet after each failure, he began a new quest. He became a schoolteacher, an editor, a real estate salesman, customs collector, and surveyor. During that time he came up with several interesting ideas that had no commercial success. His land and water vehicle nearly drowned the town elders of Galveston, Texas, on a demonstration voyage. Borden experimented with food preservation and won a gold medal at the 1851 London Crystal Palace Exposition for a dried meat biscuit, but he was unsuccessful in marketing the product. On the trip back to America, Borden was concerned about the deaths of four children on the ship caused by bad milk. This sparked some inventive thinking. How could milk be stored for long periods of time?

Borden was fifty-six years old when he devised a way to condense milk. His first attempt to produce the milk commercially was underfinanced and failed. A year later, with more financing, he tried again. The Civil War was beginning and Borden began to receive steady orders from the army. He was finally on his way to success. Borden used much of his profits to educate farmers in dairy techniques, organize schools for African Americans, build churches, and provide support for underpaid ministers, teachers, and students.

CONSIDER THIS: If you think you have the "right stuff" to make it, keep trying, keep seeking until opportunity comes, then grab it for all it's worth!

Feeling the Part

"From what we get, we can make a living; what we give however, makes a life." — Arthur Ashe

There is a lot of truth to the old saying "clothes make the man." When Florenz Ziegfeld brought his popular Follies to the stage, he made the showgirls wear silk undergarments because he said the lingerie made the performers feel beautiful. And when they felt beautiful, they acted beautiful, and that aura was conveyed to the audience. Many businesses have instituted some form of dress code, not just for the sake of presenting a good image to the public but also to give employees a feeling of pride and belonging. Some companies are concerned about how their entire organization is "dressed." The image of companies such as McDonald's is enhanced by their squeaky clean restaurants. That spic-and-span reputation also conveys a message that says "Our food is also prepared with care" and that the customer deserves a clean place in which to enjoy a meal.

People who make a living buying businesses have developed a practical method for determining a good buy. When a business such as a retail store is being managed poorly, evidence can be found in merchandise that is out of place, trash in the parking lot, improperly maintained displays, and employees who are slow to help customers. Such visible evidence is often indicative of poorly managed finances, little emphasis on performance or employee incentives, and a poorly served customer base. Such a business usually has the potential for a better bottom line if the details of image and morale are properly addressed.

CONSIDER THIS: Image not only makes a difference to customers, it is also a good gauge of management's effectiveness.

Monopoly

"Public opinion in this country is everything."
— Lincoln

It was a bleak winter in 1933. The weather and the economy were both bad. Charles Darrow of Germantown, Pennsylvania, longed for the trips he had made to Atlantic City, New Jersey, but the depression left him with little money for such frivolity. Perhaps as the next best thing to being there, Darrow concocted a little diversion. He devised a game based on the streets of Atlantic City: Boardwalk, Park Place, Baltic Avenue, Marvin Gardens, and the rest. He called his new game Monopoly, and it was all about making and spending money, something everyone wanted to do during the depression. Darrow showed the game to a few friends, and they liked it enough to want copies. Darrow made a few copies by hand, and thinking that he had a good idea, showed the game to Parker Brothers. But the Parker company considered the game too complicated to ever be successful.

Not willing to stop because of a single "no," Darrow managed to raise enough money to have some sets printed and offered them to Wanamaker's Department Store in Philadelphia. Soon Monopoly was the rage of the city. People who normally went to bed by nine o'clock would find themselves still trying to buy Boardwalk at two in the morning. Something about the game was addictive. After the successful showing at Wanamaker's, Parker Brothers took a second look and acquired the rights to the game in 1935. Today, Monopoly is licensed in over eighty countries and in twenty-three languages. It is a worldwide pastime that even boasts a "world series" of Monopoly that is played each year.

CONSIDER THIS: If you have an idea you think will sell, you may have to cough up the original marketing investment yourself and prove that you have a winner before getting a major company to help you out.

Bank of America

"Above the cloud with its shadow is the star with its light.   — Victor Hugo

During a disaster, we often find out who can be trusted and who really cares. Such was the case in the days following the massive earthquake of April 28, 1906, that nearly destroyed San Francisco. At 5:12 a.m., the city was rocked by a temblor. Although much of the financial district survived the quake intact, numerous blazes were kindled as ruptured gas lines ignited, and the city's water systems failed. Amades Peter Giannini, the founder of the small Bank of Italy on Montgomery Street, traversed the seventeen miles from his home in time to reach the bank before the fire did. Since the bank had no vault, Giannini had to hide $80,000 in cash under orange crates in a wagon, which he then drove to his home so that he could hide the money in his fireplace.

Many banks expected to remain closed for months, but Giannini reopened his bank on a wharf, loaning money for reconstruction and spearheading an effort to buy shiploads of lumber. Loans were made on a handshake basis. Soon, the bank began to get deposits, which before long outnumbered the loans. Giannini had an abiding faith in the people and ran his bank that way. It was his customers' bank, a place where they could feel appreciated. Giannini thought banking should be simple and that transactions should be done quickly. He introduced branch banking throughout California and eventually offered a variety of services around the world. Giannini was proud of his achievements in making banks more user-friendly. The tiny makeshift bank on a San Francisco wharf eventually become the Bank of America, one of the largest financial institutions in the world.

CONSIDER THIS: When you open a business, make it simple and convenient for people to get the services they need.

There's Gold in Those Hills

*"Gold! Gold! Gold! Gold! Bright and yellow, hard
and cold."* — Thomas Hood in "Her Moral"

People often have no idea how close they have come to attaining a goal—until after they have already given up. At some point in our lives, nearly all of us have abandoned a goal that we had wanted to achieve. Perhaps we had worked for days, weeks, or even years trying to reach our goal but finally found it was just too difficult to keep going. We had become burned out. It was time to quit. We had lost all hope of making a decision that would be right. Later, we asked ourselves, "Why didn't I hold on for just a little longer?" In *Think and Grow Rich*, author Napoleon Hill tells the story of R. U. Darby, who discovered gold in the Colorado hills. It seemed that the vein of gold ore was huge, until it suddenly ran out. Frantically, the drillers searched to pick up the vein again, but to no avail. Finally, Darby gave up and sold the remaining assets to a junkyard dealer.

The owner of the junkyard called in a mining engineer who was an expert in the area of mineral deposits. The engineer surveyed the situation and calculated that the gold vein would start up about three feet from where the others had stopped digging. The expert had a thorough knowledge of geology and understood how rock formations often shifted. He had the tools and training to determine where the vein would likely be found—and he was exactly right! The mine was reopened, and the junkyard owner took millions of dollars worth of gold from the previously abandoned vein.

CONSIDER THIS: Before you give up, cover all the possibilities. Ask for advice from those who know more than you. Your pot of gold may be only a few feet away.

The Strategy of Leadership

*"Reason and judgment are the qualities of
a leader."* — Tacitus

Leadership is something every organization has to have. It is something that everyone agrees is good to have but that no one really knows how to find. In researching their book *Leaders*, authors Warren Bennis and Burt Nanus interviewed ninety leaders from a variety of professional fields in an attempt to find common threads in leadership behavior. Although most people agree that there is no singularly correct way to lead, there are some underlying leadership principles that can be identified. By analyzing the character and personality traits of the ninety leaders, Bennis and Nanus were able to discern four distinct traits that most leaders share:

1. Leaders bring attention to their agenda (vision).
2. Leaders communicate, although not necessarily in conventional ways.
3. Leaders trust people. They put themselves at risk by giving other people the power to act.
4. Leaders believe in themselves and keep their eyes on the positive side of their goals.

A business leader's worth does not necessarily come from technical knowledge of the industry. A leader must encourage others to act, help them visualize their goals, and cheer them on when things look bleak. A strong leader is part visionary, part cheerleader, and part warrior.

CONSIDER THIS: How do you measure up as a leader? Are there personal strategies you should change to become a more effective leader?

Success Takes Work

"In the sweat of thy face shalt thou eat bread."
— Genesis 3:19

Ray Kroc looked for success for a long time. As a fifty-six-year-old salesman of malt mixers, he was curious about a small restaurant that needed to make lots of malts at the same time. That is how Kroc "discovered" the McDonald brothers' restaurant. He knew that the operation had real franchising potential. The brothers were reluctant, however, and Kroc had to convince the pair that he could help develop their concept into a national restaurant chain. Kroc took McDonald's from obscurity to stardom and in the process relied on this inspirational message that was placed in every executive office of his company:

> Nothing in the world can take the place of persistence.
> Talent will not; nothing is more common than unsuccessful men
> with great talent.
> Genius will not; unrewarded genius is almost a proverb.
> Education will not; the world is full of educated derelicts.
> Persistence, determination alone are omnipotent.

Ray Kroc was well over the age of fifty before he realized his American Dream. Kroc knew the value of continuing to move forward in the face of problems and temporary failures. He also knew that it was his own hard work that eventually helped him establish the most successful restaurant chain in history.

CONSIDER THIS: Good ideas are fine, but long-term success will always be preceded by persistent work.

Whitman Sampler

"Keep your eyes and ears open, if you desire to get on in the world." — Douglas Jerold

A good company cannot remain the same forever. It must change with the times. It must retain those ideas and products that continue to be popular while daring to experiment with new concepts and new products. Since 1912 the Whitman Sampler assortment of chocolate candies has been a favorite gift to give and to receive, but it was not the Whitman company's original product. The enterprise's tradition goes back to 1842, when Stephen Whitman opened a small candy shop in Philadelphia. The Market Street store was located near the city's wharves, where Stephen bought exotic nuts and fruits to include in his chocolates. In the early days, Stephen sold his customers an empty box that they could then fill with candies from the store.

Stephen's candies became popular, and to take advantage of the increasing demand, he began prepackaging them in fancy boxes. By the turn of the century, Walter Sharp was running Whitman's candy business. While on a visit to his grandmother's house, Sharp noticed an embroidered box that he recognized as a potential candy box. He produced a likeness of the box, and it instantly became a popular addition to his line. The Whitman Sampler that can be seen on store shelves today (with some minor changes) is patterned after that same box. Experimentation and adaptation are the lifeblood of any growing organization.

CONSIDER THIS: Keep your eyes open for the idea with the potential to become a legend. Even if what you now have is successful, don't be afraid to experiment with new ideas.

Richard Snyder's Cool Millions

"He helps others most, who shows them how to help themselves." — A. P. Gouthey

Being in the right place at the right time helps, but you must also be prepared to act quickly when opportunity knocks at your door. Richard Snyder worked as an executive in the Climate Control Division at Singer when rumors began to circulate that the company might sell off the division in order to concentrate on the more glamorous aerospace industry. Snyder saw an opportunity to buy the division himself, and in order to be ready if Singer did decide to sell, quietly began to arrange the necessary financing. Over the next seven months, Snyder talked to ninety-four banks and venture capital companies. During the 1981 recession sales were poor, and the book value of Climate Control was $54 million. Snyder could never find the money to buy it at that price, but when Singer, in an effort to get rid of the failing business, offered it at $27.5 million, he was able to get the loans.

The new company was named SnyderGeneral. The enterprise slashed expenses, accelerated its inventory turnover, and dramatically reduced the average amount of time needed to collect payments from customers. Within three years, Snyder had paid off the original loans. Operating his own company motivated Snyder to expand his business. He encouraged his executives—many of whom were lured away from the competition—with high earnings that were keyed to the company's growth. He also acquired smaller companies to enter new climate-control markets. Richard Snyder took a dead-end business and, through motivated management, turned it into the darling of the industry.

CONSIDER THIS: Do you want people to perform? Give them the incentive to do so. Make them feel that they are a vital part of the organization. Make their success keyed to the bottom line.

Intel's Beginnings

"All your strength is in union, all your danger is in discord." — Longfellow

So many leaders in the computer and electronics fields have been employed at some point in their careers by Fairchild, a pioneer in the semiconductor industry, that they have become known as "FairChildren." Three of those former employees were Robert Noyce, Gordon Moore, and Andy Grove. In the mid-1960s, tension was running high at Fairchild and morale was sinking lower as the company went through three CEOs in a year. Noyce and Moore, both brilliant research scientists, were spending more time on administrative tasks than on research. They believed that their talents were being wasted and were certain that their American Dream was not to become corporate bureaucrats. In 1968 Noyce and Moore left Fairchild, were soon joined by Grove, and together formed Intel, which was named for a combination of the words "integrated electronics."

Intel set out to make computer memory chips. Many of its early attempts did not work well, and when something finally did work, it called for a champagne celebration. To convince visiting customers of the company's ability as a supplier, Intel's management would move workers from area to area during plant tours to make it appear that the business had more employees. Customers liked what they saw at Intel, and the company eventually was responsible for developing such important electronic components as the primary chip in the successful line of IBM personal computers. Not only has Intel made pioneering advancements in the computer industry, it has produced a company culture that can only be described as family.

CONSIDER THIS: Is your organization likely to encourage employees to leave, or to join in a family struggle to make the company grow?

Mack Trucks

"You don't have to focus on everything to be successful. But you do have to focus on something."
— Al Ries

While other mechanics were busily inventing passenger automobiles, Jack and Augustus Mack had a different idea. At the dawning of the age of the horseless carriage, the brothers reasoned that there also would be a need for large trucks and passenger wagons. The Macks began experimenting with vehicle construction as early as 1892. First they tried constructing steam-driven and electric-powered wagons but were dissatisfied with the results. In 1900 the brothers built an unusually rugged vehicle, christened "No. 1," which began its life as a bus that carried passengers around Brooklyn's Prospect Park. "No. 1" was later converted into a truck and, in all, was used for seventeen years—not bad for a first-of-a-kind vehicle.

In the following decade, the Macks produced a number of buses and trucks that became known for their durability. Vehicle No. 9 became a sightseeing bus, and it remained in use until the 1950s, recording more than a million miles. Of course, other automobile manufacturers were also building trucks and buses, but for most of those companies, the larger vehicles seemed only to be a sideline business. Mack Trucks Inc. retained its focus. In 1910 it built a special vehicle that was America's first motor-propelled hook-and-ladder fire truck. The firm's 1918 "AC" model was popular during World War I. Its unique blunt-nosed design reminded British troops of a bulldog, and the truck's tenacious character made the analogy stick and inspired the bulldog logo used by Mack today.

CONSIDER THIS: Find your niche in the marketplace and become the best there is. Focus on what you do best.

Coming Back After Loss

"When you have exhausted all the possibilities, remember this: You haven't."

— Robert Schuller

Robert Schuller remembers a family tragedy in his book *Tough Times Never Last But Tough People Do*. It was 1933, some four years into the Great Depression, and things had been difficult on the Iowa farm owned by Robert's father. Besides the poor economy, the family's crops were failing and there had been no rain. One day there was a spark of hope as clouds appeared on the horizon. But as the clouds approached, an ominous funnel dropped out of the sky and headed for the farm. The Schullers jumped into the family car and made a hair-raising dash out of the tornado's path. When they returned, nothing was left of the farm. It was as if the entire area had been vacuumed clean.

Twenty-six years of backbreaking work was gone in a matter of minutes. The mortgage on the house was due, and the elder Schuller was nearing the age of retirement. When the family examined the spot where the house had been, all they found was part of a molded plaster motto that had hung in the kitchen. It originally had said "Keep looking to Jesus," but now it read "Keep looking." The Schullers took the sign back to the car, and it became their inspiration to continue trying and not give up. Two weeks later, they began rebuilding. Working harder than ever, the Schullers paid off their entire mortgage in five years. That tragedy inspired Robert Schuller, who became a noted evangelist, to believe in the power of "Possibility Thinking." With faith in God, belief in your own capabilities, and with hard work, you can make the impossible possible.

CONSIDER THIS: Circumstances are not your enemy; what is holding you back are your own shallow beliefs and defeatist attitude. When setbacks occur, regroup and move forward.

Olga's Slips

"He started to sing as he tackled the thing that couldn't be done, and he did it."

— Edgar A. Guest

We are a country of immigrants seeking a better life. American Dreams are often conceived in other countries around the world in the hope that they may eventually take root in the fertile soil of free enterprise. Olga and Jan Erteszek were married in Poland during World War II. To escape Nazi oppression, they emigrated to the United States and moved to California. Jan was trained as a lawyer but could not practice in the United States, so Olga decided to bring in money by sewing. Her mother had been a corsetiere, but Olga knew little about design. With $10 she rented a machine and bought fabric. After spending long hours sewing and modeling in front of the mirror, Olga had made several samples of garter belts. Jan took them to a local department store and was able to obtain an order for more. The items proved popular, and the stores soon placed additional orders.

The small business grew during the war, and Olga continued to design new items of intimate apparel. Her secret, she claims, is that she serves as her own model. Olga wears everything she makes and also fits the apparel to live models, rather than templates. Her unique feminine touches are original, since she refuses to look at what the competition is doing. Jan and Olga love to hear about things that are "impossible" to do, since they enjoy the challenge of devising ways to accomplish those very feats. Their creativity and drive to do what no one else can do has made the Olga Company one of the most successful makers of intimate apparel in the United States today.

CONSIDER THIS: Those who are willing to try to do the impossible are the same persons who reap the benefits when the impossible is finally accomplished.

The Louisville Slugger

*"I'd have been a .290 hitter without a
Louisville Slugger."* — Ted Williams

Pete Browning was known as the "Old Gladiator' in the American Association baseball league. Although he holds the twelfth-highest career batting average in the major leagues at .341, another aspect of his career is perhaps more lasting. Pete was fighting a batting slump during the 1884 season when he broke his favorite bat. As it happened, John "Bud" Hillerich was at the ballpark that day, playing hooky from his father's woodworking shop. Bud invited the despondent ball player to go with him to the wood shop, promising to make Pete a new bat. The two found a piece of white ash, and Bud worked late into the night trying to create a perfect bat.

During the next baseball game, Browning went three-for-three with his new bat and was immediately enamored of his custom-made slugger. However, Bud's father saw no future in the bat business, preferring instead to keep on making bedposts, tenpins, and wooden bowling balls. Bud continued to make bats on the side, with ever increasing success. His early efforts were known as Falls City Sluggers, but the name was changed to Louisville Slugger in 1894. Bud continued to custom-make bats to players' exacting specifications, and they soon became legendary. To identify the bats, players' names were often carved into the handles. For bats created for general distribution, Bud came up with a unique marketing idea. In 1905, Bud signed Honus Wagner to a contract and put the popular player's signature on Louisville Sluggers, thus beginning the era of endorsement advertising.

CONSIDER THIS: Solve someone's problem by giving him a better tool to perform his job. There is always a demand for the best.

Jim Henson

"The only way the magic works is by hard work."
— Jim Henson

Jim Henson begged his family to get a television set, and in 1950, when Jim was fourteen, they bought one. Jim was fascinated with the medium's sights and sounds and wanted to be a part of the magic. He got his first opportunity in 1954, when, as a member of his high school puppet club, he heard that a local TV station, WTOP, was looking for a puppeteer. Jim applied for the job and soon began working on the *Junior Good Morning Show*, but the program was canceled after three weeks. Jim entered college and planned to develop his talents as a cartoonist, but he quickly got a job performing a five-minute puppet show for WRC-TV. He used the opportunity to create new puppet ideas and also learned how to make people laugh.

Jim melded traditional marionette and hand puppets into his own creations, called Muppets. In 1956, through his work at WRC, he was given the opportunity to garner national exposure for his Muppets by appearing on NBC's *Tonight Show*. That led to appearances on such popular programs as *The Ed Sullivan Show* and *The Jimmy Dean Show*. In 1969 Jim Henson's Muppets became part of a new educational show on the Public Broadcasting System called *Sesame Street*. The program was a hit, but the major networks still would not give Jim his own show. Finally, in 1976, an English businessman provided the funding to produce *The Muppet Show*. The series made superstars of Kermit the Frog, Miss Piggy, et al. When asked about his secret for success, Henson replied: "Follow your enthusiasm. It's something I've always believed in. Find those parts of your life you enjoy the most. Do what you enjoy doing."

CONSIDER THIS: Your most creative energy is released when you do what you love the most.

Chopping Down the Cherry Tree

"I can't tell a lie, Pa; you know I can't tell a lie. I did cut it with my hatchet."

— George Washington

The story of George Washington and the cherry tree has been told to generations of children. According to the fable, young George received a new hatchet and merrily chopped away at some "pea sticks" before looking for something more substantial. When George's father found that his favorite sapling cherry tree had been chopped down, he confronted his son. George confessed, and his father congratulated him for telling the truth. The story illustrates the strength of character that is basic to American integrity. It is also one of the factors that solidified Washington's status as one of America's great heroes.

Mason Locke Weems was a preacher and bookseller who lived in Virginia, not far from Mount Vernon, Washington's home. Weems may have preached occasionally at the church where the Washington family worshipped. Months before George Washington died, Weems began to collect anecdotes about the hero, and a few weeks after the former president's death on December 14, 1799, finished an eighty-page book, entitled *The Life and Memorable Actions of George Washington*. The book was so well received that it became the nation's best seller for several years and went through numerous revisions and reprints. The cherry tree story appeared in the 1806 fifth edition, entitled *The Life of Washington*. Even today, in newly created cartoons and children's books, the story's message continues to define an American ideal.

CONSIDER THIS: Truth never goes out of style. In times of confrontation, our integrity and character are put to the test. Are you ready for that test?

TV Guide

*"Do not suppose opportunity will knock twice at
your door."* — Sébastien Chamfort

The idea hit him like a ton of bricks. It was obvious that it would be a success, but others might just beat him to the punch. The year was 1952, and Walter H. Annenberg of Triangle Publications had seen a newspaper advertisement for a new weekly magazine called *TV Digest*, which was to contain information about local television shows. Annenberg reasoned that such a magazine could be put together on a national basis. It would include local program listings plus feature stories that would have national appeal. Convinced that such a publication offered enormous possibilities, Annenberg vigorously began to research the market. He found that there were already local television magazines in many major cities, and he moved quickly to buy them all.

Annenberg put together a staff of writers and began planning the first issue. The most popular show of the day was *I Love Lucy*, so star Lucille Ball was designated to appear on the first cover. Inside, there would be stories about Lucy, husband Desi Arnaz, and their new baby, who had already garnered considerable television and newspaper attention. The first issue of *TV Guide* came out in April 1953 with ten local editions, and its success seemed assured. But as summer approached and people began pursuing more vigorous activities than watching television, the publication's circulation started to drop. To bolster its sagging circulation, *TV Guide* devoted an issue to the new fall lineup of shows, thus beginning the publication's Fall Preview tradition. Today, *TV Guide* is one of the most widely read magazines in America.

CONSIDER THIS: When an idea comes, do something about it right away, or it may be too late. Don't let someone else beat you to the punch.

Land's End

*"There will always be a frontier where there is an
open mind and a willing hand."*
— Charles Kettering

This Christmas literally thousands of items will be ordered
from the Lands' End mail-order catalog. For many Americans,
the company's catalog has replaced shopping malls as a source
for better clothing. For Gary Comer, it is the realization of his
American Dream. Gary started his career as a copywriter with
the Young & Rubicam advertising agency. He won awards for
his work, but his heart belonged to sailing. As a result, he left
the agency in 1962 to become a salesman for a sailmaking company in Chicago. A year later, he started Lands' End as a mail-
order company specializing primarily in equipment for persons
involved in the sport of sailing. The catalog proved to be mod-
erately successful.

As a copywriter, Gary Comer enjoyed a heyday as he used
his catalog as an opportunity to write interesting stories and to
attract customers with dreamy descriptions of his offerings. He
noticed that the clothing section of the catalog was becoming
quite popular and that he was receiving an increasing number
of requests for additional apparel items. Realizing that clothing was less seasonal than sailing, Comer eventually dropped
sailing equipment altogether. He brought in talented executives to effectively plan and control his company's growth, and
he began to offer traditionally styled casual clothing that appealed to active people across the country. Recognizing the
unique position of mail order and its possible pitfalls, Comer is
also careful to offer an exceptionally high level of friendly and
efficient service.

CONSIDER THIS: Be prepared to allow your original ideas to
be molded by the needs of the marketplace.

Timex Watches

"They take a licking and keep on ticking."
— Timex advertisement

Norwegian Joakim Lehmkuhl first came to America to study engineering at Harvard and MIT. He returned to Norway in 1919 to apply his newly acquired skills to shipbuilding, but in the wake of Hitler's rise, he fled first to England, then to the U.S. in 1940. Using his engineering background to help in the war effort, Joakim and others bought the Waterbury Clock Company, where they made fuses and timers for munitions. After the war, the company began to look at other markets where it might make use of the new techniques and materials discovered during the conflict. In 1949 Lehmkuhl helped to design a simple and reliable watch mechanism, but when Timex watches were introduced in 1950, they were not runaway sellers.

With virtually no advertising, however, sales of the watches slowly increased. But it was a unique advertising campaign that eventually made Timex a huge success. The legendary Ben Hogan was "recruited" to test a Timex watch by wearing it while making 100,000 golf swings. Mickey Mantle performed similar tests with a Timex strapped to his wrist. Some of the most memorable advertisements in U.S. history involved "torture tests" performed by John Cameron Swayze on live television. The tests were conducted under some the most difficult conditions imaginable and always produced a watch that "takes a licking and keeps on ticking." One of the early torture tests seemed to be a disaster when the watch accidentally came free from the outboard motor propeller to which it had been attached. But when the Timex was recovered from the bottom of the test tank, it was still ticking.

CONSIDER THIS: Inexpensive and built to survive rigors beyond everyday life-that is what consumers are looking for!

Tiffany's

*"[Tiffany's] calms me down right away, the
quietness and the proud look of it; nothing very
bad could happen to you there."*
— Truman Capote in *Breakfast at Tiffany's*

In 1837 Charles Lewis Tiffany borrowed $1,000 from his
father and went to New York, where he partnered with John
Young and opened a small store on lower Broadway. The store
carried all manner of interesting items but had little jewelry.
But in 1848, with a revolution in Europe and jewelry prices
falling, Tiffany decided to enter the market. During the California gold rush of the following year, the entrepreneur added
precious metals to his line. Tiffany pioneered a one-price system and touted the concept in advertising: "Every article is
marked in plain figures, upon which there will not be the
slightest variation."

Tiffany & Company was incorporated in 1868 and continued
to grow until the depression of the 1930s began to erode profits. The company was "rescued" in the mid-1950s by Walter
Hoving, who owned the Bonwit fashion-apparel store adjoin-
ing Tiffany. Getting rid of leftover "white elephants" with a
half-price sale, Hoving brought in the best jewelry and china
designers to upgrade the store's merchandise and also brought
in professionals to attractively decorate Tiffany's store windows. Unlike the previous owner, who shunned publicity, Hoving encouraged Tiffany's notoriety via ads in the *Wall Street
Journal* that blasted poor taste in all its forms, from tattooing to
a "loud and vulgar" Christmas tree on Park Avenue. Tiffany's was
back and setting a high standard for good taste. In its first
decade under Hoving, profits increased over 900 percent.

CONSIDER THIS: No public enterprise can exist in health
without a healthy love for the public.

Scrabble

*"Nothing is invented and brought to perfection all
at once."* — Thomas Cole

To Americans, family time is often game time. Most games
are sold during holiday periods, and the two games that sell
best are Monopoly and Scrabble. Both were invented during
the depression, when people who otherwise would have been
at work had time to devote to playing games. In 1931 Alfred
Butts, an unemployed architect, developed a game consisting of
100 wooden tiles, each with a letter of the alphabet printed on
one side. The object of the game was to select letters from the
pool of tiles and form a word, with each word receiving a score
based on the number of tiles used to form it. Alfred worked on
his game for a decade, perfecting it and changing the way it was
played. He added a playing board and gave each letter a point
value. The board allowed players to create words in much the
same way as they would fill in a crossword puzzle.

In 1948, Alfred Butts and his wife decided to market the
game, which they named Scrabble. The couple set up a workshop and began to produce the playing equipment. Selchow &
Righter noticed an early version of Scrabble and agreed to manufacture the boards, believing that the game was interesting but
probably nothing more than a fad. But as the years passed, orders continued to increase, and in 1953 Selchow & Righter acquired complete manufacturing rights. More than fifty years
after its debut, Scrabble continues to sell as many copies as it
did in its "heyday."

CONSIDER THIS: Do you have some "invention" to promote? The best way to sell it to a company is to prove that it
will sell. Is your company looking for the next million-dollar
seller? Keep your eyes open for the small idea that could turn
into a huge success.

Jessica McClure's Rescue

"I was in need, and you helped me."

— The Bible

It was a warm day in Midland, Texas, and Jessica McClure and her friends were playing in the backyard. As the children ventured into an overgrown area, eighteen-month-old Jessica suddenly disappeared down a hole. The hole proved to be an abandoned water well, and the youngster had become trapped some twenty feet down an eight-inch pipe. Jessica's story quickly became international news and a national obsession. Oil drillers from the area arrived and began to dig a hole nearby in order to reach the toddler. Not far down, however, they hit super-hard caliche rock, which shattered drill bits and slowed progress to just inches each hour. Twenty-four hours passed, then thirty-six, then forty-eight. Every newscast carried the story, and special newsbreaks updated people about progress, new hope, or new problems.

Midland's economy was depressed due to falling oil prices, but the rescue attempt seemed to spark new life into the city's residents. Drillers donated $1,200 bits, knowing that they would last only a short while before breaking. Experts flew in from all over the country to donate their time, and people throughout the region did what they could: they prayed. Fifty-six hours after the ordeal began, Jessica was pulled from the hole and carried to safety as throngs of people cheered. The celebration was repeated in homes, restaurants, football stadiums, and almost everywhere else as word spread that little Jessica had been saved. So many people cared. So many people worked, hoped, and shared. This is America at its best.

CONSIDER THIS: The American Dream is opportunity for all people. From helping one little child, to helping an entire community in need, America is bent on giving every person the chance to make his or her life count.

Building on the Ideas of Others

"Ideas are a dime a dozen." — American adage

There are many examples of people who have founded companies, organizations, or movements with ideas they adopted from someone else. The originator of an idea often does not have the wherewithal to make the idea a success. For example, the McDonald brothers needed Ray Kroc to make it big. Without Asa Candler, Coca-Cola may have remained a modestly popular local product. Wham-O Manufacturing Co. turned a Frisbie pie pan (a college student's flying toy) into its own patented Frisbee flying disc. The ingredients for Vicks VapoRub had been available for years, but it was Lunsford Richardson who mixed them together and created the successful product. Likewise, the lowly peanut was nothing new, but the genius and hard work of George Washington Carver turned it into a money crop. Two hungry veterans named Larry Deusch and Lloyd Rigler discovered a "secret" ingredient used at a steak house, and the result was the successful Adolph's meat tenderizer.

Clarence Crane developed Life Savers as only as a summer sideline, but advertising salesman Edward Nobel saw the candy's potential and bought the rights to make and market the product. Whitcomb Judson patented his "clasp locker," but the device had problems. Twenty years later, an engineer named Gideon Sunback solved the problems, and the zipper became an everyday part of our clothes. Paul Galvin heard about someone installing custom radios in automobiles. His company, which ultimately became Motorola, improved on the idea to develop the first car radio suitable for the mass market.

CONSIDER THIS: There are plenty of ideas. What is really needed is someone with the insight to make the ideas work.

The Close Shave

"I always entertain great hopes."

— Robert Frost

Until the turn of the century, shaving was performed with a straight-edged razor. King Gillette changed that. In 1901 Gillette introduced the safety razor, which proved successful and came into particular prominence as standard issue for American soldiers during World War I. The doughboys had to be clean-shaven for their gas masks to fit properly. The safety razor became an American institution because of the war, but Jacob Schick was not impressed. The razor worked well enough when hot water was available, but Schick was stationed in Alaska. Every morning he had to crack a layer of ice to get to the water to shave. The wheels of invention began to turn.

After his discharge from the service, Schick decided to invent a "dry razor." His biggest problem was the lack of a small electric motor sufficient to power his invention. Schick worked for five years to develop a workable motor, which he patented in 1923. However, that success did not solve all of his problems. Schick could not find any financial backers. After all, who needed an electric shaver when the safety razor was so good? Schick mortgaged everything in sight to bring his razor to to the marketplace in 1931. The $25 price tag seemed high, particularly during the Great Depression, but he managed to sell 3,000 of the devices. His novel razor began making money, and Schick reinvested all of his profits in advertising. As a result, by 1937 Jacob Schick had sold almost two million electric razors.

CONSIDER THIS: Few people find instant success. For most people, success comes after commitment, hard work, and determination to see the project through to completion.

Macy's

"It is easier to go down a hill than up, but the view is best from the top."　　— Arnold Bennett

Macy's department store is an American tradition. When people visit New York, they go to the Statue of Liberty, the Empire State Building, and Macy's. It is doubtful that Rowlan Macy could have conceived the full extent of his venture. In fact, he failed quite a few times before finding any success in the retail business. The Nantucket Quaker left home as a teenager and spent four years aboard the sailing ship *Emily Morgan*. In 1844 Macy started a needle and thread shop in Boston, but it failed. He went to California during the gold rush, tried to make a go of another store in Massachusetts, and eventually tried again by selling ribbons and lace from a small store on Sixth Avenue in New York. Macy subscribed to the Quaker principles of one price, true value, and all cash transactions. Macy's New York store made a profit, and he began a policy of expansion that has never stopped.

By the modern era, Macy's store was so big that small problems were magnified a thousandfold. Most customers believed that Macy's carried everything. Once, when Macy's advertised a book entitled *One Million Islands for Sale*, the sales staff had their hands full explaining that the store did not actually sell islands. To handle the problem of occasionally misdelivered baby furniture, Macy's arranged for a permanent emergency supply and a special delivery truck. A staff of writers answers letters, a laboratory tests thousands of potential items, and an army of secret shoppers compares prices to make sure Macy's price is lower.

CONSIDER THIS: Rowlan Macy could have quit after his first failure—or his second or third. A dreamer continues his quest until the dream is in hand.

It's a Wonderful Life

*"Every time you hear a bell ring, it means that
some angel's just got his wings."* — Clarence

The first movie that Frank Capra and Jimmy Stewart made together after World War II portrayed George Bailey's struggle as he searched to define his own American Dream. *It's a Wonderful Life* opened in 1946 and lost over a half-million dollars. It lay virtually forgotten in film vaults until the video and cable revolution sparked a renewed interest in older films. When the film sprang to life again as a Christmas television film, it quickly became a beloved classic.

In the movie, George Bailey dreams of traveling the world and seeing mysterious and exotic places. Unfortunately, his plans always seem to be thwarted by circumstances. George "postpones" his travels to help his family's small savings and loan bank protect townspeople from a greedy banker. When George falls in love with Mary Hatch, they plan an elaborate honeymoon, only to have their plans shattered when there is a run on the bank. Then, when his Uncle Billy misplaces an $8,000 deposit just as bank examiners arrive, George faces certain ruin and humiliation. He wishes he'd never been born. An angel second-class, Clarence, grants his wish and lets George see what his hometown would be like if he'd never been born. George finds formerly pastoral Bedford Falls filled with mean, poor, and unhappy people. He desperately begs to return to his family, even if it means he must face the grim consequences. When Clarence grants his wish, George returns home and learns that his friends have banded together to replace the missing bank funds. He realizes that true wealth is not measured in possessions, but in faith, family, and friends.

CONSIDER THIS: Wealth and power are fleeting. Faith, Hope, and Love are the true building blocks of a lasting and wonderful life.

Christmas

*"I have come to give you life, and to give it
more abundantly."* — Jesus Christ

Christmas celebrates the birth of the one person who has
contributed more to our culture and societal beliefs than any
other. Christ's divine presence on earth not only gave the world
a path to spiritual salvation, it has also influenced the dreams
and lifestyles of billions of followers. American Dreams, like
the dreams of people in many nations, have to do with living a
fulfilling life free from war and tyranny, and helping others find
fulfillment. We honor as heroes those people who excel, who
save us from war, who fight injustice, and who give their lives
in the service of helping others. The teachings of Christ have
formed our own expectations of what it means to live a life that
really matters.

Christ articulated and modeled the Golden Rule. Human relationships are second in importance only to the love of God
Himself. Christ modeled a plan of leadership that has seen His
organization (the church) prosper for 2,000 years (even though
it has often deviated from Christ's ideals). Christ demonstrated
positive thinking, possibility thinking, and management. He
rewarded those who used their talents and condemned those
who took the easy way out. He showed anger toward those
who took advantage of the poor and praised those who shared
their wealth with others. He demonstrated the strength of faith
that can overcome failure, despair, hate, and ridicule. His
model is being actively followed by corporate leaders, sports
figures, statesmen, shopkeepers, and multitude of others in virtually every field of endeavor.

CONSIDER THIS: It is worth your time to discover Jesus
Christ for yourself. Any person with that much influence is
worth getting to know.

Self-affirmation

"The only thing we have to fear is fear itself."
— Franklin D. Roosevelt

People who are successful have the ability to believe in themselves. Often, they are not born with capacity for self-affirmation; it is something they worked to acquire. Like many of us, they had to change their belief from "I can't do it" to "I can." William Danforth was a sickly schoolboy and a weakling until a teacher challenged him to become the healthiest, strongest boy in the class. Danforth took the challenge, changed his life, founded Ralston Purina Company, and devoted much of his time and fortune to helping youngsters "take a dare."

Teddy Roosevelt came out of the same "weakling" mold as Danforth. Recognizing the need for change, he decided to do everything he was afraid of doing, and thus developed a strong belief in his own capabilities. It was clothing that "made the man" in the case of Bill Zanker, who founded the successful Learning Annex. His agent refused to work with him unless he "looked the part." Zanker was told to buy a $1,000 suit of clothes, a challenge that cost him just about everything he could muster. But when he put that suit on, his whole concept of himself underwent a significant change. Zanker looked like a success, he thought like a success, and he became a success. Bernie Kopell was a door-to-door vacuum cleaner salesman trying to break into acting. At the end of a frustrating day, his boss turned on some positive-thinking records—and their message began to soak into Kopell's brain. His attitude about his own capabilities changed, which enabled him to become a successful actor.

CONSIDER THIS: The first key to success in any enterprise is believing in yourself—forging ahead in the face of opposition, circumstance, fear, and frustration.

The Importance of Others

*"Do unto others as you would have them do
unto you."* — The Golden Rule

When James Cash Penney began his Golden Rule stores, the name of the business reflected his commitment to serving his customers. Various restatements of this rule are the guiding force behind many successful enterprises, from Digital Equipment Corporation to Mary Kay Cosmetics. Although "the customer is always right" is a familiar concept in our society, it is frequently paid only lip service. Organizations that actually adhere to that principle find themselves establishing a long list of loyal customers. The Sears guarantee is the cornerstone of the company's long-term success. Mail-order services such as Land's End and L. L. Bean would find it difficult to exist if they didn't offer a firm guarantee. Joe Girard, the "world's most successful salesman," admits that a customer occasionally will take advantage of service, but in the long run, the willingness to trust the customer will pay dividends.

The entire movement of excellence begun by Tom Peters and Robert Waterman Jr. hinges on the powerful word "listen." Levi Strauss listened to the needs of miners, and invented blue jeans. Bette Nesmith listened to the complaints of secretaries trying to correct typing mistakes and invented Liquid Paper. Procter and Gamble listened to customers and began to promote Ivory as "the soap that floats." Kleenex was marketed as a cold-cream wipe until Kimberly-Clark listened to customers who said the tissue was also a convenient handkerchief. One reason Arthur Fiedler became the most popular orchestra conductor in America was his ability to give people the music they wanted to hear.

CONSIDER THIS: Serving people should be the motivating concept behind every organization. People are drawn to those organizations that want to serve.

Alka-Seltzer

"Try it, you'll like it!"
— Alka-Seltzer advertisement

Many people over-indulge during the holidays and as a result suffer from pounding headaches and upset stomachs. But whether the cause of their distress is too much food and drink or the common cold, it is the "plop-plop, fizz-fizz" of Alka-Seltzer that will be the remedy of choice for millions of people. In fact, it was during a flu epidemic in December 1928 that A. H. Beardsley got the idea for Alka-Seltzer. Beardsley was president of the Dr. Miles Laboratories and was always on the lookout for new remedies for diseases. While visiting a local newspaper plant one day, Beardsley was surprised to find that the entire crew was healthy when most of the nation was suffering from influenza. The editor, Tom Keene, explained that whenever any of his workers appeared to be coming down with a cold, he put them on a regimen of aspirin and bicarbonate of soda until they were well.

When Beardsley returned to his office, he instructed his chief chemist to develop a tablet containing aspirin and soda. The new concoction was used successfully by workers in his office, and Beardsley also conducted a "field experiment," sharing the preparation with his fellow passengers while on a cruise to the Mediterranean. The tablets seemed to be effective for everything from seasickness to the common cold. Alka-Seltzer was introduced to the public in 1931 and was extensively advertised throughout the depression in an effort to make the product a household word. When television came along, the tablets were promoted on that medium with equal intensity. As a result, Alka-Seltzer is a common sight in virtually every medicine cabinet in America.

CONSIDER THIS: Old family cures, wives' tales, and legends may have some substance. Maybe they shouldn't be dismissed without a try.

Conquering the
Mousetrap Syndrome

*"No man is great in and of himself. He must touch
the lives of other great men who will inspire
him, lift him, push him forward and give
him confidence."* — Milne

Why is it that two people can have the same idea, but only one can turn it into a success? Many people have the misconception that products and services sell themselves. Some call this the "build a better mousetrap" syndrome. Literally millions of small businesses have started and failed because they could not sell their "better idea." Some entrepreneurs develop a service or product and enjoy an initial burst of success, then can only watch as their business grows out of control and fails. It is a rare individual who can start a business and bring to it all the skills necessary to make it a success through consistent and controlled growth.

On his gravestone Andrew Carnegie claimed that his success was the result of surrounding himself with people smarter than he. More than fifty people had "invented" the typewriter, but it never made it to the marketplace until businessman and promoter James Dunmore took the idea to Remington, which had the marketing expertise to sell the idea to the public. Mo Siegel had a sound idea when he started Celestial Seasonings, and he was smart enough to hire experience from the nation's biggest food companies to catapult the company to national success. In the fierce microcomputer wars, companies like Dell, Compaq, and Apple became successful in part because they filled their top ranks by hiring away the "best and brightest" people from such successful companies as Revlon, Pepsi, IBM, and others.

CONSIDER THIS: The smartest people are the ones who know when to seek the help of others. How can you multiply your own capabilities by using the skills of others?

Single-mindedness

"The sluggard craves and gets nothing, but the desires of the diligent are fully satisfied."

— Proverbs

There can be no doubt that formal education plays a role in success. There are basic skills that you must possess to be able to succeed in any venture. However, there is a point at which schooling does not provide the tools for success. As Karl Wallenda walked the high wire, he blocked out the possibility that he might fall. But one day he became afraid and fell to his death. President Kennedy's goal of a manned landing on the moon was beyond the grasp of the day's technology, but emotion and pride overcame practicality. The signers of the Declaration of Independence essentially signed their own death warrants, but their desire for freedom overcame their fear. No one would give an old man with a chicken recipe much chance for success, but Colonel Sanders kept selling his idea until someone listened.

How can a person ignore reality and cling to the vapor of a dream? How can personal drive overcome the fear of failure? What drives a person to work eighty hours a week for a dream when he or she would balk at working such hours for a boss? Why do some people quit when others continue? The answer lies in the age-old conflict between the reality of your own faith and the realities of the world. God has given you the ability to dream great dreams, but circumstance, education, personal doubts, and the ridicule of others challenge your goals. A single-minded concentration on discovering your own soul is paramount in defining your own success. You alone are responsible for your life and what you do with it.

CONSIDER THIS: What you make of your life is entirely up to you. Choose carefully to expend your energy only on those ideas that mean the most.

Begin Now, Don't Delay

"A trip of a thousand miles is begun with a single step." — Chinese proverb

If you are not making mistakes, you are not traveling the road to success. If you are waiting for the time to be right to begin, you will never begin. It is true that mistakes are costly and that the timing must be right, but it is also important to know that inertia is hard to overcome. Our American "jackpot" mentality makes us eager for a quantum leap into success, but success more often is a result of many, many small wins (sprinkled with a generous helping of failures). Success is more a journey than a destination. If you are not now making progress on your own journey, you will never find success. You must take the risk to enjoy the prize. An old American adage says that you must climb out on the limb to get the best apples.

H. Ross Perot had an idea about selling computer services but took no action to carry his idea to fruition. Then one day as he was waiting in the barbershop, he picked up a *Reader's Digest* and read a quote from Thoreau: "The mass of men lead lives of quiet desperation." Perot made the decision of his life, and that was the moment EDS "began." For many years, Gail Borden invented all sorts of unmarketable things, taking odd jobs to eke out a living. It was not until he was fifty-six years old that he developed condensed milk. All of Borden's previous inventing "failures" had given him the developmental tools to devise his new product. Even that venture failed the first time out, however; but he kept trying until it succeeded.

CONSIDER THIS: Begin your journey to success today. Write down the details of your plan of action. Begin doing the little things that will prepare you to take advantage of new opportunities as they come along.

Index

3M, 39,152, 164, 172, 265
Aaron, Henry, 260
ABC Nightly News 46
Academy Awards, 14, 119
"Acres of Diamonds," 36
Adelson, Sheldon, 179
Adolph's Meat Tenderizer, 84
aerobics, 121
Alamo, 34
Aldus Corporation, 127
Alka-Seltzer, 43, 375
Allen, Paul, 77
aluminum foil, 207, 302
American Way Association
    (Amway), 213,239
American Youth Foundation,
    111
American Zoetrope, 14
Amos, Wally, 17
Andersen, Elmer, 115, 338
Anderson, Harlan, 303
Anderson, Walt, 287
Andy Griffith Show, The, 151
Annenberg, Walter H., 362
Änsa Bottles, 200
Apple Computer, 50, 127,
    273, 376
Arlen, Roy, 248
Armstrong, Thomas, 100
Armstrong World Industries,
    Inc., 100
Arnold, Stanley, 171
Ash, Mary Kay, 269
AT&T, 204, 229
Austin, Nancy, 187
automobile radio, 254

Bachelor, Charles, 18
Bachman Company, 327
Baekeland, Leo, 71
Bakelite, 71
Ball, Lucille, 362
Band-Aid bandage, 45, 207
Bangham, Dick, 284
Bank of Italy, 349
Bartocci, Barbara, 322
BASIC, 77
Bauer, Eddie, 104
Baum, Lyman Frank, 163
Baxter Travenol Laboratories,
    63
Beardsley, A. H., 375
Bell, Alexander Graham, 68

Benji, 344
Bennis, Warren, f25, 199,
    233, 351
Bere, James, 91
Berkshire Hathaway, 194
Berlin, Irving, 217
Berry College, 216
Berry, Martha, 216
Bettger, Frank, 150
Bible, The, 31, 52, 97, 208,
    238, 256, 301, 367
Birds Eye frozen foods, 117,
    270
Birdseye, Clarence, 117, 270
Bissell Carpet Sweepers, 293
Bissell Company, 293
Bissell, Melville and Anna,
    293
Blanchard, Kenneth, 341
Black & Decker Company,
    143
Black, S. Duncan, 143
Blanc, Mel, 307
Bloch, Henry, 267
Bloch, Richard, 267
Bloom, Benjamin, 105
Blount, Inc., 185
Blount, Winton, 185
bluejeans, 66, 173, 374
Blumkin, Rose, 188
Bolton, John, 292
Bono, Sonny, 13
Boone, Daniel, 157
Borden, Gail, 241, 346
Borg-Warner, 91
Boston Pops, 203
Boys Town, 192
Brack, Reg, 323
Brainerd, Paul, 127
Bricklin, Dan, 273
Bringing Out the Best in People,
    55
Brinker, Norm, 211
Brinklin, Dan, 273
Brinks Coffee Shop, 211
Brooks Brothers Clothiers,
    308
Brooks, Henry, 308
brown paper bag, 316
Brown Shoe Company, 175
Browning, Pete (Old
    Gladiator), 359
Bryant, Lane, 313

Buck, Pearl, 329
Buffett, Warren, 194
Bundy Used Cars, 291
Burnett, Leo, 86, 234
Bush, John, 175
Buster Brown Shoes, 175
Butts, Alfred, 366

Caldwell, Phillip, 67
Calvin Klein Ltd., 20
Camp, Joe, 344
Campbell, Bill and Nickie,
    200
Canadian Broadcasting
    Corporation (CBC), 46
Candler, Asa, 235, 272, 368
Cannell, Stephen, 135
Carnegie, Andrew, 9, 81,
    216, 288, 318, 376
Carnegie, Dale, 37, 96, 223
Carlson, Curt, 191
Carrier air-conditioning
    system, 317
Carrier, Dr. Willis, 317
Carter, Jimmy, 278
Carver, George Washington,
    51, 304, 368
Cary, Bess, 48
Castro, Bernard, 295
Castro Convertible, 295
Cathy, Truett, 136
CB radio, 155
Celestial Seasonings, 210,
    340, 376
Celluloid, 71
Channing, Carol, 137, 164
Chaplin, Charlie, 283
Chevrolet, Louis, 206
Chevrolet Motor Company,
    33, 38, 43, 206
Chick-fil-A, 136
Christmas, 372
Chrysler, 38, 93, 218
Chrysler, Walter Percy, 93
Churchill, Winston, 107, 242
Civil War, 58, 142, 205, 253,
    346
Claiborne, Liz, 296
Classic Driving School, 306
Clemens, Sam, 336
Climate Control Division,
    354
CNN, 53

Coca-Cola Classic, 43, 112, 210, 235, 272, 278, 368
Cochraine, Josephine Garis, 161
Collar, 292
Collins, Marva, 255
Colton, Chrales Caleb, 148
COMDEX, 179
Comer, Gary, 363
Communications User, magazine 179
Compaq Computer Corporation, 220, 376
ComputerWorld magazine, 209
Connor, Gen. Fox, 41
Continental Bakeries, 243
Conwell, Russell, 36, 100
Cook and Baker's School, 19
Cooper, Dr. Kenneth, 121
Coppola, Francis Ford, 14
Corbin, Lt. Howard J., 59
Cornell Aeronautical Laboratories, 233
Cox, Edwin W., 311
C. R. Walgreen Company, 320
Cracker Barrel Old Country Store, 156
Cracker Jacks, 72, 165
Crane, Clarence, 248, 368
Creek, Joel, 294
Crosby, Phillip B., 158
Crowley, Mary, 208, 275
Crum, George, 214
Cullinane Software, Inc., 335
Cullinane, John, 335
Cullinet Software, 335
Cumberland Gap, 157
Cunningham, Harry, 32

Dahl, Gary, 169
Danforth Foundation, 111
Danforth, William H., 111, 330, 373
d'Arbeloff, Alex, 286
Darby, R. U., 350
Darrow, Charles, 348
Data General, 56
deCastro, Edson, 56
Decker, Alonzo, 143
Deere, John, 236, 332
Dell Computers, 229, 376
Dell, Michael, 229
Delta Air Service, 231
Delta Air Lines, 231
Delta faucets, 155

Demming, W. Edward, 176
Democratic National Convention, 46
DePree, D. J., 83
desktop publishing, 127
Desmore, James, 212
Deusch, Larry, 84, 368
Developing Talent in Your Children, 105
DeVoss, Richard, 213
Dewar, Jimmy, 243
DeWolf, Nick, 286
Dickson, Earle E., 45
Diesel, Rudolph, 184
Digital Equipment Corporation (DEC), 56, 280, 303, 374
Discovery Toys, 239
Disney theme parks, 25, 128, 219
Disney, Walt, 128, 207, 210, 219, 223, 236, 277, 344
Dodge Brothers, 93
Doolin, Charles, 95
Dove Candy shop, 309
DoveBar, 309
Downs, Hugh, 96
Drucker, Peter, 222, 236, 291
Durant, W. C., 93, 206
Dwarf House restuarant, 136

Earhart, Amelia, 168
Eastern Onion, 258
Eastman, George, 60, 345
Eastman Kodak, 60
Ebony magazine, 74
Edison Electric Light Company, 18
Edison, Thomas, 18, 71, 193, 202, 241
Edmonds, Jim, 85
E. G. Otis Company, 73
Eisenhower, Dwight, 41
Eisner, Michael, 219
Electronic Data Systems (EDS), 147
Elliott, Alan C., 35, 223, 260, 272
Emerson, Ralph Waldo, 85, 97, 104, 124, 172, 215, 300, 337
Emmy Awards, 99, 225
Enthusiasm Makes the Difference, 116
Entrepreneurial Megabucks, 181
Erie Insurance Exchange, 331

Erteszek, Olga and Jan, 358
Eversharp, 16
Evinrude Detachable Row Boat Motor, 48
Evinrude, Ole, 48, 184
Evins, Dan, 156
Executive Breakthrough, The, 171

Falls City Sluggers, 359
Famous Amos Cookies, 17
Fashion Institute of Technology, 20
Federal Express, 43, 226, 264
Federated Department Stores, 190
Federation of Women's Clubs for Civic Improvement, 103
FedMart Corporation, 131
Fiedler, Arthur, 203, 374
Field, Marshall, 102
Fields, Debbi, 277
Fitzgerald, Ella, 113
Flanagan, Father Edward J., 192
Flatt, Mary, 258
FlightSafety International, 148
Foley's, 190
Foot-Eazer, 26
Forbes, Malcolm, 268
Ford, Henry, 195, 202, 216, 236
Ford Motor Company, 38, 67, 195, 222
Franklin, Benjamin, 9, 118, 259, 330
Frankston, Bob, 273
Freemont Canning Company, 182
Freeware, 218
Frisbee flying disc, 207, 228, 319, 368
Frisbie Pie Company, 319, 368
Fritos Corn Chips, 95
Fry, Art, 164, 172
Fuller, Harvey Benjamin, 115, 338
Fuqua Industries, Inc., 189
Fuqua, John Brooks (J. B.), 189, 271

Galvin Manufacturing Company, 35
Galvin, Paul, 254, 368

Gamble, James, 130
Garis-Cochraine, 161
Gate of Opportunity, The, 216
Gates, Bill, 77
General Electric (GE), 90, 193
General Foods Company, 117, 210, 270
General Motors, 38, 127, 206
General Staff School, 41
Gerber, Dan, 182
Gerber Products Company, 182
Getting into the Mail-order Business, 240
Giannini, Amades Peter, 349
Giles, Robin and Carol, 64
Gillette, King, 369
Girard, Joe, 33, 374
Glendinning, 57
Goddard, Robert, 289
Goethe, Johann Wolfgang von, 45, 145, 258, 307, 317
Going for It!, 162
Goizueta, Roberto, 278
Gold Bond Stamp Company, 191
Golden Rule stores, 230, 374
Goodyear, 250
Grace Church (Philadelphia), 36
Graham, Billy, 343
Graham, William B., 63
Grammy Awards, 88, 99, 281
Grandy's restaurants, 221
Green Bay Box & Lumber, 266
Green Bay Packaging, Inc., 266
Green Bay, Wisconsin, Chapter of the American Foundation of Religion and Psychiatry, 266
Griffith, Andy, 151
Groad, Mary Dr., 328
Grove, Andrew, 77, 355
Guideposts, 31
Guinness Book of World Records, 33, 99

H & R Block, Inc., 267
Haapoja, Jim, 284
Haley, Alex, 186
Hall Brothers, Inc., 89

Hall, Col. George, 78
Hall, Joyce Clyde and Rollie, 89
Hallmark Cards, 89
Haloid Company, 263
Hanson, John K., 132
Harvey, Paul, 261
Hay, John, 340
H. B. Fuller, 115, 338
Healing of Persons, The, 252
Heflin, Becky, 164
Henson, Jim, 360
Hepburn, Katharine, 137
Herman Miller, Inc., 83, 236, 325
Hershey, Milton, 241, 262
Hewitt Associates, 62
Hewitt, Edwin, (Ted) 62, 215
Hewlett-Packard, 145, 152, 193, 276
Hill, Napoleon, 97, 125, 326, 350
Hill, Paula, 138
Hobart company, 161
Hodgson, Peter, 118
Holiday Inn, 149
Home Interiors, 208, 275
Homebrew Computer Club, 50
Hooper, Grace, 174
Hoover, William, 184
Hope, Bob, 298
Horan, John, 54
Horchow Collection, The, 190
Horchow, Roger, 190, 218
House, Chuck, 276
How I Raised Myself from Failure to Success, 150
Hudson, Edward, 237
Huff Daland Dusters company, 231
Hula Hoop, 228
Hyatt, Wesley, 71

I Dare You, 111, 330
Iacocca, Lee, 37
Ideal Toy Company, 314
Industrial Light and Magic, 14
Ingram, E. W., 287
Intel, 355
Interface Group, The, 179
International Business Machines (IBM), 34, 56, 72, 77, 127, 127, 145, 147,

174, 180, 193, 202, 220, 229, 241, 280, 303, 324, 355, 376
International Data Group (IDG), 209
It's a Wonderful Life, 371
Ivory Soap, 130, 374
Ivy League clothing, 59

Jack-in-the-Box restaurants, 211
Jackall, Robert, 197
James, Richard, 196
James, William, 83, 109, 186, 200, 315
Jantzen, Carl, 133
Jantzen Knitting Mills, 133
Jantzen Swimwear, 133
Jarvis, Anna, 142
JCPenney, 32, 87, 230
Jeanloz, Claude and Donna, 279
Jemison, Dr. Mae, 29
Jenkins, George Washington, 329
Jennings, Peter, 46
Jesus Christ, 23, 31, 72, 210, 230, 372
Jobs, Steve, 50
Joe Jacobs's Drug Store, 235
Johnson & Johnson, 45
Johnson, Edward, 45, 221
Johnson, James, 45
Johnson, John H., 74
Johnson Publishing, 74
Johnson, Robert, 45
Jolt Cola, 112
Jones, Quincy, 281
Jordan, Michael, 154
Jordan, Vernon, 141
Judson, Whitcomb, 250
Juicy Fruit gum, 42

K-Mart, 32
Kampgrounds of America, 98
Kauffman, Ewing M., 52
Keller, Helen, 57, 79, 111, 201, 256
Kellogg's cereals, 101
Kellogg, Will, 101
Kelly, Russell, 242
Kelly Services, 242
Kenton Corporation, 190
Kentucky Fried Chicken, 19, 75
Kiam, Victor, 162

King, Jr., Dr. Martin Luther, 27
Kilby, Jack, 146
Kimberly-Clark, 159, 374
Kirchmeier, Jim, 306
KitchenAid, 161
Klein, Calvin, 20
Kleiser, Grenville, 76, 304, 339
Kleenex tissues, 159, 207, 374
Knerr, Rich, 228, 319
Knox gelatin, 103
Knox, Rose, 103
Kodak camera, 60, 71
Kojak, 166
Kopell, Bernie, 232
Kraft Foods Inc., 340
Kresge Company, 32
Kress, George, 266
Kroc, Ray, 15, 34, 84, 352, 368

Lady Fredrick, 28
Land, Edwin, 39
Landry, Tom, 69
Lane Bryant, 313
Lane Cedar Chest, 237
Lane, John, 237
Lasorda, Tommy, 321
Lauder, Estee, 282
Lazarus, Emma, 312
Lazarus store, 190
Leaders, 125, 199, 351
Lear Jet, Inc., 35
Lear, William P., 35
Learoscope, 35
Lehmkuhl, Joakim, 364
Leininger, Steve, 50
L'Engle, Madeleine, 238
Leno, Jay, 70
Leo Burnett Agency, 86, 234
Leonard, Stew, 223, 297
Levi Strauss & Company, 173
Life Savers, 248, 368
Lincoln, Abraham, 55, 97, 119, 160, 205, 210, 253, 290, 308, 323, 327, 348
Lindbergh, Charles A., 334
"Little Red Hen, The," 249
Liquid Paper Company, 124, 374
Lister, Joseph, 45
Liz Claiborne, Inc., 296
Louisville Slugger, 359
Love Boat, 232

Lowen-Stern, Walter, 300
Lower, Elmer, 46
Lucas, George, 14

Mac World magazine, 209
Macintosh personal computer, 127
Mack, Jack and Augustus, 356
Mack Trucks Inc., 356
Macy, Rowlan, 370
Macy's department store, 370
Magna Carta, The, 183
Managing Management Time, 82
Manoogian, Alex, 155
Manoogian, Richard, 155
Mao Tse-tung, 107
Marchant, Henry, 112
Marcus, Herman, 126
Marion Laboratories, 52
Marketing Corporation of America (MCA), 57
Marsalis, Wynton, 88
Marshall Field and Company, 102
Martin, Steve, 70
Mary Kay Cosmetics, 193, 239, 269, 374
Mary Kay, Inc., 269
Masco Screw Products Company, 155
Maugham, W. Somerset, 28, 180
Maxwell House Coffee, 294
Maxwell House Hotel, 294
Maxfield, Robert, 300
Maxwell Motor Company, 93
Maytag, Fred, 170
Maytag washers, 86, 170
McClure, Jessica, 367
McColough, Peter, 263
McDonald, Eugene, 74
McDonald, Richard and Maurice, 152
McDonald's restaurants, 15, 25, 34, 70, 84, 86, 167, 248, 347, 352, 368
McGinnis, Alan Loy, 55
McGovern, Patrick, 209
McGowan, William, 204
McLean, Malcom P., 160
McManus, James, 57
McNair, Robert, 29
Method of Reaching Extreme Altitudes, A, 289
Melin, Spud, 228, 319

Merck & Co., 54, 301
Merck, George, 301
Method of Reaching Extreme Altitudes, 289
Microsoft, 77
Microwave Communications Inc. (MCI), 204
microwave oven, 251
Miller, Herman, 83, 325
Milne, A. A., 191, 217, 247, 313, 328, 376
Minnesota Keystone Club, 191
Model T automobile, 49
Monopoly, 348, 366
Monsanto, 122
mood ring, 227
Moog, Bill, 233
Moog Inc., 233
Moonlighting, 225
Moore, Gordon, 355
Moore, Sam, 110
Moreno, Rita, 99
Morrison, Fred, 319
Mother's Day, 142
Motorola, 35, 254, 368
Mrs. Fields Cookies, 277
Mullikin, Harry, 339
Muppet Show, The, 360
Murphy, John, 40
Murto, Bill, 220
Musser, Warren (Pete), 92

Nanus, Burt, 125, 199, 351
National Book Company, 110
Nebraska Furniture Mart, 188
Negro Digest, 74
Neiman, Carrie and Al, 126
Neiman-Marcus, 126, 190, 282
Nemeth, Lane, 239
Nesmith, Bette, 124, 374
New Coke, 278
Newberry Medal, 238
Nobel Prize, 116
Noble, Edward, 248, 368
NonStop computer, 145
Noyce, Robert, 355

O'Donnell, Rosie, 246
Olga Company, 358
Olsen, Ken, 280, 303
Olympic Games, 114, 259
Oncken, Jr., William, 82
Oprah Winfrey Show, The, 119

Organizational Dynamics, 108
Orteig, Raymond, 334
Oshman, Kenneth, 300
Otis, Elisha G., 73
Otis elevators, 73
Outcault, Richard, 175

Packard, Dave, 236 276
PageMaker, 127
Pan American World
  Airways, 148
Parker Brothers, 348
Parker, George S., 16
Parker Pens, 16, 215
Pasteur, Louis, 173, 202
Pastime Washer, 170
Patron Power, 197
Patton, Gen. George S., 22,
  44, 58, 174
Patton's Principles, 22
PC Limited, 229
PC World magazine, 209
PDP-1 computer, 303
Peale, Norman Vincent, 31,
  116, 266
Pemberton, Dr. John, 235,
  272
Penn, William, 137
Penney, James Cash, 230,
  374
Perdue, Arthur, 257
Perdue, Frank, 257
Perot, H. Ross, 147, 378
Pet Rock, 169
Peters, Tom, 108, 144, 187,
  374
Pepperidge Farms, 153, 210
Peters, Tom, 341
Phillips 66, 123
Phillips, Frank 123
Phillips Petroleum, 85, 123
Phillips-Van Heusen
  Corporation, 292
Pilgrim, Aubrey, 51
Pilgrim, Bo, 51
Pilgrim's Pride, 51
Pillsbury, C. A. & Company,
  285
Pillsbury, Charles, 285
Pillsbury, John, 285
Pitney-Bowes, 94
Plexiglas, 71
"Pluto Platter," 319
Plymouth, 93
Polaroid Land camera, 39
Post-it Notes, 39, 172

potato chips, 214
Power of Positive Thinking, The,
  31
Powertron, 204
Price Clubs, 131
Price, Sol, 131
Pro Football Hall of Fame, 69
Procter and Gamble, 57, 130,
  191, 374
Procter, Harley, 130
Publix Supermarkets, 329

Quad/Graphics ,341
Quadracci, Harry, 341
Queeny, John F., 122

Ralston Purina Company, 57,
  111, 373
Rapp, C. J., 112
Raytheon Company, 251,
  280
Read, Jim, 299
Reader's Digest, 247, 322, 378
Remington shaver, 162,
Remington typewriter, 212,
  376
Rempp, Adolph, 84
Reid, James, 310
Renovators Supply, 279
Rent-A-Wreck, 291
"Rest of the Story, The," 261
Reynolds Metals Company,
  207, 302
Reynolds, R. S., 302
Richardson, Lunsford, 245
Richeson, Eugene, 300
Rigler, Lloyd, 84, 368
Rockefeller, John D., 140
Rockford Files, The, 135
Rockola, David C., 134
Rockola jukebox, 134
Roebuck, Alvah C., 305
Rogers, Will, 342
ROLM Corporation, 300
Roosevelt, Theodore, 47, 55,
  216, 294, 314, 338, 373
Roots, 186, 281
Rough Riders, 47
Rudkin, Margaret, 153
Rudolph, Wilma, 259
Rueckheim, F. W., 165
Running Things, 158
Rutan Aircraft Factory, 224
Rutan, Burt, 224
Rutan, Dick, 224
Ruth, Babe, 55

saccharin, 122
Safeguard Business System,
  92
Sanders, Col. Harland, 75,
  84, 322, 377
Sanders, Rex, 221
Saratoga Chips, 214
Savalas, Aristotle (Telly), 166
Schick razor, 369
Schick, Jacob, 369
Scholl, Billy, 26
Schuller, Robert, 357
Schwab, Charles, 81, 116
Schwartz, Dave, 291
Scrabble, 366
Sea-Land Services (SLS), 160
Secrets of Successful Selling, 40
Seabury & Johnson, 45
Sears, R. W., Watch Co., 305
Sears, Richard, 305
Sears, Roebuck and Co., 305,
  374
Sewell, Carl, 34, 49
Sewell Village Cadillac, 25
Shakespeare, William, 20, 23,
  153, 346
Shareware, 218
Sharp, Walter, 353
Shaw, Bill, 221
Shepherd, Cybill, 225
Sherwin, Dunham, and
  Griswold, 244
Sherwin, Henry, 244
Sherwin-Williams, 244
Sholes, Christopher, 212, 248
Siegel, Mo, 210, 340
Silicon Valley, 50
Silly Putty, 118, 207
Silver, A. David, 181
Simon, Julian L., 240
Sleeper, George, 214
Slinky, 196, 207
Sloan, Alfred P., 206, 236
Smith, Fred, 226
Smucker, Jerome, 61
Smucker's, 61
SnyderGeneral, 354
Snyder, Richard, 354
Software Arts, Inc., 273
Sohio, 177
S. O. S. Pads, 311
Spahr, Charles, 177
Spencer, Dr. Percy, 251
Spielberg, Steven, 109, 164,
  281
Spirit of St. Louis, 334

Standard Products Co., 310
Stanley Arnold & Associates, 171
Stanley, Professor Thomas, 333
Star Trek, 29
Starship Enterprise, 29
Star Wars, 14
Statue of Liberty, 312
Staubach, Roger, 274
Steak & Ale, 211
Stefanos, Leo, 309
Steinway & Sons, 21
Steinway, Heinrich, 21
Steinway Village, 21
Stillwell, Charles, 316
Strauss, Levi, 66, 173, 241, 374
Sullivan, Anne, 79, 256
Sunback, Gideon, 250, 368
Sunday, Billy, 23
Super Bowl, 274

T-Ball Jotter, 16
Sysco, 34
Tandem Computers, 145
Tandy Radio Shack, 50
Tappan, 251
Teddy bear, 314
Teflon, 71
telephone, 68
Telnack, Jack, 222
Temple University and Samaritan Hospital, 36
Teradyne Inc., 286
Texas Instruments, 220
Theresa, Mother, 315, 337
Tiffany & Company, 365
Tiffany, Charles Lewis, 365
Time, Inc., 323
Timex watches, 364
Think and Grow Rich, 97, 350
Thomas, Dave, 19, 211
Thomas Nelson Publishers, 110
Thoreau, Henry David, 147, 314, 324
Tonight Show, The, 70
Tough Times Never Last But Tough People Do, 357
Tournier, Dr. Paul, 252
Trammell Crow, 25
Treybig, Jim, 145

Truman, Harry S, 34, 139, 343
Tubman, Harriet, 205
Tupper, Earl, 76
Tupperware, 76, 239
Turner, Ted, 52
TV Guide, 362
Twain, Mark, 103, 196, 336
Twinkies, 243
typewriter, 212

Ueberroth, Peter, 114
Ueltschi, Al, 148
Uncle Sam, 253
Underground Railroad, 205
United Business Company, 267
Upton, Francis, 18
User-supported Software, 218

Van Andel, Jan, 213
Van Camp's Baked Beans, 326
Van Camp, Frank, 326
Van Heusen, John, 292
Veeck, Bill, 144
Vicks VapoRub, 245, 368
Viking Freight, 284
VisiCalc, 273
Voit, William, 80
Voyager, 224

Wallace, DeWitt, 247
Wallenda, Karl, 24, 377
Wal-Mart, 87, 152
Walgreen, Charles, 320
Walgreen Company, 320
Walton, Sam, 87, 152
Wang, Dr. An, 202
Wang Laboratories, 202
Warner Bros., 307
Washington, Booker T., 178
Washington, George, 65, 107, 361
Waterbury Clock Company, 364
Watson, Thomas, 34, 68, 180, 193, 210, 236, 241, 324
Webb, Chick, 113
Webster, Daniel, 65, 97
Weems, Mason Locke, 361
Welch, Jack, 90
Welch, Joseph, 327

Wendy's, 19
Wernick, Marvin, 227
Westin Hotels and Resorts, 339
Weyerhaeuser, Frederick, 120
Wham-O Manufacturing Co., 228, 319, 368
Wheeler, Walter, 94
White Castle restaurants, 287
"White Christmas," 217
Whitman Sampler, 353
Whitman, Steven, 353
Whitney, Eli, 290
William Morris Agency, 17, 151
Williams, Edward, 244
Williams, Ted, 359
Williamson, Porter, 22
Willys Overland Company, 93
Wilson, Kemmons, 149
Wilson, Samuel, 253
Wilson, Woodrow, 107, 142
Winchester, Oliver, 58
Winchester rifle, 58
Winfrey, Oprah, 119
Winnebago Inc., 132
Wise, Earl, 214
Wise Potato Chips, 214
Wonderful Wizard of Oz, The, 30, 163
Wooden, John, 129
Woolman, Collett Everman (C. E.), 231
Wordtemps, 98
Wozniak, Steve, 50
Wrigley, Bill, 42
Wrigley's Spearmint gum, 42
Wrinkle in Time, A, 238
WTBS, 53

Xerox, 263

Ya-hoo Cake, 299
Yeager, Jeana, 224

Zehntbauer, John and Roy, 133
Zenith, 74
Ziegfeld, Florenz, 106, 347
Ziegfeld Follies, 106, 217
zipper, 250
Zipper Boots, 250